Evening Standard
LONDON PUB GUIDE

Evening Standard
LONDON PUB GUIDE

'96

1996

ANGUS McGILL

PAVILION

*For all telephone numbers in the Review section
of the Guide which do not have a code,
please dial 0171 before the number listed.*

First published in Great Britain in 1995 by
PAVILION BOOKS LIMITED
26 Upper Ground, London SE1 9PD

Text copyright © Evening Standard 1995
Cartoons copyright © Frank Dickens 1995
Maps and design copyright © Pavilion Books 1995

Designed by
THE BRIDGEWATER BOOK COMPANY

Commissioning Editor for the *Evening Standard*: Joanne Bowlby
Associate Editor: Edward Sullivan

Additional reporting by Brian Angel, Chris Bond, Nicholas Bond,
Richard Bruton, Joan Cawston, Ben Colman, James Hughes-Onslow,
Robert Jennings, Peter Morrison, Ann Morrow, Kenneth Hughes,
Tom Pocock, David Weston, Peter Williams.

The moral right of the author has been asserted.

All rights reserved. No part of this publication may be reproduced,
stored in a retrieval system, or transmitted, in any form or by any
means, electronic, mechanical, photocopying, recording or otherwise,
without the prior permission of the copyright holder.

A CIP catalogue record for this book is
available from the British Library

ISBN 1 85793 735 X
Typeset in Baskerville
Printed and bound in Great Britain by Butler & Tanner Ltd,
Frome and London

2 4 6 8 10 9 7 5 3 1

This book may be ordered by post direct from
the publisher. Please contact the Marketing Department.
But try your bookshop first.

Corporate editions and personal subscriptions of the
Evening Standard London Pub Guide are available.
Call us for details. Tel: 620 1666

ALSO PUBLISHED IN THIS SERIES:
the *Evening Standard London Restaurant Guide*
by Fay Maschler and the *Evening Standard London
Wine Guide* by Andrew Jefford.

CONTENTS

Maps · 8

REVIEWS · 16

Eros Awards · 219

Pubs with Theatres · 220

Gay Pubs · 220

Riverside Pubs · 221

Pubs with No-smoking Areas · 221

Pubs with Live Music · 222

Pubs with Outdoor Seating · 223

THE EVENING STANDARD LONDON PUB GUIDE

This is a book crammed from cover to cover with pubs, and let me tell you something straight away. You aren't going to like them all, not by a long shot. Still, they are all someone's favourite pub. Well, nearly all. Some pubs not even the landlord could love.

Their variety is what I like most. If you don't care for the pub you are in, if you are the only customer in a three-piece suit, if you don't understand anything the stand-up comic says, if the music is turned up so high it flattens your nose, try the one across the road. It was put there for just such an emergency. Brixton, for instance, is a musical borough. Several of its robust pubs are in this book. But it also has one in which no music of any sort is allowed. Even the music in the fruit machine is turned off.

So I hope you will browse a while in this forest of pubs, taking your time, going 'tsk' on occasions no doubt, but here and there coming across one that promises exactly what you have in mind. This, as we all know, is a drink and a chat with the love of your life. Pubs specialize in these three items, particularly the drink, which has never been as interesting. English cask ales, rescued from oblivion by CAMRA, are enjoying a brilliant renaissance and can be found in just about every single pub in this book, extraordinary beers some of them. You will find one pub here selling an ale called Dog's Bollocks. No, I didn't try it actually, another time perhaps, but I have tried a great many others and lagers from all over. Good heavens, those Trappists; and there's the alcoholic lemonade that gets the kids going; and as for the things you can do with vodka…Those who fancy making Absolut Mars Bar will find the recipe within.

So browse, that is my message, see the lengths London's pubs will go to to amuse you. They fix giant television screens in the bar. They sell kangaroo steaks. They provide ice-hockey fans with buckets of chicken wings and lay on live jazz every night of the week, also reggae and country, and western and rap, ska and rhythm and blues. They keep vast sandwiches coming all day long and there's a whole new breed of born-again foodie pubs, with young chefs in the kitchens producing the sort of sunny food you used to get only on holiday. Mod Med they call it now, or sometimes pleb Med. There are lots of these pubs here. There are also pubs with other things in mind, ones in which comely young women take their clothes off, every stitch except – pub floors being what they are – their shoes. In others it is the young men who strip. One has different male strippers every two hours all through Sunday. Which reminds me...

At the height of the long, hot summer the rules we live by shifted. Pubs were, for the first time, allowed to stay open all day on Sunday. Couples running pubs were often sorry to lose their Sunday afternoons, and not all did. Some pubs sold so little beer on that first Sunday afternoon that they went back to the old hours the very next week, and others have not made their minds up even now. But customers by and large seemed happy with the change and, as sunny Sunday followed sunny Sunday, these were happy days for pubs with gardens, terraces or even a couple of tables on the pavement.

Meanwhile it has been a year of major restoration, of money sloshed around, and now that the British weather is more or less itself again, people are finding that pubs of all degrees are more comfortable and generally more agreeable than at any time they can remember. These are great days for pubs.

MAP 1 • Greater London

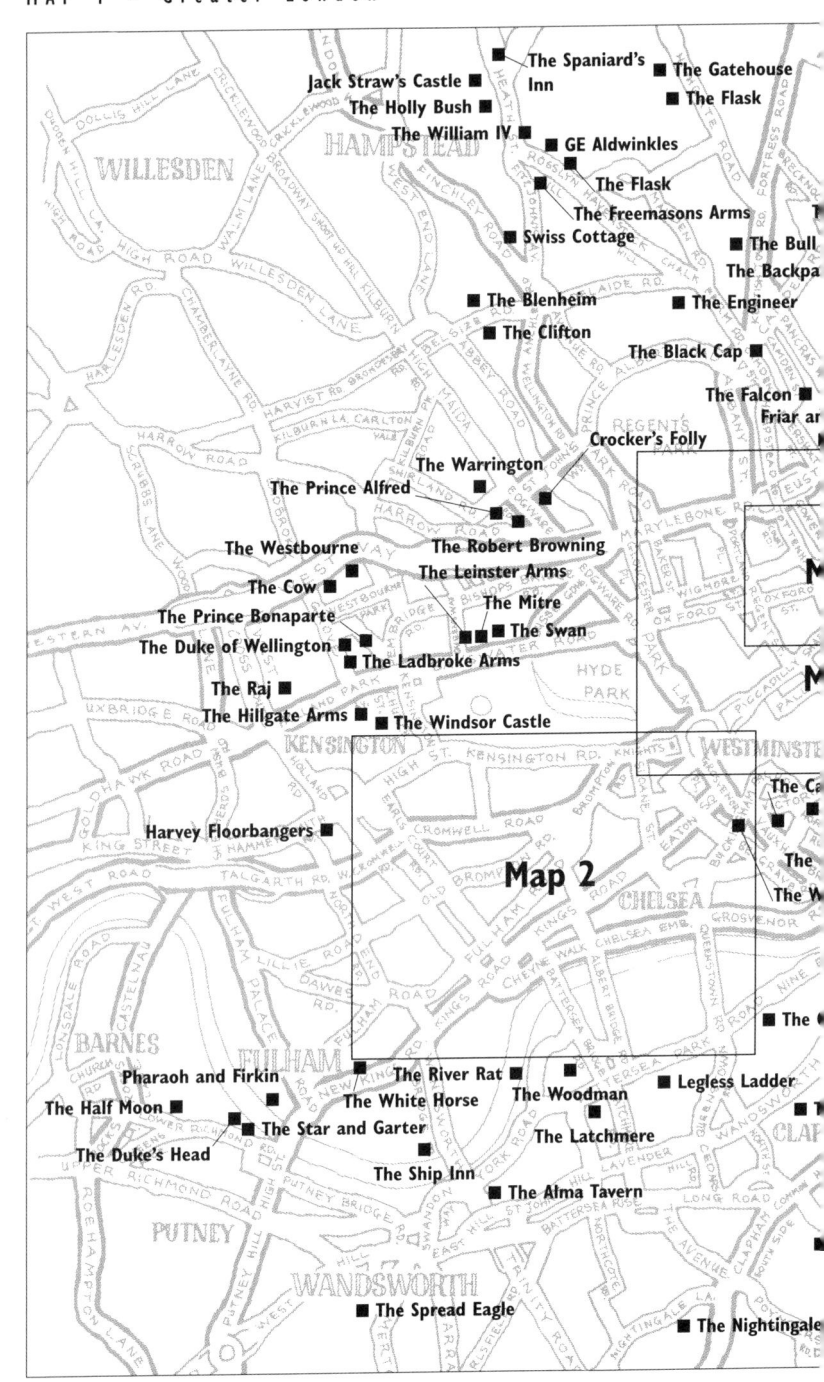

Greater London • MAP 1

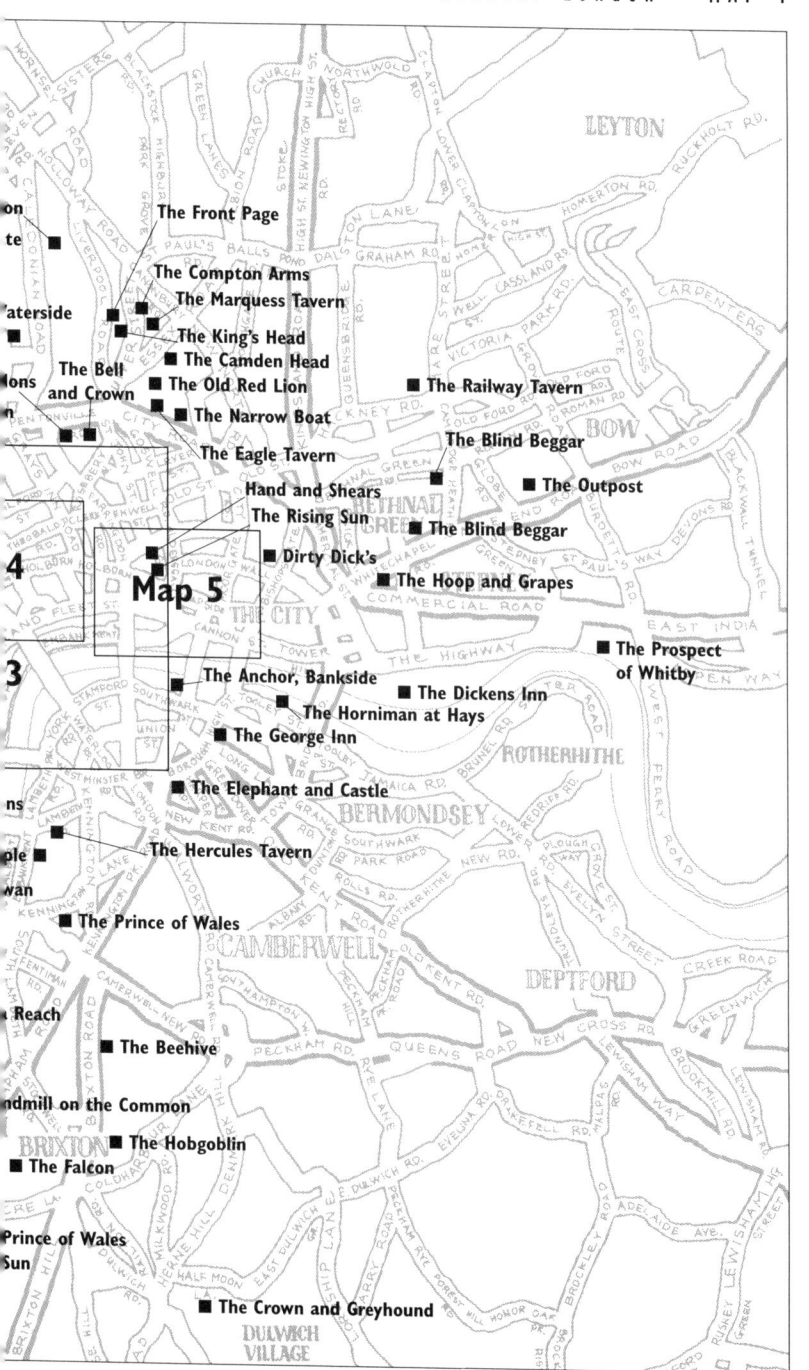

MAP 2 • West London

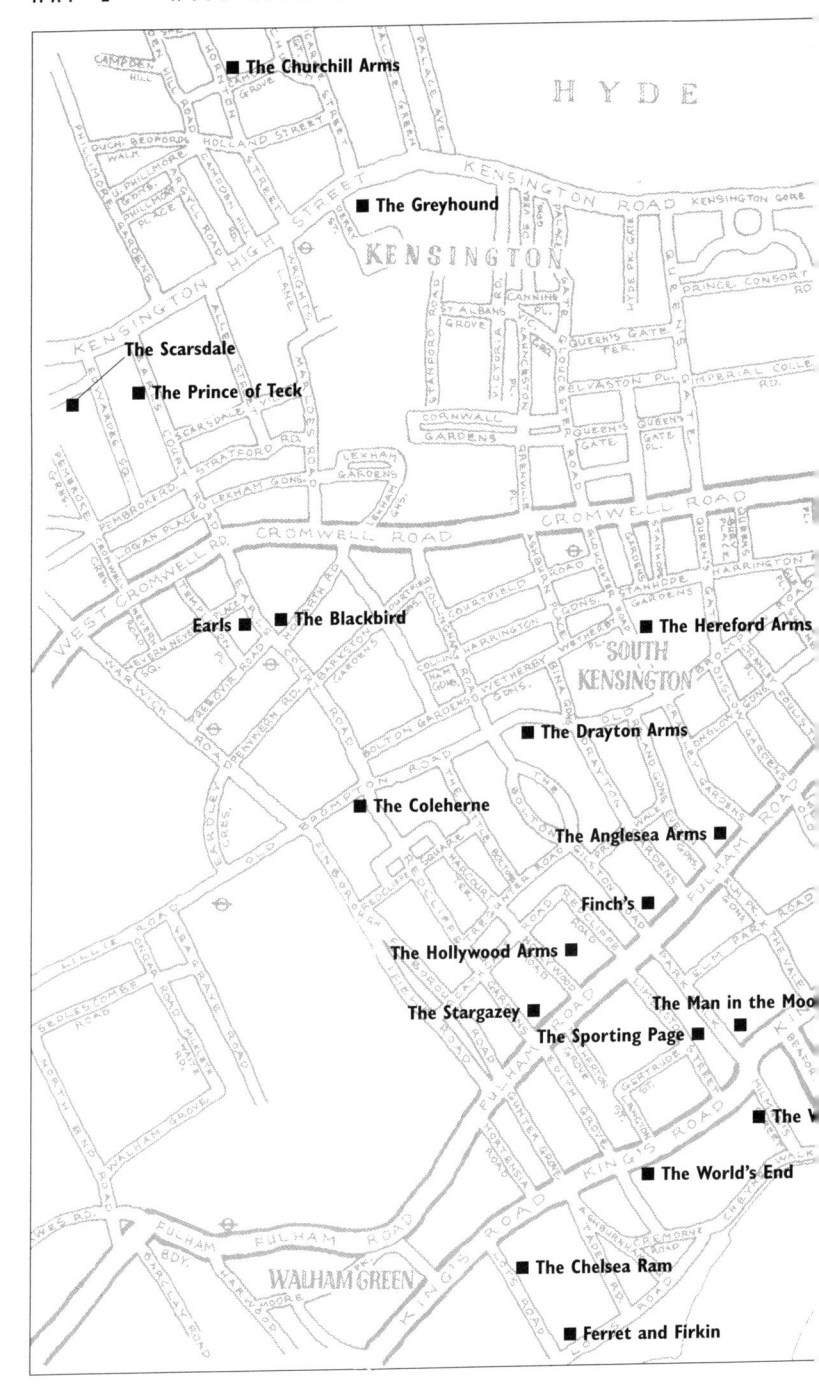

West London • MAP 2

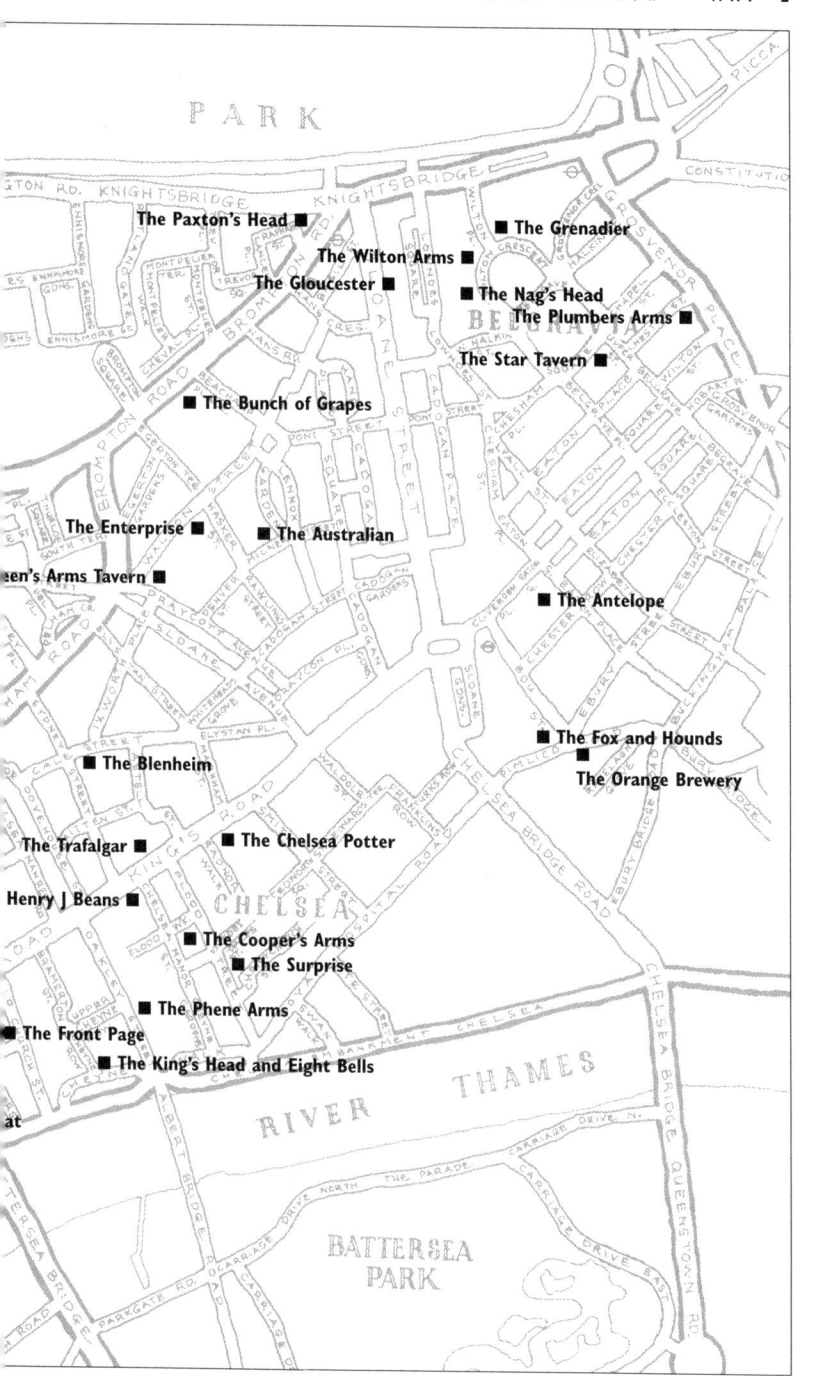

MAP 3 • Central London

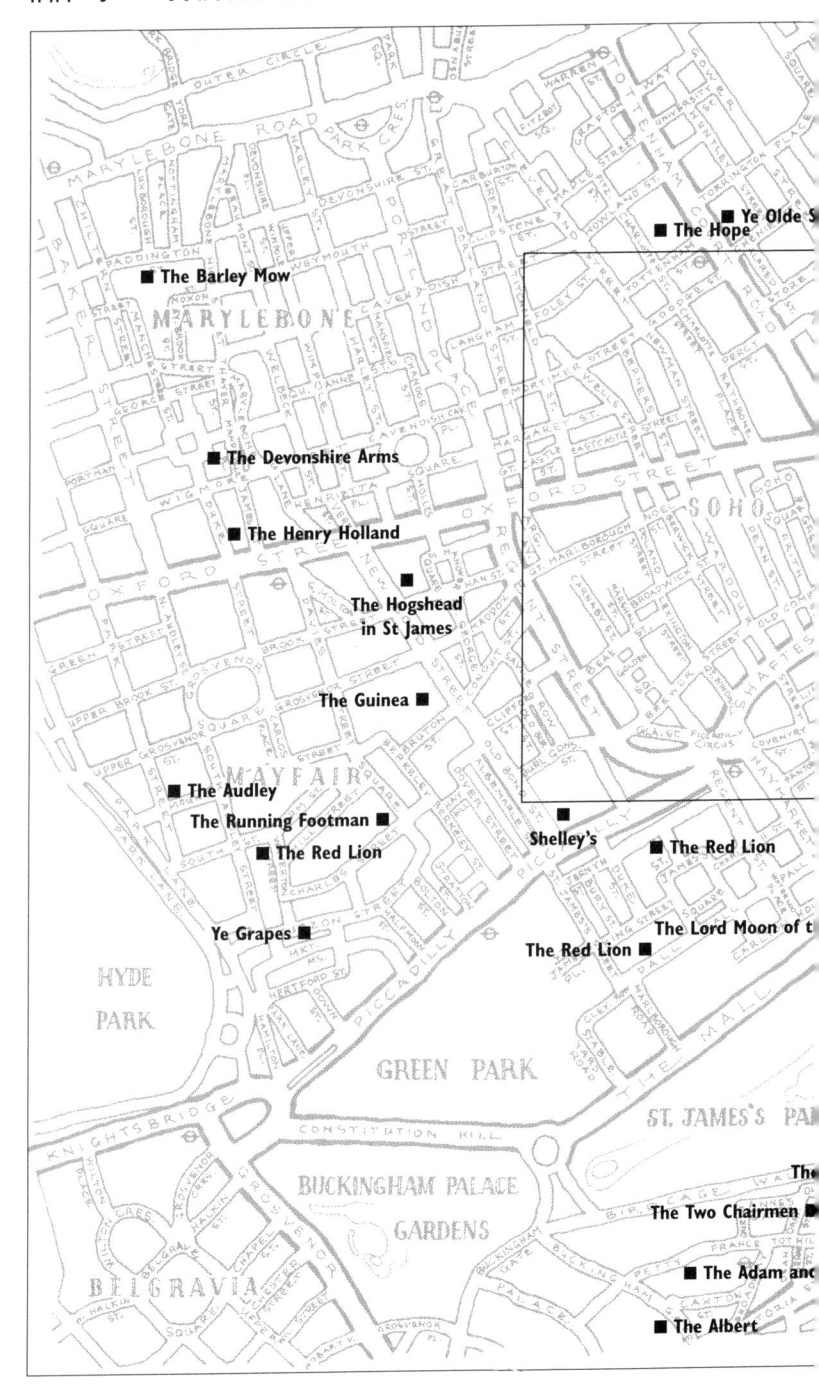

Central London • MAP 3

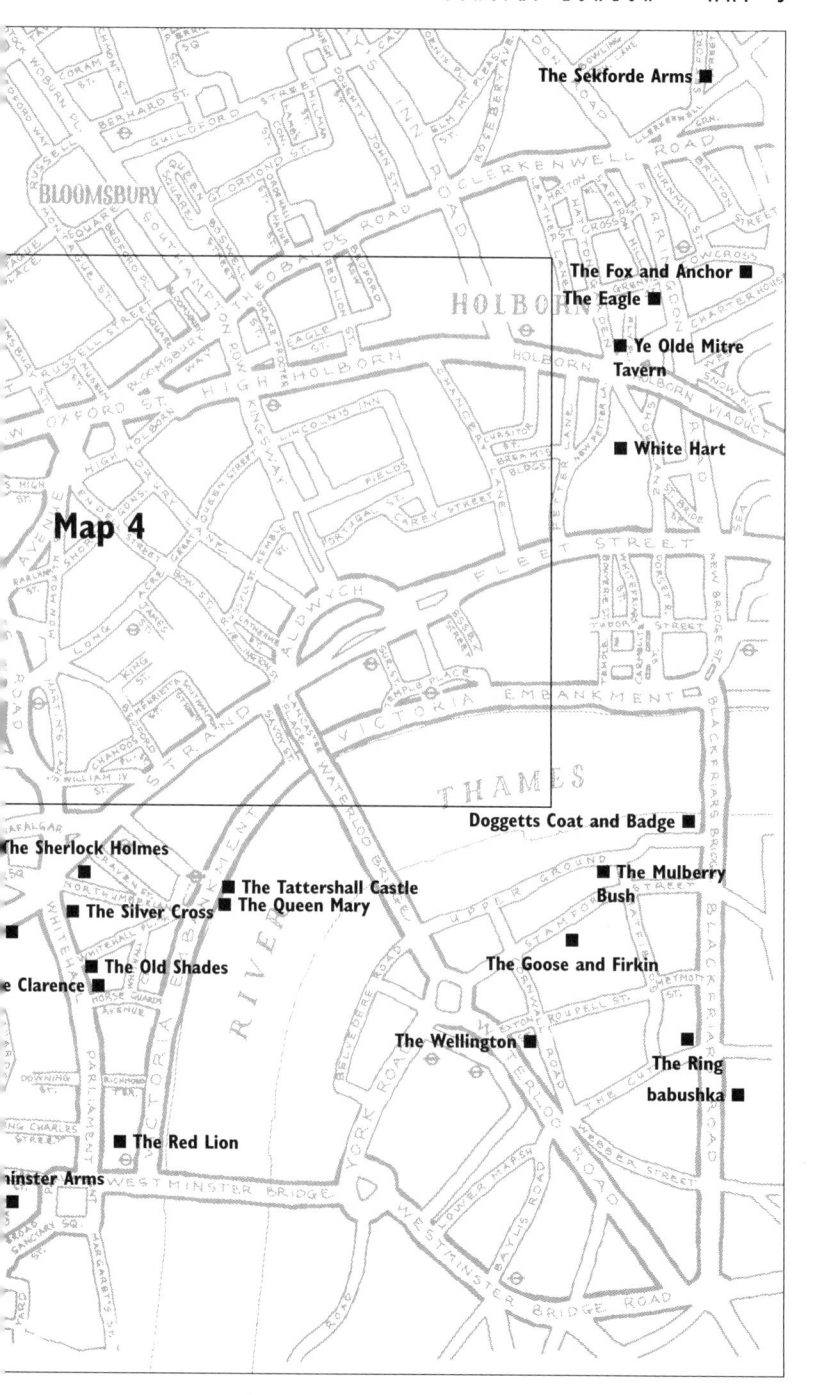

MAP 4 • The West End

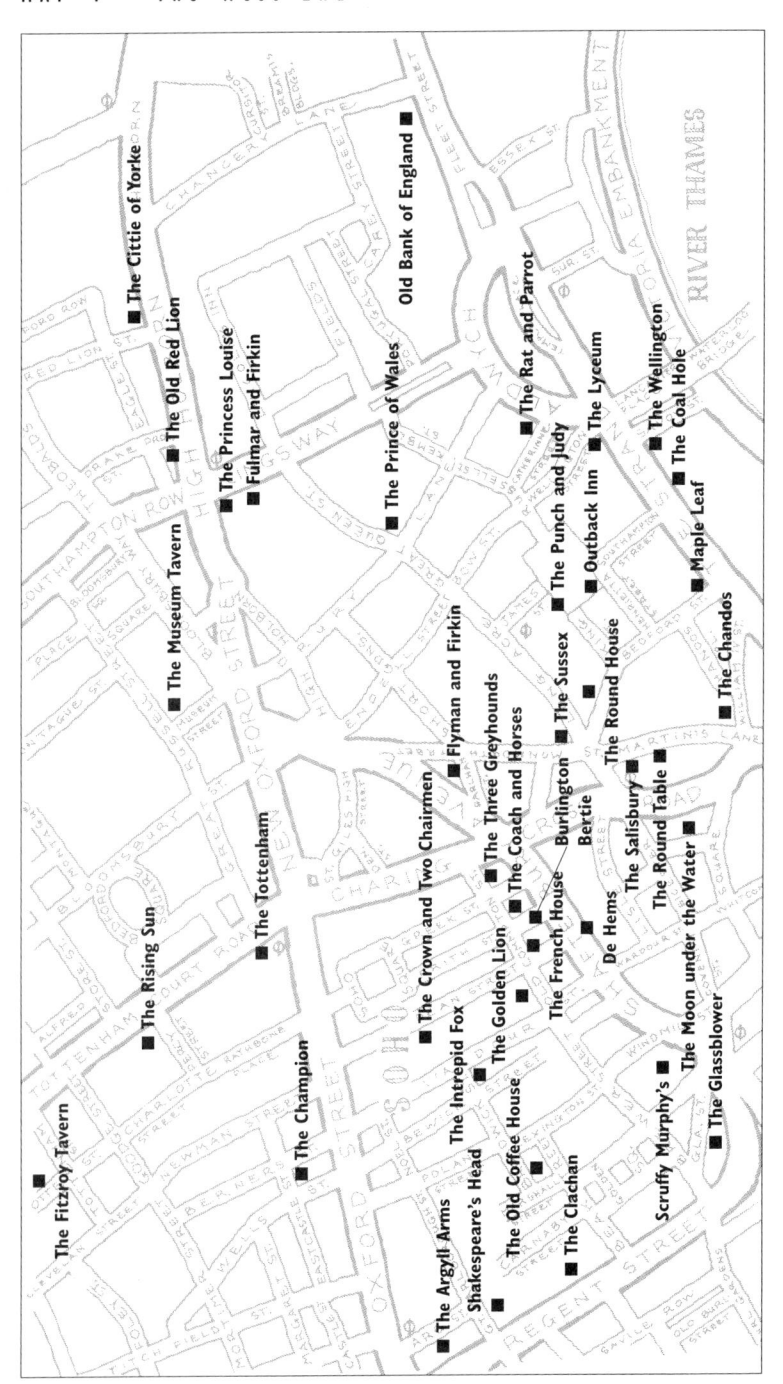

14

The City • MAP 5

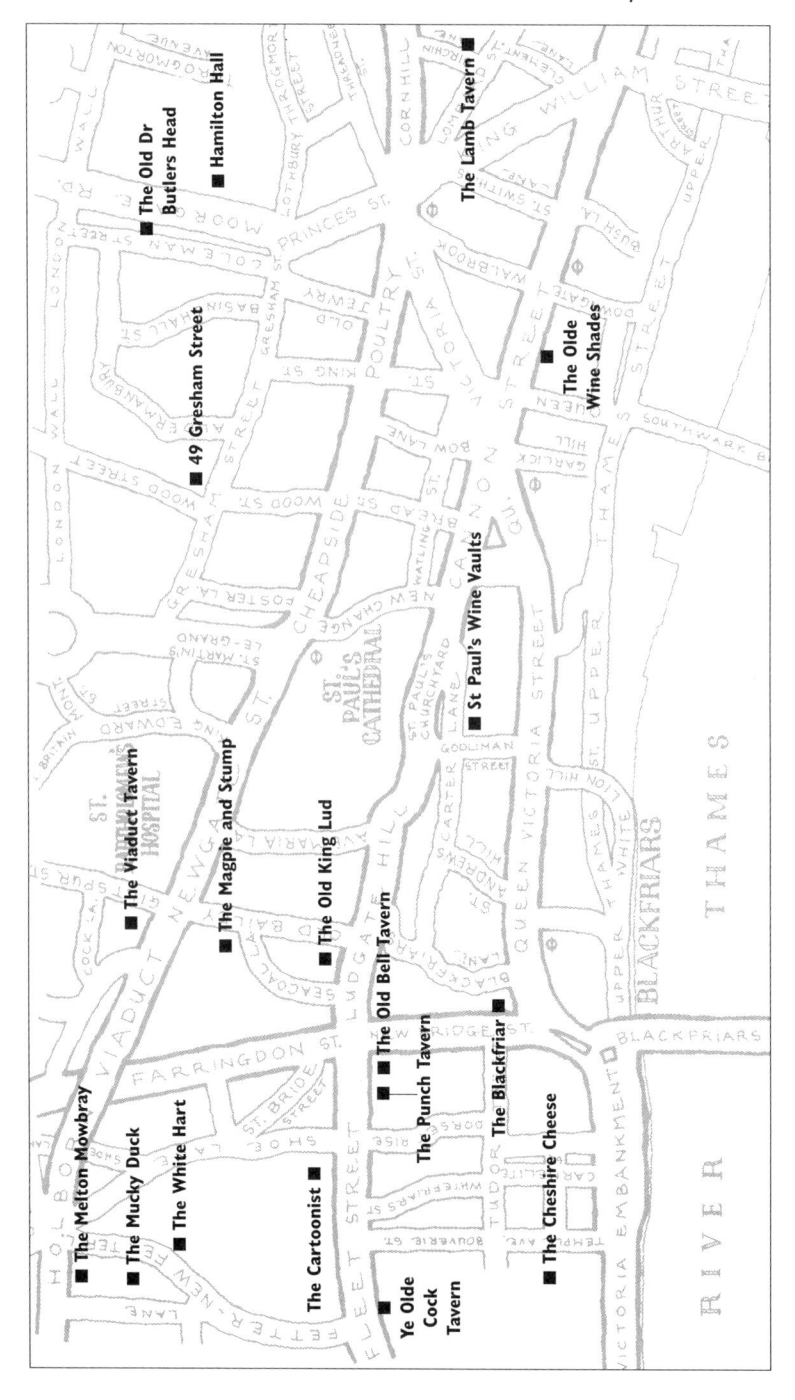

· THE ADAM AND EVE ·

81 Petty France, SW1   **222 4575**

'If you haven't been to this little pub lately it may surprise you'

Petty France is where you go to change your passport. It's all quicker these days but there is still time to kill and forms to fill so what we want here is some positive thinking. Think of the holiday ahead. Think of the Adam and Eve waiting for you just along the street.

If you haven't been to this little pub lately it may surprise you. It has had a complete personality change. It used to be a fair to middling lager house. Then the new owners, Scottish and Newcastle, closed it for six weeks, and when it reopened, hey presto it was one of their new real ale houses, bare boards, quick pies with flaky pastry lids and all.

It has eight cask beers on the hand pumps and these now account for 60 per cent of its turnover. New regulars are settling in nicely.

Open
All Week
Hours
11.00–23.00
(12.00–15.00 Sun)
Closed Christmas Day, Boxing Day
Credit Cards
Visa, Access
Bar Food Available
11.00–22.00
(12.00–14.00 Sun)
Special Features
Wheelchair Access
Private Room seats 15
Beers Available
Theakston, Courage Best, Courage Directors, Holsten, Foster's
Nearest Tube Station
St James's Park

· THE ALBERT ·

52 Victoria Street, SW1   **222 5577**

'A welcome respite from sore feet and history'

When it comes to Victorian values let me commend to you the Albert. It is the very model of a high-Victorian public house. No larking about here, sir, if you please.

The Albert started out in 1845 as the Bluecoat Boy, a modest sort of pub, but slummy, dissolute Victoria was in the grip of a major redevelopment, to whit, the building of Victoria Street and everyone was straightening their ties and adjusting their clothing. Was the Bluecoat Boy good enough for the grand new mansion flats? It seems not. The Artillery Brewery rebuilt it and when it reopened in 1862 it was the Albert we see today, the very essence of middle-class respectability.

Today, gleaming new towers attempt to dwarf the Albert. It remains steadfastly undwarfed. With its fine engraved windows, removed and stored during the war, its rich decorations, its gleaming bar and noble staircase, it is in splendid form.

It needs a staff of 25 to keep the Albert running smoothly, more in the summer. There is quick food in the bar and a busy carvery on the first floor. Tourists with much to see in the neighbourhood find here a welcome respite from sore feet and history.

This is New Scotland Yard's local and MPs use it a lot. With the Houses of Parliament just up the street, they appre-

Open
All week
Hours
11.00–23.00
(12.00–22.30 Sun)
Credit Cards
All major cards accepted
Food Available
Bar 11.00–22.30
Carvery 12.00–22.00, fixed-price 3 courses, coffe and service £13.95
Special Features
Wheelchair Access (bar only, not lavatory)
Private room seats 24
Beers Available
Theakston Best Bitter, Theakston XB, Ruddles, Webster's, John Smith's, Wadworth, Guinness, Holsten, Budweiser, Foster's, Miller
Nearest Tube Station
St James's Park

ciate the division bell in the restaurant and, after a drink or two, may well start to think that one day their picture may join the portraits of Prime Ministers, from the Marquis of Salisbury to John Major, lining the broad staircase. Mrs Thatcher unveiled her portrait herself.

The pub sign in Victoria Street shows the young Prince Consort in pensive mood, holding a rose. The route has been changed now, but when the Queen met heads of state at Victoria Station she would often point it out to her guests as they bowled along Victoria Street in the state landau. Albert was her great-great-grandfather.

·THE ALBION·

10 Thornhill Road, N1   **607 7450**

'Worth any number of detours'

Nice old Thornhill Road with its Georgian houses and little shops is a bit bothered by all the cars, but then just about everyone in this agreeable bit of Islington has one, if not two, and they spend a lot of time squeezing past this graceful ivy-covered coaching inn that belongs to a quieter, more rural time. People drinking at the oak tables in front of the pub whenever it's not actually raining take no notice.

If going to the Albion means a detour then make it, though of course if you do you will be increasing the traffic in Thornhill Road. It is an elegant, prosperous pub. The roomy bar has a restaurant area with an open fire in winter and smaller panelled rooms behind, one for non-smokers. Hearty home-cooked lunches and suppers emerge from a busy kitchen. Beware fattening old-fashioned puddings covered in custard.

The star turn at the Albion, though, is the beer garden at the back – big, quiet and extraordinarily pleasant in the summer with its trellis and roses and picnic tables. This really is worth any number of detours.

Open
All Week
Hours
11.00–23.00
(12.00–22.30 Sun)
Credit Cards
All major cards accepted
Bar Food Available
12.00–21.30
(12.00–22.30 Sun)
Special Features
No-smoking Area
Wheelchair Access (including lavatory)
Beer Garden seats 180
Beers Available
Theakston Best, Theakston XB, John Smith's Bitter, Carlesberg, Holsten, Molsen, Becks, Budweiser, Foster's
Nearest Tube Stations
Angel, Highbury and Islington

·THE ALEXANDRA·

33 Wimbledon Hill Road, SW19   **0181-947 7691**

'An institution in the busy town centre of Wimbledon'

The Alex is one of Young's flagships – number one for liquor sales, they say in ringing tones. My man in Wimbledon is not surprised.

He writes: 'The Alex is an institution in Wimbledon, a busy town centre pub, classically Victorian and over recent years it has been very carefully refurbished. The old public

Open
All Week
Hours
11.00–23.00
(12.00–22.30 Sun)
Wine bar licensed till 1.00 am Fri and Sat
Credit Cards
All major cards accepted

**Bar and Restaurant
Food Available**
12.00–15.00 and
19.00–22.00

Special Features
No-smoking Area
Wheelchair Access
(but not lavatory)
Tables outside seat 85

Beers Available
Michelob, Rolling Rock,
Castle Lager, Peroni, all
Young's, Budwar,
Budweiser, Becks,
Molson, Labatt

Nearest Tube Station
Wimbledon

bar, for instance, is the Wine and Ale Bar now, all beams and brickwork and huge barrels to put plates and glasses on, an open log fire spit-roasting beef and turkey and a staircase leading to the new roof garden where you may well encounter Wimbledon's first rooftop marquee.

'A no-smoking bar leads to the Green Bar, now predominantly red actually. Go past the counter where pub meals are served and you are in the wine bar, Young's first, where you can eat and drink till 1.00 am on Friday and Saturday nights.

'It is, as it always was, a place where people do business, do lunch, recover from shopping. The station is only a few minutes' walk away and some regularly break their journeys to the farther-flung outposts of Network Southeast for a little something at the Alex. They can always catch the next train. Or the one after that...'

· THE ALMA TAVERN ·

Open
All Week

Hours
11.00–23.00
(12.00–22.30 Sun)

Credit Cards
All major cards
accepted

Food Available
Restaurant
12.00–15.00 and
19.00–21.30
(12.00–14.30 and
19.00–22.00 Sun)

Special Features
Wheelchair Access
Private Room seats 70

Beers Available
Young's Bitter, Young's
London Pride,
Castlemaine, Oatmeal
Stout, Beamish, Stella
Artois

Nearest BR Station
Wandsworth Town

499 York Road, SW18   0181-870 2537
'Hôtel de la gare'

Every Victorian schoolboy knew what the Alma was. Alma, battle of; famous victory; Crimean War, 1854. The Alma Tavern was built 12 years later, a hotel at first but now a much admired Victorian pub.

It stands directly opposite Wandsworth Town station, and after victory or defeat at Twickers rugger buggers bound for Waterloo see the Alma's elegant Frenchified dome and pour off the train and straight into the bar. They tend to get home a little later than intended.

The Alma is a prosperous pub faced by shiny glazed tiles, bright green, and inside there are lovely painted mirrors, gold mosaic medallions, a classical plaster frieze and a fine mahogany staircase leading out of the bar. They have all been scrupulously restored. In winter a fire blazes in the art deco fireplace, and a handsome 1920s range heats the separate dining room.

There are morning papers on the bar, a huge baker's dough table and a little French cash kiosk in the dining room. They cultivate Frenchness at the Alma, sell croques monsieur and croques madame, also a lot of wine. Indeed they have now taken to printing 'hôtel de la gare' on the menus. 'Tongue in cheek,' says Charles Gotto, the licensee.

The Alma has become a big rugger pub, and rugby nights are terrific occasions there. Doesn't the pub fear for the health of its painted mirrors? 'Why?' says rugger fan Gotto. 'They are as good as gold.'

· THE ANCHOR, BANKSIDE ·

34 Park Street, SE1 **407 1577**

'Not a pub you can leave quietly'

Bankside has certainly gone up in the world. In Shakespeare's day it was all slums and stews but look at it now, a riverside walk, the new Globe Theatre and a famous old inn, immaculate in every particular.

Dr Johnson often supped here with his good friend Mrs Thrale, whose husband owned it and the brewery next door. It became a sort of Groucho Club with Oliver Goldsmith, David Garrick and Edmund Burke holding court.

Today's Anchor cannot always offer conversation on quite such a level but it is a fine old pub with five bars, a minstrels' gallery, a private 18th-century dining room, a new riverside terrace with serried ranks of picnic tables, a garden terrace, a barbecue and a most superior restaurant. Sam Wanamaker often ate here when his wonderful Globe was taking shape nearby. He always had table 7, the one in the window.

It is not a pub you can leave quietly. In the creaking Olympics the Anchor's floorboards would take gold.

Open
All week

Hours
11.00–23.00
(12.00–22.30 Sun)
Closed Christmas Day, Boxing Day, New Year's Day

Credit Cards
All major cards accepted

Food Available
Bar 11.30–15.00 and 17.30–21.00
Restaurant 12.00–14.30 and 18.00–21.30

Special Features
Wheelchair Access (but not lavatory)
Beer Garden seats 200
Private Room seats 50

Beers Available
Anchor Bitter, John Smith's, Courage Directors, Courage Best, Adnams, Ruddles County, Kronenbourg, Foster's, Budweiser, Old Speckled Hen

Nearest Tube Station
London Bridge

· THE ANGEL ·

101 Bermondsey Wall East, SE16 **237 3608**

'Haunt of pirates, smugglers, press-gangs, bawds'

There has been an inn here in Rotherhithe, built on piles at the water's edge, since the 17th century, perhaps much earlier, always in the thick of things, around it a warren of tenements, workshops, boatyards, and general riverside carrying-on.

There were at least four little bars on the ground floor, the haunt of sailors, pirates, smugglers, press gangs, bawds, I suppose bawds, there were always bawds. Pepys knew it well; it appears in his diaries. Judge Jefferies, they say, watched the hangings on Execution Dock from the balcony. Sometimes he watched the hangings in one pub, sometimes in another, but, disagreeable to the last, he appears to have chosen the Angel to haunt. There is still a balcony, very narrow. Standing room only, even for hanging judges.

The Angel has been rebuilt a few times in its day, but it has done well to survive at all what with hard times and the Blitz and sundry disasters. In more recent years it was a busy

Open
All Week

Hours
11.00–15.00 and 17.30–23.00
(12.30–15.00 and 19.00–22.30 Sun)
Closed Christmas Day, Boxing Day

Credit Cards
All major cards accepted

Food Available
Bar 12.00–14.00
Restaurant 12.00–13.45 and 19.00–21.45
(19.00–21.45 Sat; 12.00–13.45 Sun)

Special Features
Private Room seats 50

Beers Available
Courage Best Bitter, Courage Directors, Webster's, Adnams, Foster's, Kronenbourg, Beamish, Guinness

Nearest Tube Station
Rotherhithe

and popular dockers' pub, but they too have gone now and the Angel looks a bit lonely in its historic place on the river bank.

But the bar is where old Bermondsey and Rotherhithe residents meet the new incomers and start to mingle, and there is a serious restaurant upstairs with an ambitious menu, venerable and formally dressed waiters and a fine view of Tower Bridge. This attracts business lunchers from the City, not far off, and is open in the evening too.

Almost at the front door is an outcropping of ruin in the centre of a field and a notice telling us that this is the remains of Edward III's moated manor house, begun in 1353. Edward III was A Good Thing, 'the greatest warrior king in Christendom' in Antonia Fraser's view. He had nothing at all to do with the Angel Tavern.

· THE ANGLESEA ARMS ·

Open
All Week

Hours
11.00–15.00 and 17.00–23.00 (12.00–22.30 Sun) Closed Christmas Day, Boxing Day

Credit Cards
Visa, Access accepted

Bar Food Available
11.00–15.00

Special Features
Wheelchair Access
Beer Garden

Beers Available
Adnams, Harveys, Boddingtons, Brakspear, Dorset IPA, London Pride, Young's, Flower's Original, Grolsch, Red Stripe, Foster's, Guinness, Murphy's

Nearest Tube Stations
South Kensington, Gloucester Road

15 Selwood Terrace, SW7   **373 7960**

'Lady Joseph's pub'

When, not long ago, Lady Joseph died the Anglesea Arms lost the best possible owner. It had been a personal gift to her from her husband, Sir Maxwell Joseph, chairman of Grand Met. She loved it and would have no changes made.

It passed to her family which, happily, sees things as she did, so the Anglesea remains wonderfully reassuring with its armchairs and buttoned leather settles, its deeply polished woodwork, its pictures and shaded lights. Everything is substantial, nothing too smart, on all sides evidence of tender loving care. There are no juke boxes, no fruit machines, no television. The hours are unchanged too, time called at 3.00 pm so that the bar gets a clean and a rest in the afternoon.

The Anglesea is an early-Victorian free house, an integral part of a prosperous South Kensington terrace. There is a large saloon bar and a smaller bar down some steps, known as the cubby, very cosy with a fire in winter. Then there is a stretch of forecourt that some would say was the jewel in its crown. It is a hugely popular place to drink in the summer.

The Anglesea, immaculately run by Pat and Mary Timmons, was the *Evening Standard* Pub of the Year in 1988.

· THE ANTELOPE ·

22 Eaton Terrace, SW1   **730 7781**

'Deeply traditional'

The residents of Eaton Terrace are twice blessed. They live in Eaton Terrace and they have the Antelope on their doorsteps.

It is a charming old pub, gentlemanly and understated. It doesn't want to swank but there was an inn on the site for, oh, ages, and the present building goes back to at least 1780, which means that modern Belgravia grew up around it.

When the houses arrived the Antelope obligingly provided two front doors, one for the grander household staff led by the butler, the other for lowlier persons. Once inside, partitions kept them decently apart. There are still the same number of front doors. Fewer butlers, though.

The Antelope is deeply traditional. One tradition is good plain cooking. Roast beef, home cooked, is on the menu every day. Fanny Craddock said its little panelled restaurant recaptured the flavour of the old chop-house, and that is still the aim.

Some things change. For many years customers stood outside on the pavement every summer, enjoying a drink in the sun. There were complaints and they have to stay inside now. Shame.

Open
All Week
Hours
11.00–23.00
(12.00–15.00 and
19.00–22.30 Sun)
Credit Cards
All major cards accepted
Bar and Restaurant Food Available
12.00–15.00
Special Features
Wheelchair Access
(but not lavatory)
Private Room seats 40
Beers Available
6 types of real ale,
Tetley, Nicholson's,
Adnams, Castlemaine,
Wadsworth 6X, Burton
IPA, plus a guest
Nearest Tube Station
Sloane Square

· THE ARCHERY TAVERN ·

4 Bathurst Street, W2   **402 4916**

'Once in a while an archer might come in'

The Archery Tavern is a pretty country pub tucked away behind Bayswater Road, the archer's pub, rooted in the great days. It was built in 1839 on what used to be Thomas Waring's archery range and he is the fine chap drawing his bow on the inn sign. Well he was a famous archer in his day, a celeb.

Waring is still there but I'm sorry to say he is just about the only archer who is. It is not that there aren't any archers these days. There are archery clubs all round London; in fact, the London Archers are just across the park. They shoot three or four times a week on a strip of land attached to Kensington Palace. But, well, let's face it, there are any number of much nearer pubs. The London Archers go to them.

So the Archery Tavern has to depend on drinkers with other interests, and it has no problem there. People love it. It is so genuinely old-fashioned and it has such interesting

Open
All Week
Hours
11.00–23.00
(12.00–22.30 Sun)
Closed Christmas Day
Credit Cards
Access, Visa, AmEx,
Diner's Club
Bar Food Available
11.00–23.00
Special Features
Tables outside seat 30
Beers Available
Vice Beer, Tanglefoot,
Badger's Best,
Wadworth, Blackadder,
Eagle, Hoffbrau lagers
Nearest Tube Station
Lancaster Gate

beers. Badger. Tanglefoot. Blackadder. There's champagne at £2.95 a glass and oysters to go with it in season.

Still the Archery Tavern stays loyal to the *idea* of archery. It keeps its name, Thomas Waring goes on drawing his bow and there are pictures of old archery occasions all over the walls. And once in a while, an archer might come in.

·THE ARGYLL ARMS·

18 Argyll Street, W1   734 6117

'Victoria Regina!'

Open
Mon–Sat

Hours
11.00–23.00

Credit Cards
All major cards accepted

Bar Food Available
11.30–19.30;
hot salt-beef sandwiches all day

Special Features
No-smoking Area
Wheelchair Access (but not lavatory)
Private Room seats 60

Beers Available
Tetley, Nicholson's Best, Wadworth 6X, Pedigree, Greene King IPA, regular guests, Wells Bombardier Best, Everards Tiger Best

Nearest Tube Station
Oxford Circus

Round the corner from Oxford Circus, actually squashed up against the side of the Underground station, is this spectacular Victorian pub. It gets packed at lunchtime. It is busy in the afternoon. You can't move in the evening. The Victorians knew about pubs all right.

This Argyll is the business. First of all it looks so great from the front, all that decoration, all that show, so of course you go in and Victoria Regina! You are in a glittering mirrored corridor with etched-glass partitions opening on to small numbered bars. Straight ahead is the big saloon bar, bags of space, bags of swank, and behind that is the dining room, every room full of people talking.

The small bars at the front are lovely. They give you your own bit of counter and, more important, your own space. People liked that in 1868 and they like it now, but all over London grand Victorian pubs like this one have had the partitions they were born with taken away.

They haven't done it at the Argyll, so cheers for it and back to our tour. Up the massive mahogany staircase and you are in another big bar, Victorian pastiche up here, recently done but in the spirit of things, comfortable, plush with lamps and low partitions and a fine view of the London Palladium just across the road. That is where Argyll House stood, the Duke of Argyll's London home, a great mansion that came down in the 1860s. The original Argyll Arms came down too and this one went up in its place.

Nicholson's get high marks for keeping it in such sparkling nick. They always seem to be fitting new carpets, there is hidden air conditioning at work, and they recently spent £50,000 on the loos.

You might suppose a pub so near Oxford Circus to be on the front line, particularly on Saturday nights, but there is very little trouble. Mike Tayara, the landlord, has a dress code. He asks for 'an acceptable standard of dress' and puts the general absence of aggro, even on Saturday nights, down to this. Others put it down to the large man on the door.

· THE AUDLEY ·

41 Mount Street, W1   **499 1843**

'Heart of Mayfair'

Pubs do not come grander than the Audley. Mount Street, the heart of Mayfair, Berkeley Square at one end, Park Lane at the other. Even Lady Bracknell might have approved of that.

We have the first Duke of Westminster to thank for it. In the early 1880s he was having Mount Street rebuilt and his architects included drawings for a large glitzy public house. He sent them right back, giving them clearly to understand that a gin palace was not what he had in mind. So the Audley was built in red brick and pink terracotta, neo-French Renaissance like the rest of the street. In the opinion of the Duke this would not offend the sensibilities of the most fastidious gentleman's gentleman.

It is, indeed, very imposing, and when the British Tourist Board wanted a pub for its London brochure the Audley was the one it chose.

Like all pubs of its generation the Audley mirrored the class divisions of the world outside. It was cut up into a parish of separate bars, each with its own social nuances. Mahogany and etched-glass partitions hid each group of customers from each other, while narrow hinged screens hid customers from staff.

The screens and partitions have long gone, of course. It is one big open bar now and we can see, as the first customers could not, all of the superb plaster ceiling and the whole of the bar itself, and very splendid it is. The original chandeliers have survived, so have the clocks, so has its general air of being rather a cut above, which, indeed, while in the Audley, we all are.

It is the perfect pub to take oversees visitors. It appears on the schedules of all up-market tours and sometimes in the summer it fills up with lively and appreciative American ladies. At other times Japanese, French or German groups take over. The panelled dining room upstairs is a great attraction for them all. You eat formally and substantially here in the well-known English manner – several courses, Stilton, port. The roast beef always goes well, as does the distinctly superior fish with chips.

Open
All Week

Hours
11.00–23.00
(12.00–15.00 and
19.00–22.30 Sun)
Closed Boxing Day

Credit Cards
All major cards accepted

Food Available
Bar 11.00–21.30
Restaurant
12.00–15.00 (Sun–Fri)
and 17.30–21.30
(Mon–Sat)

Special Features
Wheelchair Access
Tables outside seat 30
Private Room seats 40

Beers Available
Courage, John Smith's, Holsten, Kronenbourg, Miller, Budweiser

Nearest Tube Stations
Green Park,
Marble Arch

· THE AUSTRALIAN ·

29 Milner Street, SW3 **589 6027**

'A golden age'

Open
All Week
Hours
11.00–23.00
(12.00–22.30 Sun)
Credit Cards
All major cards except AmEx and Diner's Club
Food Available
Bar 12.00–14.30
(12.00–15.00 Sat);
traditional Sunday lunch £5.95
Special Features
Wheelchair Access (but not lavatory)
Beers Available
Tetley, Nicholson's, Wadworth, Brakspear, Adnams, Lowenbrau, Carlsberg, Castlemaine
Nearest Tube Stations
Knightsbridge, Sloane Square

Brief cricketing interlude... In 1878 Australia, on its second tour, played two matches on the smart new cricket pitch on Prince's Green, now occupied by Lennox Gardens. The first was against the Gentlemen of England. All three Grace Brothers turned out for the Gentlemen, who won by an innings and one run. The Australians then played the Players of England. The match was unfinished.

It was a golden age. Dr Grace was in his prime, everyone was playing for the fun of it, England nearly always won, and Australian cricketers far from home found a refreshment stop much to their liking in the wide, leafy street that led directly to the cricket ground.

The pub they adopted later renamed itself the Australian, and successive licensees have filled the place with cricketing memorabilia. There are early banana-shaped cricket bats, antique cricket balls, a replica of the urn in which the ashes are kept, cigarette cards, an ancient box of Blakey's Cricket Spikes, a terrific carved figure of Don Bradman. Photographs of great cricketers are everywhere.

It is a fine-looking pub built with the rest of Milner Street in the 1850s, a three-storey building covered in Virginia creeper with well-used tables on the pavement. It had an expensive refurbishment recently and is now a lot less Spartan than in days of old.

It is a serious beer pub with five regular ales, but Pimms is a popular local drink and they get through a lot of champagne. Cricket remains an abiding interest, and the food is substantial and very English. You used to be able to eat outside but neighbours objected, sigh. So in came the tables. There are still benches outside. You can sit on them until 9.00pm.

· BABUSHKA ·

173 Blackfriars Road, SE1 **928 3693**

'Na zdorovye, as they say in Blackfriars Road'

Open
All Week
Hours
12.00–23.00 Mon–Wed;
12.00–24.00 Thur–Fri;
20.00–24.00 Sat
(19.00–22.30 Sun)
Credit Cards
All major cards except Diner's Club

The Old King's Head closed down a couple of years ago having lived out its natural life. It lay empty for a while. Then it reopened, a pub of a totally different kind. It was starting all over again.

The assembly of small bars had become one huge one, stripped down to its bricks and girders with Dali-esque murals replacing wallpaper, and a new name had emerged during a long night on the vodka. A babushka is Russian for grandmother. Few grandmothers, Russian or otherwise, have been seen there since.

The pub now attracts the young and hip, great numbers of which are to be spotted in Blackfriars Road making for the Ministry of Sound. The new pub has become an essential pit stop for them as it is for City moneymen getting through the Bollinger.

It is now two years old and doing very well indeed. The food, of course, is Mod Med, speedy and good.

The staff is itself hip and young. Boys and girls alike wear black, slick back their hair and set the scene, dishing out free pizza, moving to the grand piano in the corner when they've had enough of salsa, country and western, soul, hip-hop and jazz. There's a big demand for the cask ales, a choice of 50 flavoured vodkas and cocktails expertly produced by multi-gifted barmen who won't say what goes into the KGB. Na zdorovye, as they say in Blackfriars Road.

Bar Food Available
12.00–21.00 Mon–Thur;
12.00–16.00 Fri
(12.00–15.00 Sun)

Special Features
Wheelchair Access
Beer Garden seats 150

Beers Available
London Pride, Adnams Broadside, Bass, Caffrey's, Grolsch, Carling, Tennent's Extra, Staropramen, Guinness

Nearest Tube Station
Waterloo

· THE BACKPACKER ·

126 York Way, N1

'Legless Sundays'

This small pub in the grotty bit behind King's Cross station was first a local called the City of York, then a gay pub called Traffic. It is now the Backpacker, a pub famed among young Oz and Kiwi world travellers.

It keeps what other pubs may think eccentric hours, but the Backpacker knows its customers. It stays shut all week then opens with a bang on Friday night and stays open until 2.00am. It does the same on Saturday and reels on to legless Sundays.

In these three days ravenous young boozers demolish a phenomenal number of tinnies. Lager is king but there's a big run on green stuff, a Backpacker concoction of celebrated potency. It is not for contemplatives. Fortissimo is one word that comes to mind. Plastered, hammered, shickered, rat-arsed and blind are some more.

On Sunday mornings the action switches to Bagleys, an empty warehouse nearby known as the Church because it only opens on Sundays. Tickets and coupons for lager at the door, entry is Ozzies and Kiwis first, Poms last. But once inside everyone equally slams it back from 12 till 3.30 with an Oz stand-up comic, strippers, and the sort of party games you don't get in nursery school. Then, for the ones still standing, it's back to the Backpacker where the party goes on until midnight.

Open
Fri–Sun

Hours
20.00–02.00 Fri–Sat;
(Sun: The Church
12.00–15.30,
pub 15.30–24.00)

Beers Available
Australian canned lager

Nearest Tube Stations
King's Cross, Kentish Town

·THE BARLEY MOW·

8 Dorset Street, W1   **935 7318**

'The Beatles sometimes popped in'

Open
Mon–Sat
(Sat often closed
for private parties)

Hours
11.00–23.00

Credit Cards
All major cards
accepted

Bar Food Available
12.00–15.30

Special Features
Wheelchair Access

Beers Available
Tetley, Brakspear,
Marston's Pedigree,
Wadworth 6X, Adnams.

Nearest Tube Station
Baker Street

The Barley Mow must sometimes miss the old days, lowing herds winding slowly o'er the lea and so on. It still looks every inch the farmers' pub it used to be.

It is full of reminders of days gone by. Brass price lists are still countersunk in the bar counter, so worn you can hardly read them, which is as well as the prices are a hundred years out of date, and there is still an old brass tap behind the bar labelled Old Tom. It was for gin. You brought your own jug and they filled it up.

Its strong card then was English country ales and it still is. It gives you a choice of six nowadays. The main relics of the past, though, are the two pine kiosks occupying the whole of the left-hand side of the bar. Each has its own bit of counter, a pair of facing benches and a door with a lock. They are pawnbroker booths. The idea was you slunk in with the family silver under your jacket, locked the door and did a deal. Then you had a drink and left.

Pawnbrokers stopped coming years ago but the booths were left, and now they are the most popular bit of the pub. People lucky enough to find a free one tend to stay there the rest of the evening.

In late 1967 the Beatles opened their new Apple boutique round the corner in Baker Street and they sometimes popped into the Barley Mow. Well, you can see it was their sort of pub, plain, old-fashioned, unflash and, with teeny boppers out there in force, I bet the privacy of those nice old booths went down well.

·THE BARLEY MOW·

Narrow Street, E14   **265 8931**

'New roles for dockmaster and customs house'

Open
All Week

Hours
11.00–23.00
(12.00–15.00 and
19.00–22.30 Sun)

Credit Cards
All major cards, except
Diner's Club

Food Available
Bar 12.00–14.30 and
18.30–21.00
Restaurant
12.00–15.00 and
18.30–21.00
(12.00–14.15 and
19.00–20.30 Sun)

In the days when canals served most of the country, the lock at the entrance to the Limehouse Basin was the way in from the Thames to the whole system. The basin had 10 acres of water, 4 acres of quays and wharfs and the river lock, and the dockmaster controlled it all from the big customs house on the river bank.

The Limehouse Basin is a marina now and dockmaster and customs house both have new names and new roles. The dockmaster has become the harbourmaster, with new offices in the dock. The customs house has become the Barley Mow.

This is a dramatic turn of events for any building, particularly one with such an official, not to say bossy, past. It has to be said, though, that the customs house makes a surprisingly good pub.

It is a listed building – 'red brick, domestic, early 18th-century style with rusticated stucco quoins' is how the list describes it – so when Taylor Walker took it over in the late 1980s it couldn't be altered too much. Still, it provides an extra-large bar, a sizeable restaurant, a big function room upstairs and a huge riverside terrace, and there was a historic name waiting for it – the Barley Mow, after Taylor Walker's famous old brewery the Barley Mow. This was in Limehouse too. The dockmaster used to fly a blue flag if the dock was open, a red flag if it wasn't. His flagpole is still there, flagless at the moment but jaunty and optimistic as flagpoles are, and the views of the river are beyond price.

Serious carnivores may like to know that the steaks in the restaurant go from 5oz to a gargantuan 32oz. There's something for vegetarians too.

Special Features
Wheelchair Access
(disabled lavatory)
Tables outside
seat 100
Private Room seats 40
Beers Available
Tetley, Burtons,
Carlsberg,
Castlemaine,
Budweiser, Labatts
Nearest Docklands Station
Limehouse

· THE BEAUFOY ARMS ·

18 Lavender Hill, SW11   **228 9246**

'Every night is reggae night.'

This is the leading reggae pub and the sound is up to blast off.

From Lavender Hill comes this report: 'Big central bar has mixed crowd sitting and mingling. No room to move but who needs it? Dancing on the spot is normal way to appreciate sounds from the wheels of steel. There's no live music here. Strictly for reggae lovers only with elements of dancehall, ragga and the safe side of jungle.

'Every night is reggae night but Thursday is Ragga Jungle Revival Night with Trevor Sax and you pay to get in, or at least the men do. Women still get in free. Friday night has Daddy Ernie of Choice FM and other well-known reggae DJs and Saturday is revival night with reggae from the '60s, '70s and '80s. This is Bob Marley time.

'There are exotic dancers during the day hence the large mirror at waist height on the platform.'

Exotic, you may have noticed, means they take their clothes off.

Open
All Week
Hours
11.00–23.00
(12.00–22.30 Sun)
Credit Cards
None
Bar Food Available
11.00–23.00
(12.00–22.30 Sun)
Special Features
Wheelchair Access
Beers Available
Tetley, Burton's.
Carlsberg,
Castlemaine,
Budweiser
Nearest BR Station
Clapham Junction

· THE BEEHIVE ·

Open
All Week

Hours
11.00–23.00
(12.00–22.30 Sun)

Credit Cards
All major cards except Diner's Club

Bar Food Available
All day

Special Features
No-smoking Area

Beers Available
Theakston, Directors, Youngers, Becks, Foster's, McEwans, Kronenbourg

Nearest Tube Station
Brixton

407–409 Brixton Road, SW9　　　　　**738 3643**

'It even switches off the music in its games machines'

The Beehive is a busy, well-run pub in the busiest bit of Brixton and it makes a bold claim. It is, it says, the only pub in Brixton with no music. No music of any kind. It even switches off the music in its games machines.

Its customers seem to like this. They also seem to like the big non-smoking bit, something all J D Wetherspoon pubs have. At any rate the turnover constantly increases. There was a shoeshop here before.

· THE BELL AND CROWN ·

Open
All Week

Hours
11.00–23.00
(12.00–22.30 Sun)

Credit Cards
AmEx, Access, Visa

Food Available
11.00–22.00
(12.00–18.00 Sun)

Special Features
No-smoking Area
Wheelchair Access
(but not lavatory)
Beer Garden seats 30
Private Room seats 40

Beers Available
Fuller's IPA, London Pride, ESB, Chiswick Special, Hock, Mr Harry

Nearest BR Station
Kew Bridge

72 Strand on the Green, W4　　　　**0181-994 4164**

'In the summer it comes into its own'

Strand on the Green wanders for half a mile along the river bank at Chiswick, with beech trees and weeping willows and lovely 18th-century houses. As if this wasn't enough, it has three of London's most attractive pubs.

If you walk along this riverside path starting at Kew Bridge you come to the Bell and Crown first, then the City Barge, then the Bull's Head. Meanwhile you will have passed houses in which John Zoffany chose to live and later Hugh Cudlip, Nancy Mitford, Margaret Kennedy, Goronwy Rees and Dylan Thomas. Most of them will have known at least one of these pubs. Dylan Thomas, of course, will have known them all.

The Bell and Crown is marginally the biggest, a well-appointed, comfortable old pub with an air of no expense spared. The polished central counter serves a number of separate drinking areas, one around a corner, one down a flight of stairs, one over there, and there is a spacious conservatory. It seems a bit cut off in winter but in the summer it comes into its own.

Indeed, the whole pub seems to turn towards the river when the sun shines. The conservatory now becomes part of the outdoors with a terrace beneath it, under a green awning, and beneath that a patio by the tow-path filled with picnic tables. If you can't get a seat in any of these places you can sit on the river wall. People do in great numbers.

·THE BLACK CAP·

171 Camden High Street, NW1   **485 1742**
'The London Palladium of late-night drag'

Every day of the week, sometimes twice on Sundays, stars of the gay pub circuit will be performing somewhere. Elaborately wigged, extravagantly gowned, tottering on the highest heels, these starry ladies are in great demand. Some sing, belting out standards like Ethel Merman but louder. Some mime to Shirley Bassey or k. d. lang but the top stars are the stand-up comics, formidable dames not to be crossed, their banter usually the extravagant insult, the attack direct.

They have strong personalities and a large following. Wherever they play – the White Swan in Commercial Road, the Two Brewers in Clapham High Street, the Royal Oak in Hammersmith, the Salmon and Compasses in Islington, the Gloucester in Greenwich, the Father Redap in Camberwell Green, the Royal Vauxhall Tavern in Kennington Lane, the Queens Arms in Lewisham – they get a welcome that would not disappoint Miss Bassey herself.

The Black Cap in Camden Town is the London Palladium of late-night drag. Years ago the ground floor of this Victorian pub had a public and a saloon bar, snugs and taprooms too, I shouldn't wonder. Now it has one long cabaret bar that opens at 9.00 pm and closes at 2.00 am, the music turned up to the threshold of pain. It is dimly lit and crowded, with a bar counter running most of its length, stopping to make room for a wider open space and a stage at the far end. The audience – mostly gay men, some gay women – pack the space in front of the stage as midnight approaches.

Upstairs is Shufflewicks Bar, a pleasant bar with unpublike hours during the week – 1.00 pm to 2.00 am. It has pub hours on Sunday, though, noon to 10.30 pm. It is named after Mrs Shufflewick, aka Rex Jameson, one of the great drag artists who often appeared downstairs. His LP A Drop of the Hard Stuff was recorded live at the Black Cap. He died at 58 in 1983. There is no one today to touch him.

Open
All Week
Hours
13.00–02.00 Mon–Thurs
13.00–03.00 Fri–Sat
(12.00–24.00 Sun)
Credit Cards
None
Bar Food Available
All opening hours
Special Features
Wheelchair Access
(but not lavatory)
Beers Available
Worthington, Grolsch, Tennent's Extra, Tennent's Pilsner, Carling Black Label, Staropramen
Nearest Tube Station
Camden Town

·THE BLACK LION·

2 South Black Lion Lane, W6   **0181-748 7056**
'Alas for skittles!'

Walk along the river from Hammersmith Bridge, first the Lower Mall and then the Upper, and you pass five very different and very interesting pubs. This is the fifth one that you will come to.

Open
All Week
Hours
11.00–23.00
(12.00–22.30 Sun)
Closed Christmas Day,
Boxing Day

Credit Cards
Visa, Mastercard

Bar Food Available
12.00–14.30 and
18.00–22.00

Special Features
Wheelchair Access
(but not lavatory)
Beer Garden seats 100
Private Room seats 44

Beers Available
Theakston, Courage
Best, Foster's,
Kronenbourg, Holsten
Export, Guinness,
Newcastle Brown Ale

Nearest Tube Stations
Ravenscourt Park,
Stamford Brook

The Black Lion appears in A P Herbert's The Water Gypsies, lightly disguised as the Black Swan, and is, like the others, old. Like the others it has lovely views of the river and provides a pleasant place to eat and drink outside. In the Black Lion's case it is a garden shaded by a massive chestnut tree even older, they say, than the pub.

But things can change even at the most historic old pub. For as long as anyone can remember the Black Lion had a skittle alley. This is where A P Herbert used to play. In his day there were still skittle alleys in at least 50 London pubs, but slowly, remorselessly the number dwindled. The Black Lion's alley, a particularly good one, was one of the few survivors, but it was well known and seemed safe enough. Alas for skittles! It too has now been scrapped, replaced, sadly, by a few extra tables. It wasn't making money, says the new manager, not a chap to beat about the bush.

What will the pub ghost make of this? There have been reports of a ghost at the Black Lion for a good 200 years, some quite recent. Down-to-earth Australian barmen heard it clumping round on the top floor, and the manager of the day told me he had actually seen it.

He did not mind ghosts, differing in this regard from Mr Francis Smith, an excise officer, who set out to investigate the Black Lion ghost in 1804. He laid in wait for it, his fusee primed and loaded. At midnight the phantom appeared and Mr Smith shot it. Beneath the apparition's shroud was found the dead body of Mr Thomas Milward, a bricklayer. The hauntings, for the moment, ceased.

·THE BLACKBIRD·

Open
All Week

Hours
11.00–23.00
(12.00–22.30 Sun)

Credit Cards
Visa, Mastercard

Food Available
14.00–21.00
(12.00–15.00 and
19.00–21.00 Sun)

Special Features
No-smoking Area
Wheelchair Access
(but not lavatory)

Beers Available
Chiswick, London Pride,
ESB, Heineken

Nearest Tube Station
Earls Court

209 Earls Court Road, SW5   **835 1855**

'No blackbird pies, I notice'

Customers of the Earls Court Road branch of Barclays Bank who were not paying attention got a surprise when they popped into their bank. It had turned into a pub.

Fuller, Smith and Turner, the Chiswick brewer, is doing this to banks. It has launched a new chain of Ale and Pie houses and has found redundant banks ideal for its purpose. Nat Wests in Fulham Road and Surbiton are now the Stargazey and the Denby Dale; the Martins in Tottenham Court Road has blossomed into the Jack Horner; and the old Bank of England in Fleet Street has become, you will never guess, the Old Bank of England. Your bank next.

To look at it now you would never guess that the Blackbird had ever been anything but a pub. The builders knew, though. They had a terrible job converting it. The walls were feet thick and reinforced. Down the stairs and their troubles redoubled. It took one man eight days to cut a reasonable opening between two vaults to make one decent-sized beer cellar. The kitchens are down here too and the manager's office. This is the old bank safe. There isn't a window, but he keeps the big steel door propped permanently open.

Upstairs in the banking hall, I beg your pardon, the saloon bar the original pillars are in place and the mahogany panelling, but the rest is a 1990s version of the 1890s, the golden age, say the designers, of pub interiors.

That is just the building. You may think that what it sells is the important thing, the Fuller's beer and the new pie-and-ale pies. The best seller pie-wise is the steak and ale pie, though the chicken and bacon pie is close behind. There are no blackbird pies, I notice.

· THE BLACKFRIAR ·

174 Queen Victoria Street, EC4   **236 5650**

'Jolly monks have the time of their lives'

The Blackfriar is a famous, much-photographed pub, an outstanding example of art nouveau and funny with it.

It is the wedge-shaped building opposite Blackfriars station, built in 1875 on the site of the old Dominican monastery you hear about and it is still a monastery of sorts. That must be the Abbot, hands folded over his tummy, beaming down over the front door while jolly junior monks exuberantly point the way in. Inside, in a treasurehouse of multicoloured marble, you find their brother monks having the time of their lives, drinking, singing, fishing, sleeping it off. Theirs, clearly, are the mock-serious wise saws. 'Wisdom Is Rare', 'Industry Is All', 'A Good Thing Is Soon Snatched Up'.

It is a leisurely pub with comfortable hours – 11.30 am to 11.00 pm, bar snacks lunchtime only. Office workers pop in for a drink on their way home so it has a busy time early in the evening, and on warm evenings a happy crowd in suits, collars and tie gathers on the pavement outside.

The Blackfriar doesn't open at all at weekends. As the monks say, industry is all.

Open
Mon–Fri

Hours
11.30–23.00
(11.30–22.00
Mon–Tue)
Closed Bank Holidays

Credit Cards
Visa, Access accepted

Bar Food Available
12.00–14.30

Special Features
Wheelchair Access
(but not lavatory)

Beers Available
Brakspear, Tetley,
Adnams, Wadworth,
Lowenbrau, Carlsberg,
Guinness, Labatts,
Molsen, Tennent's
Pilsner

Nearest Tube Station
Blackfriars

·THE BLENHEIM·

27 Cale Street, SW3 **349 0056**

'Famous victories'

Open
All Week
Hours
11.00–23.00
(12.00–22.30 Sun)
Closed Christmas Day
Credit Cards
All major cards accepted
Bar Food Available
11.00–23.00
Special Features
Wheelchair Access
(but not lavatory)
Tables outside seat 12
Private Room seats 35
Beers Available
Wadworth 6X, Badger, Tanglefoot, Hard Tackle, Hofbrau, Premium Export, Pilsner, Guinness
Nearest Tube Stations
Sloane Square, South Kensington

London seems to have been particularly taken with the Duke of Marlborough's distant exploits. So many Blenheim Closes, Crescents and Gardens. Eighteen Blenheim Roads, several pubs. Here is one built in 1824 and called the Blenheim 120 years after the famous victory.

This Blenheim is a handsome four-storey Georgian pub tucked away in a quiet back street and life has not been easy. The first floor has been a bar, a pool room, a Thai restaurant. It is now used for private parties. The back bar was a mortuary at one time and the great gale of 1987 did its best to make it one again, sending the chimney crashing through the skylight. The pub seemed to go into a serious decline after that and when its lease reverted to the Cadogan Estates in 1991 it closed down.

Two years later a local entrepreneur bought the lease and spent a lot of money putting it to rights. He made a good job of it but the business failed and the pub closed again.

Its latest chapter seems promising. Badger Inns has it now and Tony and Lynn O'Neill are running it. The place has a buoyant, cheerful air.

·THE BLENHEIM·

21 Loudoun Road, NW8 **328 5884**

'No beer'

Open
All Week
Hours
10.00–23.00 Mon
11.00–23.00 Tues–Sat
(12.00–22.30 Sun)
Credit Cards
AmEx, Visa, Mastercard, Switch
Restaurant Food Available
12.00–15.00 Tues–Sat
18.00–23.00 Mon–Sat
(17.30–22.30 Sun)
Special Features
Outside terrace seats 50
2 function rooms seat 20 and 30
Parking

The Blenheim in Loudoun Road is in an unusual situation for a pub. No beer. No beer on tap, that is, no draught beer. Lager in bottles it has. Beer in casks it has not. 'People round here,' says Marcus Leaver, indicating the elegant houses of St John's Wood, 'don't drink a lot of beer.'

Marcus Leaver, a young entrepreneur going places, took over the Blenheim in January 1995 and closed it down. It was a big good-looking old pub built in 1830 and Leaver had plans for it. He set about turning it into one of the most ambitious of the new born-again foodie pubs of London.

It took him five months. The Blenheim is a listed building, which means you can't do much to the outside but you can take out most of the inside, and this he did. It reopened last summer with hardly any of its original insides left. Instead there was a big restaurant filled with tables, a gleaming kitchen and a smallish bar counter busily keeping the tables supplied with drinks, also anyone who might just look in, as one does in a pub.

Some still do, but mostly people go to the Blenheim to eat and a meal for two can cost £50 including wine. Wine is what the Blenheim sells most of. Its old beer cellar is full of wine, neatly racked, and other subterranean chambers no doubt hold the house aperitifs, which are also admired. No beer, though. There isn't a barrel in the place. 'I don't see the point of going through the palaver of having beer on tap and selling just three pints a week,' says Leaver.

Is it still a pub then?

Beers Available
Krombacher Pils, Castle, San Miguel, Stein Lager, London Pride, Samuel Adnams, Franziskaner, Pete's wicked lager, Pete's wicked ale
Cider: Various

Nearest Tube Station
St John's Wood

· THE BLIND BEGGAR ·

337 Whitechapel Road, E1   247 6105

'Well, look who's here'

On 8 March 1966, George Cornell of the Richardson gang was drinking in the Blind Beggar in Whitechapel Road when Ronald Kray walked into the bar and shot him dead.

It is a scene that has passed into legend: the crowded bar, the Walker Brothers' hit on the juke box, the shots in the air from Kray's minder, customers diving for the floor, the two gangsters facing each other for a long moment. 'Well, look who's here,' Cornell said, whereupon Kray raised his Mauser 9mm and shot him through the forehead.

The Blind Beggar already had a place in the history of the East End. In 1865 the young evangelist William Booth had spoken at an open-air meeting on the pavement outside. This was the genesis of the Salvation Army. Parties of Salvationists regularly arrive on William Booth tours, but alas, it is the other event that holds centre stage.

The Blind Beggar has been refurbished time and again. A big conservatory has been added and a beer garden tacked on at the side and people drinking in the comfortable modern bar with its button-backed sofas and red-shaded wall lights talk of other things. All the same, almost 30 years later, the Blind Beggar is still the pub where Ronnie Kray, hearing that George Cornell had called him a fat poof, sought him out and shot him down.

The Blind Beggar is up for sale as I write, has been for three years. The tenant is asking £100,000 for a 17-year lease.

Open
All Week

Hours
11.00–23.00
(12.00–22.30 Sun)
Closed Christmas Day, Boxing Day

Credit Cards
None

Bar Food Available
11.30–14.30 Mon–Fri;
18.00–21.00 Sat
(12.00–14.30 and
18.00–21.00 Sun)

Special Features
Wheelchair Access
Tables outside seat 100

Beers Available
Ruddles County, Ruddles Best, Webster's Yorkshire Bitter, Courage Best, Budweiser, Foster's, Holsten, Carlsberg

Nearest Tube Station
Whitechapel

33

· THE BLUE ANCHOR ·

13 Lower Mall, W6   **0181-748 5774**

'Someone seems to have left their oars behind'

Open
All Week
Hours
11.00–23.00
(12.00–22.30 Sun)
Credit Cards
None
Bar Food Available
12.00–14.30 and
18.00–21.00
(phone pub for Sunday hours)
Special Features
Wheelchair Access
(but not lavatory)
Tables outside seat 60
Private Room seats 38
Beers Available
Courage Best Bitter, Courage Directors, Wadworth, Sol, Molson Dry, Newcastle Brown Ale, Kronenbourg, Brody, Budweiser, Victor Bitter, Diamond White, Holsten Pils, Carlsberg Special Brew, Foster's
Nearest Tube Station
Hammersmith Broadway

The Blue Anchor is the first of the pubs on Hammersmith's riverside, a handsome old place at least 300 years old. There have, of course, been changes along the way, not least to its name. It started out as the Blew Anchor and Washhouses, but as time passed it gave up washing and its spelling improved. The Victorians installed a host of partitions, our generation took them down and so it goes on. The old panelling survives, though, as does the beautiful pewter bar counter.

The Blue Anchor is popular with the rowing club next door and goes in for old rowing photographs. Someone seems to have left their oars behind. There is a rather sombre collection of World War I artefacts – helmets, gasmasks and so on – and banknotes of many lands are pasted up over the bar counter.

This is a busy pub in the summer. Its customers fill the picnic tables lining the river wall and there are cool marble-topped tables for them to relax around inside. The Georgian bow window has a view of the bridge, the river and the riverside path, a view which used to be much enjoyed by Gustav Holst who taught at the St Paul's Girls School in Hammersmith for 35 years. Indeed, it is said that he was inspired to write his Hammersmith Prelude and Scherzo for Military Band while sitting at this window admiring the view.

· THE BULL AND GATE ·

389 Kentish Town Road, NW5   **485 5358**

'Comfort-free zone'

Open
All Week
Hours
11.00–23.00
(12.00–22.30 Sun)
Special Features
Tables outside seat 25
Private Room seats 150
Beers Available
Flowers IPA, Hancock's, Webster's, Toby, Budweiser, Becks, Caffrey's, Tennent's Extra, Foster's, Carling Black Label, Newcastle Brown Ale, Kronenbourg
Cider: Scrumpy Jack, Strongbow
Nearest Tube Station
Kentish Town

A cheerfully ornate exterior hides two bars. One for customers who go for the beer, the other for the choosier ones who go for the music. They take their chances at the Bull and Gate.

A music lover writes: 'The Bull and Gate specializes in breaking new bands, with at least three playing every night of the week in a music room beyond the little bar. The music room is without chairs, tables and bar counter, a comfort-free zone that often empties between and during acts. Consequently bands can find themselves playing to two mates and a dog.

'Nirvana, Carter and Suede all played here in their early days and a hot new act still draws an excited crowd. Pick your night.'

· THE BULL'S HEAD ·

Strand on the Green, W6   **0181-994 1204**

'You don't take the Thames for granted'

The Bull's Head admires but does not altogether trust the river that runs beneath its windows at Strand on the Green. Every month it washes over the tow path. Four or five times a year it covers the benches against the pub walls. It has not got into the pub itself since New Year's Eve 1977 when it swamped the saloon bar, and the authorities promise that this won't happen again. Still, you don't take the Thames for granted.

High tide, low tide, this is a lovely site for a pub. District Line trains rattle across the railway bridge almost overhead, but it is surprising how quickly you get used to that. The swans on the foreshore take no notice, nor does the heron on the post in the river, the cormorants on Oliver Island nor, indeed, the customers of the Bull's Head.

It has been there for almost 400 years now and has been expanding lately. It took over two of the pretty cottages on its right for the staff and the one on its left for extra room but from the outside you could never tell.

There's an old plan of the interior dated 1803 on the wall, and the pub seems much the same. The main bar with its old beams and nicotined ceiling is much as it was, as are the outhouses and the entrance hall they call the games room because that is where the darts board is. There is a big flagged room next to it where people eat, and picnic tables just off the tow path for sunny days.

There is meant to be a secret tunnel to Oliver's Island that is said to have saved Oliver Cromwell's bacon during the civil war. No one lives on the little island now.

Open
All Week

Hours
11.00–23.00
(12.00–22.30 Sun)

Credit Cards
All major cards except AmEx and Diner's Club

Bar Food Available
11.00–15.00
(12.00–22.00 Sun)

Special Features
Wheelchair access by prior arrangement (but not lavatory)

Beers Available
Waddington, Wadworth, Theakston, Theakston Old Peculier, Courage Directors, Courage Best, Holsten, Budweiser, Foster's, Carlsberg

Nearest BR Station
Kew Bridge

· THE BUNCH OF GRAPES ·

207 Brompton Road, SW3   **589 4944**

'People in dirty clothing, go away!'

Visitors from foreign parts have been known to fly into Heathrow at first light, check into their hotel and make straight for the Bunch of Grapes. It is one of the London pubs in every guidebook.

Year after year it stays a very classy pub. It is a protected building, of course, and looks it – granite piers, painted stucco Corinthian columns, a cast-iron balcony and what about the spectacular painted mirrors, the etched glass and the splendid mahogany set piece in the bar, a hand-carved vine with the ripest grapes?

Open
All Week

Hours
11.00–23.00
(12.00–22.30 Sun)
Closed Christmas Day

Credit Cards
Visa, Access, Mastercard

Bar Food Available
11.00–21.00
(12.00–21.00 Sun)

Special Features
Wheelchair Access

Beers Available
Theakston Best Bitter, John Smith's, Courage Best, Courage Directors, Budweiser, Holsten, Foster's, Carlsberg, Guinness

Nearest Tube Stations
Knightsbridge, South Kensington

In its high Victorian days the Bunch of Grapes had six bars with a separate entrance to each. It still has four bars and three entrances and has kept a lot of the old partitions and a set of snob screens in good working order.

It does well with food, stalwartly English, cooked by the landlord's wife – fish and chips, steak and kidney pie – and there is a firmly worded notice on one of the doors: 'The management regrets that people in dirty clothing will not be served.'

· BURLINGTON BERTIE ·

39–45 Shaftesbury Avenue, W1   **437 0847**

'I'm Burlington Bertie I rise at 10.30'

Open
All Week

Hours
11.00–23.00
(12.00–22.30 Sun)

Credit Cards
All major cards except Diner's Club

Bar Food Available
11.00–22.00

Special Features
Wheelchair Access (disabled lavatory)
Tables outside seat 20
Private Room seats 52
Live Piano Music 19.00–23.00 Mon–Fri

Beers Available
Bass, Brakspear, Wadworth 6X, Bertie's Best, one guest beer every month, Caffrey's, Carling Black Label, Foster's, Kronenbourg 1664, Grolsch, Guinness, Budweiser, Foster's Ice, Holsten Pils, Molsen Dry; Ciders: Dry Blackthorn, Stowford Press Cider, K Cider, Diamond White

Nearest Tube Stations
Piccadilly Circus, Charing Cross

When it comes to sites for pubs it must be hard to beat the stretch of Shaftesbury Avenue sandwiched between the Gielgud Theatre and the Queens. For years it was Cecil Gee's glossy West End home. Then Mr Gee crossed to the other side of the road and in moved Burlington Bertie.

It wasn't quite as easy as that, actually. It took ages to get all the necessary permissions but Burlington Bertie finally opened in September 1994, a good-looking, roomy pub with a big bar and a Hello Dolly staircase. This takes you from the saloon bar to a broad gallery with an eye-level view of the chandelier and of upper-deck passengers in passing double-decker buses. It has a bar of its own. Upstairs and down there are comfortable armchairs and sofas, lots of pics of the naughty Nineties and a seamless flow of background music.

There is a bar in the basement too. It started out as Tilley's wine bar but that didn't seem to work. It is a cellar bar now. You can hire it for parties and on Tuesdays the Japanese-English club has it. A sandwich board on the pavement recommends Bertie's traditional fish and chips for £4.95.

Do you remember Bertie? The one who rose at 10.30 and sauntered along like a toff? Who walked down the Strand with his gloves in his hand and walked back again with them off?

Before my time.

· THE CAMDEN HEAD ·

Camden Walk, N1   **359 0851**

'The high-Victorian golden age of pub design'

The dealers of Camden Passage, one of London's nicest antique markets, have a great prize in their local, the Camden Head.

If an antique has to be 100 years old, well, the Camden Head is nearly there. It was built in 1899 with Queen Victoria nearing the end of her long reign and it is a beautiful public house, perfectly proportioned, richly appointed with lovely engraved glass and brilliant-cut mirrors.

It stands, a choice example of the high-Victorian golden age of pub design with exuberant hanging baskets and its terrace spread before it at a commanding point in the market. If whatever you search for still eludes you, there at the critical moment is the Camden Head.

You can choose between a red plush banquette and one of the stools around the imposing island bar counter, or, on fine days, return with your glass to the terrace. It may be quite a while before you feel inclined to return to the fray.

Open
All Week

Hours
11.00–23.00
(12.00–22.30 Sun)
Closed Christmas Day

Credit Cards
None

Bar Food Available
11.00–15.00

Special Features
Wheelchair Access
(but not lavatory)
Beer Garden seats 50
Private Room seats 45

Beers Available
Theakston Best,
Younger IPA, Becks,
Guinness

Nearest Tube Station
Angel

· CAPTAIN KIDD ·

108 Wapping High Street, E1   **480 5759**

'A fine addition to tourist London'

Captain Kidd is a large and exuberant theme pub built on a magnificent site on the river at Wapping just four years ago. The theme is, of course, Captain Kidd, the 17th-century privateer, and his story is graphically told on the walls of the bar in words, pictures and enlarged photostats of original documents. Here is his letter to the Lords of the Admiralty from Newgate Jail pleading for his two black children, here his death warrant...

He was cruelly and, many now think, unjustly done to death on nearby Execution Dock hard by the Town of Ramsgate. The Town of Ramsgate, small and introvert, is the genuine article. This is an exuberant modern pastiche and it is proving a great success.

A seemingly ancient archway takes you down a cobbled path to a big, cheerful ground-floor bar with a flagstone floor and genuinely brand-new 17th-century features. Above it is another bar devoted largely to bar snacks and with a slightly separate area where children can have soft drinks. On the floor above that is a serious restaurant. Each floor has fine river views, though the big river terrace at the side has the best with Canary Wharf mistily downstream.

Open
All Week

Hours
11.00–23.00
(12.00–22.30 Sun)

Credit Cards
All major cards except
Diner's Club

Food Available
Bar 12.00–14.30 and
18.00–21.30
(12.00–21.00 Sun)
Restaurant
12.00–14.30 and
18.30–22.30
(12.00–21.00 Sun)

Special Features
Wheelchair Access
(disabled lavatory)
Beer Garden seats 200
Private Room seats 60

Beers Available
Samuel Smith variants
including Old Brewery,
Museum Ale,
Ayingerbrau

Nearest Tube Station
Wapping

Captain Kidd seems to have been here for ever, massive timbers supporting the ancient structure, open-tread wooden stairs leading uncreaking from floor to floor, all bleached and split, you might suppose, by centuries of spray and sun. You would suppose wrong.

Captain Kidd is what you might call ship-shape and Sam Smith fashion and it is a fine addition to tourist London. It is sure to give the genuinely old pubs of Wapping a run for their money.

· THE CARDINAL ·

23 Francis Street, SW1   **834 7260**

'A dramatic conversion'

There's a whole college of cardinals in the Cardinal. Cardinals Pole, Mazarin, Richelieu, Manning, Bourne, Lavigerie, Newman and Beaton in copes and birettas and the St Louis Cardinals in their baseball gear occupy the walls of the bars and the stairs of this quiet, comfortable pub at the back of Westminster Cathedral.

Cardinal Hume, Archbishop of Westminster, is often glimpsed walking by but he does not call in. If he did he may find a future cardinal drinking at the bar. Young priests often look in after mass. The Bach Choir fills the place after its Monday night rehearsal in Westminster Cathedral Hall and signs direct you upstairs to the Bishop's Table Restaurant. Alas it is a humble pool room now. You eat downstairs in the back bar.

The Cardinal has not been the Cardinal all that long. It was built as the Windsor Castle in 1848 and so it remained until 1963. A most dramatic conversion then seems to have taken place and Monsignor Warlock, now Archbishop of Liverpool, unveiled its new inn sign. This showed Cardinal Wolsey on one side and a bright red cardinal bird on the other. The cardinal bird was changed to Cardinal Manning. Cardinal Wolsey remains gazing steadfastly in the opposite direction.

Open
All Week
Hours
11.00–23.00 Mon–Fri;
11.00–15.00 and
20.00–23.00 Sat
(19.00–22.30 Sun)
Closed Christmas Day, Boxing Day, New Year's Eve, New Year's Day
Credit Cards
Visa, Mastercard, AmEx
Bar Food Available
11.00–21.30 Mon–Fri
Special Features
Wheelchair Access (but not lavatory)
Beers Available
London Pride, Bass, Young's Bitter; Worthington, Carling, Grolsch, Caffrey's, Guinness
Nearest Tube Station
Victoria

·THE CARTOONIST·

76 Shoe Lane, EC4 **358 2828**
'Robert Maxwell filled the pub with his elephantine bonhomie'

Members of the Cartoonist Club of Great Britain come to this bright modern pub for get-togethers and original cartoons cover the walls of its two bars and staircase.

Enoch Powell, Margaret Thatcher, Tony Benn, Ken Livingstone, Geoffrey Archer, Frank Bruno, Terry Venables and Terry Waite (twice, once before, once after) have all been here to receive the Cartoonist Club's annual award. Robert Maxwell filled the pub with his elephantine bonhomie and shook it with the noise of his helicopter.

Open
Mon–Fri
Hours
11.00–23.00
Closed Bank Holidays
Credit Cards
All major cards accepted
Bar Food Available
12.00–21.00
Special Features
Wheelchair Access
(but not lavatory)
Tables outside
seat 130
Private Room
seats 40
Beers Available
Courage Best, Courage Directors, John Smith's, Theakston Best, Theakston XB, Holsten, Foster's, Guinness, Budweiser, Molsen, Becks, Grolsch, Newcastle Brown Ale
Nearest Tube Stations
Chancery Lane, Blackfriars

·THE CAT AND CANARY·

1–24 Fisherman's Walk, E14 **512 9187**
'Innocent visitors should not be misled by its ecclesiastical interior'

For those who have chosen or been forced to work in or around Canary Wharf, here is a refuge. You get off the Docklands Light Railway at the wharf, go down the escalator and through the North Colonnade door and there it is, a dark pubby pub that has been there for ever. Well, since June 1992. That is for ever on Canary Wharf.

Most of the woodwork is pretty old, as it happens. It came from redundant Victorian churches and includes some impressive pews and a telephone kiosk that used to be a pulpit. Innocent visitors who board the Docklands Light Railway by mistake should not be misled by the ecclesiastic interior. Let them be warned that the *Daily Telegraph*, the *Daily Mirror* and the *Independent*, each accompanied by their ravenous Sunday offspring, are all at large on Canary Wharf.

This means eventful times in the Cat and Canary and its lighter, airier competitor the Henry Addington. The Fleet Street expats divide fairly evenly between them. As the sonnet has it you can tell a man who boozes by the company he chooses.

Open
Mon–Sat
Hours
11.00–21.00 Mon–Tue;
11.00–23.00 Wed–Fri;
12.00–15.00 Sat
Credit Cards
Visa, Access
Bar Food Available
12.00–15.00
Special Features
No-smoking Area
Wheelchair Access
(disabled lavatory)
Patio seats 60
Private Room seats 25
Beers Available
Fuller's, London Pride, ESB, Chiswick Bitter, plus guest ales
Nearest Docklands Station
Canary Warf

The Cat and Canary has young joint-managers, Philip Hale and Natasha Percival. He presides behind the bar, she rules in the kitchen. There is good cask ale, bar billiards, darts and shove-ha'penny and a cosy corner known as the cuddy, said to be reserved for the exchange of rumours by the *Daily Telegraph*.

· THE CATCHER IN THE RYE ·

317 Regent's Park Road, N3   0181-343 4369

'A toast to J D Salinger'

There are two Regent's Park Roads. This one starts off as Finchley Road some miles back. Half-way along you will find an interesting new pub named after one of the great novels of our day and I propose a toast to J D Salinger, its sainted author. It can be drunk any day in one of the pub's several bars.

The Catcher in the Rye looks rather as if three small buildings had been knocked together. This is what happened actually, funny that. A shop, a solicitor's office and another shop each gave its all to this nice modern pub, which I dare say Salinger would like all right if he'd ever leave his remote cottage in New Hampshire.

Its best seller is a low-gravity beer that it has specially brewed for it in Suffolk. It is called Catchers. Low-gravity bitter? That might appeal to Salinger.

Open
All Week
Hours
11.00–23.00
(12.00–22.30 Sun)
Credit Cards
None
Food Available
12.00–15.00 and
18.00–22.00
Special Features
Wheelchair Access
(but not lavatory)
Tables outside seat 24
Beers Available
Theakston XB, Bass, Brakspear, Catchers, a weekly guest beer, Kronenbourg, Foster's, Tennent's Pilsner, Caffrey's, Guinness, Blackthorn
Nearest Tube Station
Finchley Central

· THE CHAMPION ·

1 Wellington Terrace, Bayswater Road, W2   229 5056

'Uncamp, uncomplicated gay local'

This long-established, uncamp, uncomplicated gay local in Notting Hill Gate has quietly got on with its life on this busy main road for years, hardly attracting a second glance.

Things have been happening there lately, though. The main bar has been smartened up and a cellar bar opened downstairs selling steak and chips every evening. There's karaoke there too every Tuesday and Sunday and cabaret on Saturday nights. The downstairs bar has a small courtyard, nice in the summer. Hooch, the new alcoholic lemonade, has been a huge hit.

Open
All Week
Hours
12.00–23.00
(12.00–22.30 Sun)
Downstairs bar and
courtyard 15.00–23.00
Closed Christmas Day,
Good Friday
Credit Cards
None
Special Features
Wheelchair Access
Tables outside seat 15
Beers Available
Worthington Best, Carling Black Label, Tennent's Extra, Guinness, Caffrey's, Staropramen
Nearest Tube Station
Notting Hill Gate

·THE CHAMPION·

13 Wells Street, W1   **323 1228**

'An extraordinary light'

The good news from what New Yorkers would call the garment district is that the Champion is a champion Victorian pub again, with partitions, snob-screens and 18-gallon barrels back on their perch of honour high above the bar counter.

The main thing, though, is the quite remarkable windows. When Samuel Smith bought the Champion in the 1980s the company commissioned a series of big stained glass windows from Anne Sotheran of York. They are now splendidly in situ filling two whole walls. Each celebrates a different champion – Fred Archer, Captain Webb, W G Grace… They fill the bar with an extraordinary light.

The upstairs bar, where you can get more substantial meals on weekdays, has its champions too, shire horses all. But black and white photographs of northern stallions, however distinguished, make less impression than large stained glass windows of such heroes as Edward Whymper, first man to climb the Matterhorn in 1865. Three of his companions died in the attempt.

Open
All Week

Hours
11.30–23.00
(12.00–22.30 Sun)

Credit Cards
Most major cards accepted

Bar Food Available
12.00–15.00 and 17.30–21.00

Special Features
Wheelchair Access

Beers Available
Sovereign Best Bitter, Samuel Smith Dark Mild, Ayingerbrau Pils, Prinz

Nearest Tube Stations
Tottenham Court Road, Oxford Circus

·THE CHANDOS·

29 St Martin's Lane, WC2   **836 1401**

'Wave to the burly cooper working on the ledge'

Samuel Smith, the Yorkshire brewer, took no chances on unknown, untried Southern builders when it bought this busy London pub 12 years ago. There was a lot to be done so they brought men up from Yorkshire to do it.

People hardly recognized the old Chandos when it reopened. The building seemed to have been totally refaced. It had a gleaming black and gold fascia and immaculate new stucco and it was quite different inside – new fittings, new panelling, new just about everything. Victorian mahogany drinking booths, handmade by the joiners from Tadcaster, lined the walls of the big downstairs bar. Pairs of button-back leather sofas faced each other across coffee tables in the grandly named Opera Room upstairs. The Yorkshiremen, well pleased, went home again.

The Opera Room has its own staircase to the street, opens for breakfast at 9.00 am and subsequently offers coffee, lunch, tea and supper. The bar downstairs opens at 11.00 am and stays open until 11.00 pm. Both bits stop serving food at 9.30 in the evening.

Open
All Week

Hours
9.00–23.00
(12.00–22.30 Sun)
Closed Christmas Day, New Year's Day

Credit Cards
Visa, Access

Food Available
Bar 11.00-21.30
Opera Room:
9.00–21.30

Special Features
Wheelchair Access
(but not lavatory)

Beers Available
Samuel Smith Old Brown Bitter, Museum Ale, Cider Reserve, Extra Strong Beer, Dark Mild Beer, Ayingerbrau Prinz, Pils

Nearest Tube Station
Charing Cross

·THE CHELSEA POTTER·

119 King's Road, SW3   **352 9479**

'A seat in the stalls'

Open
All Week
Hours
11.00–23.00
(12.00–22.30 Sun)
Credit Cards
Visa, Mastercard, Diner's Club
Bar Food Available
12.00–17.00
(12.00–14.30 Sun)
Special Features
Wheelchair Access
Tables outside seat 30
Beers Available
Sol, Molsen Dry, Budweiser, Becks, Special Brew, Holsten, Pils, Foster's Ice, Kronenbourg
Nearest Tube Station
Sloane Square

Since the dawn of time the Chelsea Potter has occupied a prime corner of King's Road, its two-window walls providing a seat in the stalls on the sometimes exotic passing scene.

It recently got a much-needed renovation. The inside was gutted, skips brimmed over, pub designers, pub fitters, pub decorators came and went. It is much smarter now and busier. Business has gone up 35 per cent under the new Slovenian manager Vanda Stiglic.

·THE CHELSEA RAM·

32 Burnaby Street, SW10   **351 4008**

'A pub at last'

Open
All Week
Hours
11.00–15.00 and
17.30–23.00
Mon–Thur, Sat
11.00–23.00 Fri
(12.00–15.00 and
19.00–22.30 Sun)
Credit Cards
Access, Visa
Bar Food Available
12.00–14.30 and
19.00–22.00
(12.00–14.30 and
19.00–21.30 Sun)
Special Features
Wheelchair Access
(but not lavatory)
Tables outside seat 16
Private Dining Room seats 12
Beers Available
Young's Bitter, Young's Special, Young's London, Young's Premium, Castlemaine 4X, Grolsch, Guinness
Nearest Tube Station
Fulham Broadway

When Edwardian developers were busy developing the wedge of Chelsea between King's Road and Lots Road power station they thoughtfully provided a little pub on the corner of Burnaby Street. The new residents weren't too pleased. They did not want their tone lowered, and the new pub could not get a licence. So it became a laundry, a soup kitchen, a bric-a-brac shop, a garage repair shop. Then, in 1984, Young's bought it and, after a lifetime's wait, its licence came through. The Chelsea Ram was a pub at last.

It made a nice, light, welcoming pub too, with big arched windows and two handsome bars. But it had to be admitted, it was tucked away, not much passing trade in Burnaby Street. So Young's granted a tenancy to Nick Elliott and a partner who knew just what they wanted to do with it. It is now one of the bright new up-market foodie pubs with Adam Baldwin in the kitchen cooking up a storm. 'Quintessentially English,' says James Symington, the manager, meaning food from just about everywhere.

It is still a pub. You can't book and the tables are for people having a beer as well as tucking into penne, salmon fishcakes and roasted vegetable salad with tomato salsa. The advice is go early, otherwise order at the bar and have a drink. There will be a table bye and bye.

·THE CHELSEA REACH·

Battersea Park Road, SW11 **498 3893**

'They start with their tops on'

This council estate pub on Battersea's busiest road has a special attraction. There is a go-go dancer every lunchtime. The girls, pretty as a rule, dance to a strong disco beat. They start with their tops on and take them off half way through. Lunchtime drinkers drink on. They have the air of men who have seen topless go-go girls before. There's something on every evening too. It is Oldie Night on Mondays.

Open
All Week

Hours
11.00–23.00;
(12.00–22.30 Sun)

Credit Cards
None

Bar Food Available
All day

Special Features
Wheelchair Access
Beer Garden
Tables outside seat 12
Live music every night

Beers Available
Courage, Webster's, John Smith's, Fosters, Carlsberg, Holsten, Kronenbourg, Guinness

Nearest BR Station
Battersea Park

·THE CHESHIRE CHEESE·

5 Little Essex Street, WC2 **836 2347**

'A certain amount of haunting'

This is not to be confused, as they say, with Ye Olde Cheshire Cheese, though it often is. American visitors sometimes photograph it inside and out before discovering that there is a rather better known Cheshire Cheese ten minutes' walk away.

This, though, is quite an old pub too, and a certain amount of haunting goes on. A ghost pushes the fruit machine around at night, and managers, alone in the pub at weekends, sometimes hear the dumb waiter inexplicably on its way up.

The pub closes at weekends but during the week the saloon bar stays open all day. It has Sky TV Sport. The dive bar's customers are noticeably younger. This is where the pool table and the music are.

Open
Mon–Fri

Hours
11.00–23.00

Credit Cards
Visa, Mastercard, Diner's Club, Switch

Food Available
Bar 11.30–23.00
Restaurant
12.00–14.30

Special Features
Wheelchair Access
Private Room seats 30

Beers Available
Courage Best, Courage Directors, Theakston, Foster's, Kronenbourg, Holsten, Beamish, Budweiser

Nearest Tube Stations
Temple, Charing Cross

·THE CHURCHILL ARMS·

119 Kensington Church Street, W8   **727 4242**

'Irish landlord, Thai chef and himself at his most cherubic'

Open
All Week

Hours
11.00–23.00
(12.00–22.30 Sun)

Credit Cards
All major cards except AmEx

Restaurant Food Available
12.00–14.30 and 18.00–21.30

Special Features
Wheelchair Access (but not lavatory)

Beers Available
Chiswick, ESB, London Pride, Carlsberg, Heineken, Grolsch, Castlemaine, Guinness, Murphy's

Nearest Tube Station
Notting Hill Gate

Winston would have liked this pub, very English and distinctly eccentric as it is with its Irish landlord, Thai chef and himself at his most cherubic, beaming down from the pub sign on all who pass that way.

It was called the Marlborough once but there have been some changes made, particularly since Gerry O'Brien took over 12 years ago. He replaced the backyard and garage with a conservatory that has 70 people eating in it most lunchtimes and his various collections cover the walls and ceilings. There are umpteen pictures of Winston, Winston mugs and statuettes and toby jugs, and the conservatory has a collection of mounted butterflies, 1,600 of them from all over the world. In the summer live butterflies, bought as chrysalises from the butterfly house at Syon Park, hatch out and flit among the plants. The windows are open and eventually they take their chances in Kensington Church Street.

In the bar you can't see the ceiling for baskets, hat boxes, jugs, steins, lanterns and the like, and marching above your head is a double row of chamber pots. This jokey pub has a wall covered in Prime Ministers labelled the Chamber Lane.

But what has brought particular renown to the Churchill Arms is its Thai food. The kitchen has a staff of eight, all Thais, and they have undoubtedly helped to transform its fortunes. It has been Fuller's top profit-maker now for five years running.

·THE CITTIE OF YORKE·

22 High Holborn, WC1   **242 7670**

'The great hall of a medieval manor'

Open
Mon–Sat

Hours
11.00–23.00 Mon–Sat
Closed Bank Holidays

Credit Cards
Access, Visa, Mastercard, AmEx

Bar Food Available
12.00–14.30 and 17.30–22.00

Special Features
Wheelchair Access
Private Room seats 300

When the Yorkshire Brewer Samuel Smith made its first sally into London in 1979 they bought Hennekey's, well known, long established, much respected. It thus acquired six fine London pubs. This one sold only wine for more than 100 years. It was surely the greatest prize.

It was the original Hennekey's and it was famous. It had evolved from an ancient inn built in 1430 and largely rebuilt every 200 years or so. It emerged in its present form in the 1890s and such a form. There is no pub in London quite like this one. The main bar resembles the great hall of a medieval manor rising to a soaring trussed roof and high Gothic windows. Along one wall is the famous bar, shorter than it used to be but still one of the longest in Britain. Above it huge iron-hooped wine butts sit on a stout timber gallery supported by fluted iron pillars. Each butt once held 1,000 gallons of wine. They were in active use right up to the outbreak of the last war when they were carefully drained. A well-placed bomb might have carried off the customers in a tidal wave of amontillado.

Small cubicles line the facing wall, a table and four chairs in each. They were originally kept for lawyers and their clients but they now have to take their chances like everyone else. The cubicles are very popular, as is the massive stove on cold days. It was made in 1815 and still works perfectly. Each of its three sides has an open grate and there is no sign of a chimney. That is under the floorboards.

Samuel Smith made some alterations. It made a second, smaller bar at the Holborn end and a long cellar bar downstairs and, of course, it gave it a quaint new name. Well there is a lot of ye oldery about and there was a pub called the Cittie of Yorke in these parts in times gone by. Furthermore olde Sam Smith does come from Yorke or not far offe. He brews good beer at Tadcaster and this and only this is now sold at all his London pubs. There were 31 of these at last count. As for the Cittie of Yorke it is clearly in good heart. It remains a spectacular pub.

Beers Available
Old Brewery Bitter, Museum Ale, Extra Stout, Dark Mild, Ayingerbrau Prinz, Ayingerbrau Pils; Cider: Cider Reserve

Nearest Tube Station
Holborn

·THE CITY BARGE·

27 Strand on the Green, W4 **0181-994 2148**

'Someone, incredibly, pinched Queen Elizabeth I's Charter'

I don't suppose the City Barge was a prime target during the war. Presumably the landmine that got it was meant for the railway bridge. It missed, though, and knocked down most of this nice old riverside pub instead. The authorities debated. Perhaps they should take the rest down too, but the City Barge just carried on trading so that was all right.

An elderly regular remembers arriving at the pub and finding the roof gone and rubble up to here. He got his drink as usual but, incredibly, someone pinched Queen Elizabeth I's Charter. It had been on the wall and it hasn't been seen since. The ancient fireplace with its grate raised to stop floods from putting the fire out survived, so did the bar counter and the parliamentary clock made without glass to save tax.

So the City Barge was patched up and after the war it was rebuilt on the original 1484 foundations. The pub was the Navigator's Arms in those days and Richard III was in the winter of his discontent. It is slightly bigger now, with an old bar and a new bar. You go down a few steps to the old bar, which is much as it was before the bombing – small,

Open
All Week

Hours
11.00–23.00
(12.00–22.30 Sun)

Credit Cards
Visa, Access, Mastercard

Bar Food Available
12.00–21.30
(12.00–14.30 Sun)

Special Features
Wheelchair Access (but not lavatory)
Tables outside seat 40

Beers Available
John Smith's, Theakston Best, Old Peculier, Holsten, Miller, Foster's, Guinness, Beamish

Nearest BR Station
Kew Bridge

homely, old-fashioned. The new bar is up a few steps, substantially larger with a long counter and drinking booths. They had live music up here every weekend until the neighbours complained.

Like the Bull's Head, its near neighbour, the City Barge, has Oliver Cromwell stories. It has Beatles stories too. A sequence of *Help!* was filmed here, and John, Paul, George and Ringo had a few days filming by the river. The bit where Ringo falls into the cellar was shot in the studio. The City Barge doesn't have a cellar.

The river tries to get in from time to time without much success. The old pub has a watertight ship's door on the towpath now.

·THE CLACHAN·

34 Kingly Street, W1 **734 2659**

'The old Scots word for meeting place,
and Scots do on occasions meet there'

Kingly Street must always have been a pain for Liberty's, nipping in as it does and cutting the great department store in two. The three-storey bridge that crosses Kingly Street is just Liberty's trying to get from one bit of the store to the other.

Go under the bridge and on the left is a small but perfectly formed public house, rather romantic, faintly Scottish, a turret on the corner adding a green copper dome to the skyline. This, until quite recently, was the Bricklayers, and Liberty's owned it.

What, though, was Liberty's to do with it? It did not want a pub. It wanted more space for warehousing. Perhaps...But no. The Bricklayers was a protected building as Liberty's itself is. A pub it had to stay.

So in 1983 Nicholson's bought it, smartened it up and changed its name. It is now The Clachan, the old Scots word for meeting place, and Scots do on occasions meet there. There is a large air-conditioned bar, at least six real ales on tap and a good-sized clachan upstairs called the Highland Bar.

The haggis is piped in on Burns Night and pictures of bearded highland worthies decorate the walls, but apart from this Nicholson's has resisted smothering the Clachan in tartan.

Open
Mon–Sat

Hours
11.00–23.00
Closed Christmas Day

Credit Cards
All major cards except Diner's Club

Bar Food Available
11.00–20.30

Special Features
Wheelchair Access
(but not lavatory)
Private Room
seats 36

Beers Available
Tetley, Greene King, Marston's Pedigree, Adnams, Wadworth, Timothy Taylor's, Bass, Becks, Castlemaine, Carlsberg, Guinness

Nearest Tube Station
Oxford Circus

·THE CLARENCE·

53 Whitehall, SW1 **930 4808**

'No malmsey at the Clarence. This is a real-ale house'

Ancient overhead timbers from a Thames pier, wonderful cellars under Whitehall, leaded windows throwing delicate patterns on the pale wooden floor, this is a most romantic old pub.

It has tremendous appeal for tourists. It used to provide a jester for them every summer but this seemed a bit over the top and anyway he retired. They are pleased to find the settles and benches still there and the wooden floors and the gas lights. At dusk the lanterns outside come into their own and the place looks more romantic than ever.

Inigo Jones's famous banqueting hall is just two blocks away. It was from one of its windows that Charles I stepped onto the scaffold to face the executioner. Every year Roundheads and Cavaliers mark the anniversary of this grisly event with a toast in the Clarence.

I suppose the Clarence who gave his name to the Clarence was good old William IV, the sailor king. He was Duke of Clarence at the time. But this was the king who gargled two gallons of water every morning. Is he a suitable role model for a pub? Richard III's brother, poor perjured Clarence, would be better, drowning, as he did, in a butt of malmsey.

Not that you get malmsey at the Clarence. It is a real-ale house – nine real ales on the handpumps. A butt of Brakspear's old ale now…

Open
All Week

Hours
11.00–23.00
(12.00–22.30 Sun)

Credit Cards
All major cards accepted

Special Features
Wheelchair Access (but not lavatory)
Tables outside seat 24
Private Room seats 52

Beers Available
Wadworth, Brakspear, Theakston's Best, Theakston's Old Peculier, Abbot Ale, Courage Directors, Courage Best, Ruddles County, John Smith's, Foster's, Holsten

Nearest Tube Stations
Charing Cross, Embankment

·THE CLIFTON·

96 Clifton Hill, NW8 **624 5233**

'Nooks for well-upholstered lovers'

Two stories are told about the Clifton. One is that it was a country retreat of a rich man who got fed up with his London friends galloping over to drink his drink so he got a licence and made them pay. The other is that the Prince of Wales, the one who became Edward VII, used to meet Lily Langtry there in the private bar. Well, he might have done. It is the sort of thing he did.

The Clifton is a substantial Georgian villa in a particularly pleasant street in St John's Wood. It has been a pub since 1834 and in recent years it has been beautifully restored and refurbished. The style is Edwardian, of course. It is all pine panelling, polished floors with Persian rugs and it is full of quiet corners for well-upholstered lovers to hold hands.

Open
All Week

Hours
11.00–23.00
(12.00–22.30 Sun)

Credit Cards
All major cards accepted

Food Available
12.00–14.30 and
18.30–21.30

Special Features
Tables outside seat 72

Beers Available
Young's, Tetley, Nicholson's Best, Adnam, Lowenbrau, Carlsberg, Castlemaine XXXX, Sam's Stout, Guinness

Nearest Tube Station
St John's Wood, Maida Vale

In 1985 it was the *Evening Standard* pub of the year, the unanimous choice of the judges, and that year too an extremely nice conservatory was added. This is the restaurant now. There is a sunny terrace at the back and tables in the garden flanking the street, and in the winter it is particularly inviting with fires in each of the main rooms.

Edward VII would probably have liked it even more now. For one thing there are pictures of him everywhere. There are even more of his shapely mistress. There is even one of his wife.

·THE COACH AND HORSES·

29 Greek Street, W1   **437 5920**

'YOU'RE BANNED!'

Open
All Week
Hours
11.00–23.00
(12.00–22.30 Sun)
Credit Cards
None
Special Features
Wheelchair Access
(but not lavatory)
Beers Available
Burton Ale, Tetley, Dorchester Bitter, Castlemaine, Lowenbrau, Carlsberg, Guinness
Nearest Tube Station
Leicester Square

The Coach and Horses, now one of Soho's most celebrated pubs, stands opposite Kettners on the corner of Romilly Street and Greek Street and it looks sober enough. Inside, though, its red plastic stool covers, black Formica table tops and Basic Food Hygiene Certificate announce that this is a pub for serious drinkers.

It owes its new-found fame to the painter Francis Bacon, to the cartoonist Michael Heath, to the staff of Private Eye, but mostly to Jeffrey Bernard, serious drinker in excelsis. Bernard, of course, was the central character in Jeffrey Bernard Is Unwell, and wherever it is performed there is the Coach and Horses on the stage, Bernard himself – locked in – and its irascible proprietor Norman Balon a powerful off-stage presence.

For many years Private Eye had its offices opposite the pub, which became a haunt of Richard Ingrams, Peter Cook, William Rushton, Michael Heath and, of course, Jeffrey Bernard. *Private Eye* still has its fortnightly lunches in an upstairs room, although lunches in the pub itself have been stopped.

The Heath cartoons on the wall all feature life in the Coach and Horses. Most show a little man, in one case from the Inland Revenue, peering round the door and saying 'Jeff bin in?' The other recurring figure is Norman Balon booming at regulars "Don't you have no homes to go to?' he'll be shouting or "YOU'RE BANNED.' He claims to be London's rudest landlord and no one disputes it.

Balon is sometimes taken for Walter Matthau. This annoys him, as do most things, a discovery soon made by play-goers arriving at the pub in search of Jeffrey Bernard.

'Sorry I was so rude last night but you see I was sober,' says one of Heath's Coach and Horses characters.

· THE COAL HOLE ·

91 The Strand, WC1   **836 7503**

'The coalheavers moved on'

In the distant days of the Coal Hole's notoriety it was a coalheavers' hang-out in old converted cellars off the Strand. It was very rough. The coalheavers drank and carried on, word got round and others started going, actors and the like.

Edmund Kean, the great tragedian, liked a bit of low life and loved the Coal Hole. He started the Wolf Club there, a club dedicated to carrying on. Byron came once but didn't like it. Then there was a craze for mock trials there, described as 'clever but disgusting Judge and Jury Entertainment'. They sound nice.

The coalheavers moved on to the Ship and Shovel, also still going strong, and the Coal Hole moved farther along the Strand to proper premises in the Savoy buildings, and that is where it is today. The old Coal Hole makes the present Coal Hole seem very respectable, which, though I would not want to hurt its feelings, I believe it is.

The main bar on the Strand is high and handsome with large windows, hanging banners and marble reliefs of frisking maidens. Muses perhaps, or seasons, and a recent refurbishment made a pleasant little gallery out of what was the manager's office.

The cellar bar has been much smartened up lately. It has its own entrance on the Strand and its own lively following. It is an interesting bar, wandering off downhill a bit, and at its far reaches is a locked gate, beyond which some steps lead down to a little windowless snug.

This, they will tell you, is the coal hole. It certainly could be a coal hole. People drink in it sometimes. It is not for claustrophobics.

Open
Mon–Sat

Hours
11.00–23.00
Closed Christmas Day,
Boxing Day

Credit Cards
Visa, Access

Bar Food Available
11.30–14.30

Special Features
Wheelchair Access
(but not lavatory)
Tables outside seat 12

Beers Available
Tetley, Brakspear, Bass,
Adnams, Wadworth,
Castlemaine,
Lowenbrau, Carlsberg

Nearest Tube Stations
Covent Garden, Charing Cross

· THE COCOANUT ·

16 Mill Street, Kingston upon Thames   **0181-546 3978**

'There aren't many cocoanuts left with this spelling'

The Cocoanut, as the landlord will tell you, is the only pub with this name in the country, and there aren't many cocoanuts left with this spelling either. This, though, is how you spelled coconut in the days when they were unshipped at Kingston in large numbers bound for the local coconut matting factory. The management were moved to put up a beer shed for its workers who called it the Cocoanut. Welcome to the pub.

Open
All Week

Hours
11.00–15.00 and
17.30–23.00
11.00–23.00 Sat
(12.00–22.30 Sun)

Credit Cards
None

Bar Food Available
12.00–14.00
Set-price lunch: £3.50

Special Features
Wheelchair Access
Beer Garden seats 30
Car Park

Beers Available
Chiswick Bitter, London Pride, Mr Harry, ESB, IPA

Nearest BR Station
Kingston

The current building was begun just before the war. Then Hitler intervened with a novel planning objection and all work stopped until that little matter was settled. Eventually, the war over, the builders returned and a brand new Cocoanut triumphantly opened on Coronation Day. Hillary and Tensing were so pleased they climbed Everest.

The Cocoanut, then, is a fairly recent addition to a noticeably bosky scene, but it nestles so comfortably among pretty cottages that you hardly notice that it is so much younger than they are.

There is a homely public bar with pool, darts, crib, dominoes and even shove-ha'penny, a comfortable lounge bar and a pretty paved garden at the back with a pergola and a barbecue, and they do sandwiches just about any time.

· THE COLEHERNE ·

261 Old Brompton Road, SW5   373 9859

'No powder. No paint. Just men'

Open
All Week

Hours
11.00–23.00
(12.00–22.30 Sun)

Credit Cards
None

Beers Available
Worthington Best, Toby, Draught Grolsch, Caffrey's, Carling Black Label

Nearest Tube Station
Earls Court

The Coleherne is a cavernous Victorian pub in Earls Court. The atmosphere is macho and slightly menacing with little of the gaiety of the usual gay pub. There's a hand-written slogan over the bar. 'No Powder. No Paint. Just Men.' It is the most famous gay pub in the world.

It has two sets of customers: the ones in leather and Levis, and the rest. The dress-code men gather exclusively on one side of the big U-shaped bar. They come from all over Europe, bringing their kit with them, elaborate leather gear as a rule, biker jackets, studded belts, heavy boots. They are unshaven, sometimes heavily moustached and have their own entrance and their own loo. They stand staring straight ahead, holding bottles. A large picture of Hell's Angels glowers down.

Less flamboyant customers gather in large numbers on other side of the bar. There is not a lot of conversation even among them. The Coleherne isn't strong on conversation.

Serial killer Colin Ireland, now serving life, met his victims here. During his trial there were said to be more reporters in the Coleherne than regular customers.

In the Coleherne you either stand or lean. There are bare wooden floors and next to no furniture. The large wooden cube in the far room used to be a stage for occasional strippers. These have been dropped and the cube is just for leaning on now.

Things get a bit jollier as the main body of the pub fills up and the music gets louder. To the disappointment of tourists and reporters there is no how's your father.

· THE COMPTON ARMS ·

4 Compton Avenue, N1 — **359 2645**

'Under a friendly sycamore tree'

A quiet little country pub hidden away off Canonbury Square. There's a small cosy low-ceilinged bar where local artists show their work and benches round cask tables under a friendly sycamore tree at the back. Crib and dominoes but not a juke box or gaming machine in sight.

Open
All Week

Hours
11.00–23.00
(12.00–22.30 Sun)

Credit Cards
None

Bar Food Available
11.00–22.00

Special Features
Wheelchair Access
(but not lavatory)
Beer Garden seats 20

Beers Available
Greene King, Abbott Ale, Rayment's, Harp, Molsen, Stella, Miller, Kronenbourg, Guinness

Nearest Tube Station
Highbury & Islington

· THE COOPERS' ARMS ·

87 Flood Street, SW3 — **376 3120**

'Denis must have looked in sometimes, surely'

Good-mannered, good-natured we have here a thoroughly well-bred pub with staff and customers in complete accord. Parents may raise an eyebrow to find Justin or Julian serving behind the bar but it is usually an enjoyable interlude, to be dined out on later. For the moment the City can wait…

A massive buffalo head, a gift from a customer, presides over the bar, a baker's dough table occupies an extravagant amount of floor space, a splendid LMS long-case clock looks as though it had been made for the end wall, and two massive air filters on the ceiling keep the air clear and smokers and non-smokers in harmony. The brasserie-style food is a major attraction.

Upstairs is a useful room for special occasions, graced by a magnificent 17ft table, originally a draughtsman's table from a Jarrow shipyard.

Lady Thatcher used to live in Flood Street. This, then, was her local. No one recalls seeing her in the Coopers' Arms but Denis must have looked in sometimes, surely.

Open
All Week

Hours
11.00–23.00
(12.00–22.30 Sun)
Closed Christmas Day,
Boxing Day

Credit Cards
All major cards except Diner's Club

Bar Food Available
11.00–15.00 (Mon–Sun)
and 18.00–21.00
(Mon–Fri)

Special Features
Wheelchair Access
Private Room seats 30

Beers Available
Young's, Castlemaine, Budweiser, Holsten, Lowenbrau, Becks, Labatts, Rolling Rock, Stella Artois, Red Stripe

Nearest Tube Station
Sloane Square

·The Country Pub In London·

52 Cambridge Street, SW1   **834 5281**

'A hunting horn, a saddle and old copper pans'

Open
All Week

Hours
12.00–23.00
(12.00–22.30 Sun)

Credit Cards
Visa, Mastercard, AmEx

Bar Food Available
12.00–15.00 and
18.00–21.30
(19.00–21.30 Sun)

Special Features
Wheelchair Access
(but not lavatory)

Beers Available
Boddingtons, Flowers Original, Marston's Pedigree, Fuggles IPA, Caffrey's, Stella Artois, Heineken, Konig Pilsner, Guinness, Murphy's, Strongbow, Addlestones Cask Cider

Nearest Tube Station
Pimlico

It seems that these three men, well-connected, well-heeled and rather hard to please, decided they didn't like any London pubs. The solution was clear. They would open one they did like. So they did.

This was it, an ordinary town pub called the Clarendon Arms until they took it over. They lowered the ceiling, shortened the bar counter, put in a second open fire, fitted olde beams and covered them in horse brasses, brought in dark oak tables, chairs and bar stools, hung up a hunting horn, a saddle, old prints and old copper pans and masked the windows so once inside you could not tell the time of day or season of the year. Then they fixed a new pub sign outside. 'Grosvenor's,' it said, 'the Country Pub in London'.

The name was the gift of the Hon William Grosvenor, one of the three founding fathers – recreations: shooting, fishing, golf. All agreed that Grosvenor was a jolly good name for just about anything, but after a few months there were second thoughts. Wouldn't 'the Country Pub in London' be enough?

So that is the pub's name now and it seems to be doing well with its good wine list and town and country ales. Its food undoubtedly helps too. Asparagus features quite a lot and lobster, sometimes pheasant casserole and occasionally guinea fowl stew. Well, you know the sort of thing, simple country fare.

·The Cow·

89 Westbourne Park Road, W2   **221 0021**

'Tom Conran's doing'

Open
All Week

Hours
12.00–15.00 and
19.00–22.30
(17.30–23.00 Mon;
12.00–22.30 Sun)

Credit Cards
Visa, Mastercard

Food Available
Bar until half an hour before closing time
Restaurant First Sitting 19.30, Second Sitting 21.30 Tues–Sat;
Lunch 12.30–15.00 Sat and Sun

Special Features
Tables outside seat 12

The Cow in Westbourne Park Road must sometimes think it has jumped over the moon. Not long ago it was a nondescript little boozer in a nondescript bit of Notting Hill Gate. Now it is never out of the glossy magazines and full just about every night.

This is Tom Conran's doing. He is a son of Terence Conran so when he bought a pub people were bound to notice. The builders were in for four months and when it finally opened it was a media event. You could hardly move in the bar for weeks and some nights they almost ran out of beer, the publican's cardinal sin. The new Cow has just one bar stretching from the street to the back wall and, after all that work, it still looks like a local boozer. Lino on the floor, thickly varnished bar counter, lace curtain half way up the windows, these, at any rate, are familiar in old pubs. The food, though, is a world away.

Small as it is, there are two kitchens at the Cow, one for the bar, which has oysters every day, (there are some you can eat whether there's an R in the month or not), the other for the dining room upstairs. It is on this that the reputation of the Cow depends.

It is small, homely room with a job-lot of tables and chairs, and you can only get about 24 in so you really have to book. There are two sittings and even so you may have to share a table. You get a three-course meal with no choice apart from a vegetarian option, what Fay Maschler calls the dinner party aspect, and it costs £16.50 per head plus wine and a service charge. Fay describes the cuisine as English bistro and it has been very well received so far.

This is far from what you expect in the well-mannered Cow of today, though locals who remember the Cow of yesterday make a point of congratulating the new regime on the absence of bother. 'This has the least aggro of any pub I've ever worked in,' says the manager, Alexander Thompson.

Beers Available
London Pride,
Brakspear Bitter,
Grolsch, Hoegaarden,
De Koninck, Budvar,
Becks, Liefmans,
Stella, Leffe Blond,
Chimay Red Cider:
Rich's Somerset.

Nearest Tube Station
Westbourne Park

· THE CRICKETERS ·

Maids of Honour Row, The Green, Richmond   **0181-940 4372**

'A pub to watch'

Ronnie Wood, the Rolling Stone, whose local this is, liked the Cricketers so much he tried to buy it. He and his drinking pal, snooker super-star Jimmy White, pooled their loose change and made an offer. Alas for them the owners stuck to their asking price, £400,000, and Greene King snapped it up instead.

Four hundred big ones, you may well think, was not a lot for an 18th-century Grade 1 listed building on Richmond Green, any pub's dream location. The Cricketers was not only down at heel but it was having unappealing problems with the local yobbery. That, at least, changed very quickly with the arrival of new Greene King managers. 'Our customers now tend to be more suited than booted,' says the new licensee Grant Adlam with satisfaction. 'More mature.'

That was the essential Stage 1 in the Cricketers' revival. Stage 2 has been putting in a new kitchen and improving the food. Stage 3 will be the complete refurb planned for 1996. The transformation will then be complete.

The Cricketers is a pub to watch. Let us hope Ronnie Wood and Jimmy White will still like it this time next year.

Open
All Week

Hours
11.00–23.00 Mon–Sat
(12.00–22.30 Sun)

Credit Cards
All major cards accepted

Bar Food Available
12.00–14.30

Special Features
Wheelchair Access
(but not lavatory)
Function Room
seats 25

Beers Available
Greene King, IPA,
Abbot Ale, Harp, Stella,
Kronenbourg, Guinness,
seasonal guest beers
Cider: Dry Blackthorn

Nearest Tube Station
Richmond

·CROCKER'S FOLLY·

24 Aberdeen Place, NW8 **286 6608**

*'You would have to have
a heart of stone not to feel for Mr Crocker'*

Open
All Week

Hours
11.00–23.00
(12.00–22.30 Sun)

Credit Cards
All major cards accepted

Bar Food Available
All day
Carvery 12.00–14.30

Special Features
Wheelchair Access
(but not lavatory)
Tables outside seat 40

Beers Available
Crocker's, Adnams, Brakspear, Theakston, Bass, Wadworth 6X, Abbot Ale, Greene King, Shepherd Neame, Foster's, Tennent's Pilsner, Tennent's Extra, Kronenbourg, Holsten, Grolsch, Guinness

Nearest Tube Stations
Edgware Road,
Warwick Avenue

At the height of the Victorian railway boom someone gave Mr Frank Crocker a hot tip. Marylebone Station was going to be built in Maida Vale.

Such information could make a man of energy and foresight rich, and Mr Crocker was such a man. He worked out where the station would go, built an hotel right opposite and waited for the Great Central Railway to arrive. Well, of course, we know now that Marylebone Station was built in Marylebone, but the news came as a terrible shock to poor Mr Crocker. A railway hotel without a railway station was at a peculiar disadvantage. Mr Crocker, despairing, jumped from one of the many upstairs windows.

The Crown Hotel – the name he gave it – faced difficult times but you should see it today. New owners, Regent Inns, spent £250,000 on it a couple of years ago and gave it a new name. It is called Crocker's Folly now and it is looking marvellous.

Mr Crocker was not one for penny pinching. Marble columns, marble walls, marble counters, massive baronial fireplaces, rich coffered ceilings, carved mahogany fittings everywhere, a magnificent saloon bar and a noble public bar, both with nine cask ales on the handpumps. The cellars are as roomy as everywhere else.

Then there's the carvery. This was originally the billiard room and still has the biggest of the fireplaces, a pike in a glass case and a bust of the Emperor Caracalla.

No bust of Mr Crocker, though he will surely get one some day. You would have to have a heart of stone not to feel for him. To have risked so much, spent so much, built such a building and to have met with such a disappointment. His ambition was the death of him, but he left London one of its most impressive public houses.

·THE CROOKED BILLET·

14 Crooked Billet, SW19 **0181-946 4942**

'At the heart of Cromwell's Half-Acre'

Open
All Week

Hours
11.00–23.00
(12.00–22.30 Sun)

Credit Cards
All major cards accepted

The Crooked Billet is in the tiny hamlet of that name hard by Wimbledon Common, and it has been slipping in and out of local records for nearly 500 years. It first appears in 1509: a brewery and inn. Then we hear of Walter Cromwell, the father of Henry VIII's Lord High Chamberlain, retiring to the inn in 1513 and dying there. His bit of land gets called Cromwell's Half-Acre. A few years pass and the old inn is being rebuilt a little way off, then rebuilt again. The builders seem hardly to have been out of the place.

The latest lot emerged only on Good Friday 1994, having given the old pub a thorough going over. When they finished, the settles in the new no-smoking area were the only original fittings left, and breath was held while the oldest regular inspected his new local. The best he'd seen it, he said.

His view of the food is not recorded, but the restaurant at the back got quite adventurous for a while. It has now returned to more traditional ways. The refurbished bar has proved popular, as have the seats outside, but in fine weather people do as they have done for centuries. They sit with their drinks on the green opposite the Crooked Billet, enjoying the sunshine at the heart of Cromwell's Half-Acre.

Restaurant food available
12.00–14.30 and
18.30–22.00
Mon–Sat

Special Features
No-smoking Area
Wheelchair Access
(but not lavatory)
Tables outside seat 20

Beers Available
Rolling Rock, Labatts, Stella Artois, Red Stripe, Budweiser

Nearest Tube Station
Wimbledon

·THE CROWN AND GREYHOUND·

73 Dulwich Village, SE21   **0181-693 2466**

'One of the great pubs of south London'

In the Dulwich of Queen Victoria you were no one unless you were a member of the Dulwich Club. It held its dinners in the Greyhound, the grandest pub south of the river, and Charles Dickens, naturally, was often a guest. So impressed was he by Dulwich that he had Mr Pickwick retire there.

Alas for the Greyhound, its story is one of pride before a fall. There were two pubs in Dulwich village but the Greyhound was the only one that mattered. It was the one with the ballroom and the pleasure grounds, the one with stables for 15 horses and six coaches. The London–Sevenoaks stage stopped there twice a day. The Crown, the small pub on the other side of the road, was merely for the villagers and no one thought much of it at all. Then one day in 1895 the manager of the humble Crown bought the fine Greyhound and pulled it down. Three years later a new pub went up on the site of the Crown, the imposing Crown and Greyhound. It has been a centre of village life ever since.

It is one of the great pubs of south London and hugely successful. Big as it is you can hardly budge there in the evenings. It still has four bars, one non-smoking, the others joined by the original mahogany counter, and a lot of the original furniture has survived, including high-backed Victorian settees of unusual discomfort. There is a big busy restaurant and every Saturday a wedding reception in the

Open
All Week

Hours
11.00–23.00
(12.00–22.30 Sun)

Credit Cards
All major cards accepted

Food Available
Bar food all day
Restaurant
12.00–14.30 and
17.30–21.00

Special Features
No-Smoking Room
Wheelchair Access
(but not lavatory)
Tables outside seat 200
Function Room seats 90

Beers Available
Burton Ale, Tetley, Young's, John Bull, Lowenbrau, Castlemaine, Carlsberg, Sam's Stout, Guinness Ciders: Merrydown, Old English

Nearest BR Station
North Dulwich

suite of function rooms on the first floor. Brides' parents sometimes book a year ahead. The garden is huge, sweeping round the side of the pub, full of tables. Steps take you up the nicest, greenest bit and to yet more tables under a magnificent horse chestnut tree.

The manager, Barney Maguire, first came to the Crown and Greyhound as a young barman and met the schoolgirl daughter of the landlord. When she was old enough they married and years later they came back to run the pub themselves. They have now been married 20 years.

·THE CROWN AND SHUTTLE·

Shoreditch High Street, E1 **247 7696**
'Exotically round the pool table'

Open
All Week
Hours
11.00–23.00
(12.00–22.30 Sun)
Credit Cards
None
Bar Food Available
11.00–15.00
Beers Available
Webster's, Courage Best, Holsten, Becks, Carlsberg, Foster's, Guinness
Nearest Tube Station
Liverpool Street

Respectable East End local with a popular regular feature. At lunchtime and in the early evening exotic dancers dance exotically round the pool table, taking off all their clothes except their shoes. City workers in suits watch without comment or expression and applaud politely as the dance concludes. Pool players then resume their interrupted game.

·THE CROWN AND TWO CHAIRMEN·

31 Dean Street, W1 **437 8192**
'The chairmen would have needed a drink'

Open
All Week
Hours
11.00–23.00
(12.00–22.30 Sun)
Closed Christmas Day, Boxing Day
Credit Cards
AmEx, Visa, Mastercard
Bar Food Available
12.00–15.00
Special Features
Wheelchair Access
Tables outside seat 12
Private Room seats 30
Beers Available
Tetley, Wadworth, Brakspear, London Pride, Castlemaine, Carlsberg, Lowenbrau
Nearest Tube Station
Piccadilly Circus

This is the story. Queen Anne was having her portrait painted. The painter was James Thornhill and he had a studio opposite this pub. She arrived for sittings in a sedan chair. The chairmen would put her down in Dean Street and while she tripped into the studio they would stagger into the pub.

The Queen Anne portrait in the House of Commons is by Thornhill. Perhaps that was the one. She seems to have been very stately. The chairmen would have needed a drink.

Anyway the picturesque name brings in the passing trade, and the pub flourishes.

· THE CUTTY SARK TAVERN ·

Ballast Quay, SE10   **0181-858 3146**
'People sometimes travel miles to be here'

Walk far enough along the river bank at Greenwich and you will come across a charming quay, a row of picturesque old houses, an ancient cherry tree and the Cutty Sark Tavern.

If it is fine people will be sitting on the river wall having a drink. If not they will be in the bar with its old beams and comfortable wooden furniture or in the old panelled room upstairs having red mullet, perhaps, or the traditional whitebait. People sometimes travel miles to be here. The Cutty Sark has a sort of fan club and you can see why. It is a true period piece.

It was the Union Tavern when it was built in 1804 and for most of its life it was a small working-man's pub used mainly by seafarers and riverboat men. Nowadays it belongs to an amiable entrepreneur called Sydney Haines and is a protected building – protected by him and by having a Grade II listing. 'I have resisted all advice to alter it,' he says.

He did change the name in 1954. He wanted to welcome the last of the great tea clippers to her new home in Greenwich, but such other changes as there have been have been forced upon him. There was the matter of the loos, for instance. Year after year his customers did as their fathers and grandfathers had done, went into the yard and gazed up at the stars. The local council insisted on a more up-to-date procedure and he reluctantly put up a lavatory block at the back in the 1960s.

Haines has other business interests. He has a wine bar in Blackfriars, another tavern in Dorking, a vineyard in France. But his grown-up children still live on the quay and the Cutty Sark is the apple of his eye.

Open
All Week
Hours
11.00–23.00
(12.00–22.30 Sun)
Credit Cards
All major cards except Diner's Club
Bar Food Available
12.00–14.30 Mon–Sun;
18.00–21.30 Tue–Fri
Special Features
Wheelchair Access
Beer Garden seats 60
Beers Available
Charrington, Bass, Worthington, Tennent's Extra, Caffrey's
Nearest BR Station
Maze Hill

· DE HEMS ·

11 Macclesfield Street, W1   **437 2494**
'Oranjeboom Gezondheid'

De Hems claims to be London's only Dutch pub. Does anyone doubt it? It looks Dutch. See its gable. It behaves Dutch. Proost. It's Dutch all right.

The De Hems used to be called the Macclesfield – you find it in Macclesfield Street on the very edge of Chinatown. A few more yards down the street and it could have been London's only Chinese pub, but a Dutch sailor called de Hems

Open
All Week
Hours
11.00–24.00
(12.00–22.30 Sun)
Closed Christmas Day, Boxing Day
Credit Cards
All major cards accepted

Bar Food Available
12.00–24.00
Special Features
Wheelchair Access
(but not lavatory)
Tables outside seat 16
Private Room
seats 120
Beers Available
Oranjeboom, Chimay,
Amstel, Witte Raaf,
Mort Subite, La Trappa,
Sol
Nearest Tube Stations
Piccadilly Circus,
Leicester Square

took it over in the 1920s so it's Dutch plates, Dutch photographs, Dutch old masters. '*Oranjeboom Gezondheid*' declares the mirror behind the bar, a friendly greeting apparently.

It is a very friendly pub this one. The noise level rises as the evening goes on and the evening goes on until midnight, courtesy of a music licence. The ceiling is a subtle shade of nicotine, though the ceiling fans do their best and in the summer the doors fold right back, opening the whole bar to the air and other delights of Macclesfield Street.

They call the upstairs bar '*t Oude Treffpunt*', the old meeting place, and on the first Thursday of every month many Dutchies living in London meet there for *Nederlandse Avond*, a Dutch evening. De Hems is known for its comedy club nights on Wednesdays.

You see people tucking into delicious-looking Dutch food – deep-fried savoury balls called *bitterballen*, *loempia*, which are pancake rolls, and *groteborrelhap*, a platter of various Dutch delights.

Oranjeboom means orange tree, the symbol of the Oranjeboom Brewery in Rotterdam. There's a huge Oranjeboom pump on the bar pouring out prime Dutch ale, and they now do draught Witte Raaf, one of the wheat beers the Dutch and Belgians like so much. It is served by the half pint, has a high creamy head and is so cloudy you can't see the bottom of the glass. You get a wedge of lemon with it.

·THE DEVEREUX·

Open
Mon–Fri
Hours
11.00–21.30 Mon–Wed;
11.00–23.00 Thur–Fri
Closed Bank Holidays
Credit Cards
All major cards accepted
Bar and Restaurant Food Available
12.00–14.30
Special Features
Wheelchair Access
(but not lavatory)
Private Room seats 100
Beers Available
Theakston XB, Courage Best, Wadworth 6X, Foster's, Kronenbourg, Holsten, Guinness, Beamish, Miller Lite
Nearest Tube Station
Piccadilly Circus,

20 Devereux Court, WC2   583 4562

'*Upstairs there are rooms to let, unusual in a London pub*'

Devereux Court is a quiet courtyard between the Strand and the Middle Temple. Here, in this elegant public house, lawyers gather, others too. There's a very nice restaurant, a pleasant bar, a room with books and comfortable chairs.

The pub was built in 1844, a good year for building things. It is very nice looking. It is caramel and white at the moment and suits it. Upstairs there are four rooms to let, bed and breakfast. This is unusual in a London pub. A single room with breakfast costs £40 a night, a double £50, reasonable considering.

The little mews got its name from Robert Devereux, the Earl of Essex who owned the land around here. He was played by Errol Flynn in the movie. Bette Davis, as Queen Elizabeth, gave him a tremendous slap across the face, not faking it at all. It brought tears to poor Errol's eyes. But I digress…

·The Devonshire Arms·

7 Duke Street, W1   **935 5887**

'Plates galore'

When Gareth Stones and Tony Crowe took over the Swan in Fetter Lane they renamed it the Mucky Duck and filled it with seaside postcards. When they took over the Devonshire Arms they kept the name and filled it with plates. There are plates galore, plates on every available surface, 458 plates so far. Tony Crowe, an inveterate collector, is still buying plates and, for that matter, seaside postcards. The surplus is rapidly filling his garage at home. He'll have to get another pub.

Open
Mon–Sat

Hours
11.00–23.00 Mon–Fri;
11.00–18.00 Sat
Closed Bank Holidays

Bar Food Available
11.00–23.00 Mon–Fri;
(11.00–18.00 Sat)

Beers Available
London Pride,
Worthington, Caffrey's,
Guinness, Staropranes

Nearest Tube Station
Bond Street

·The Dickens Inn·

St Katharine's Way, E1   **488 1226**

'A wonderful, well Dickensian, sight'

Dickens loved pubs and wrote about them like no one else. Here, though, is a pub he had nothing to do with, knew nothing about. It is called the Dickens Inn.

It is cashing in on his name, I suppose, but I wish he could have watched as this massive old wood-framed warehouse was lifted onto wheels and then trundled, creaking and groaning, to its new home by Tower Bridge. Think what he could have made of that.

The old warehouse now stands brimming with life on a superb site in St Katharine's Dock, a huge inn, three storeys high, each storey with a deep balcony the whole length of the building, each balcony crowded with people. It is a wonderful, well Dickensian, sight.

St Katharine's Dock with its marina crowded with yachts and dinghies is an outstandingly attractive part of London, and the Dickens Inn, there for about 25 years now, has been such a hit that they have made it a third bigger, though you would never know just by looking. It now has five separate bars and restaurants, a staff of 55 and recently it won a major battle to let its customers drink outside.

You would hardly believe it but there are people who go to great lengths to stop London drinking in the open air. Here is a rare victory for the good guys, so a hat or two in the air please for two terraces full of tables, the tables full of people whenever the sun shines.

The Dickens Inn has changed hands once or twice in its short life. Charles Forte has it now and it is a place to see. The ground floor is a vast bar, dark, low ceilinged, the windows filled with the waving masts of the marina.

Open
All Week

Hours
11.00–23.00
(12.00–22.30 Sun)

Credit Cards
All major cards
accepted

Bar Food Available
11.30–17.00
(11.30–20.30 Sat;
12.00–15.00 Sun)

Special Features
Wheelchair Access
Beer Garden seats 100
Private Room seats 110

Beers Available
Courage Best, Courage
Directors, Adnams,
Wadworth, Carlsberg,
Foster's, Kronenbourg,
Budweiser

Nearest Tube Station
Tower Hill

Upstairs and a pizzeria occupies the whole floor with tables all along the balcony. Up another floor and it's a grill and fish restaurant, the tables crisply tableclothed and again a long balcony full of people eating. Cask ales and lager compete in the bar, the views are of boats and water, cobblestones and an apple tree pergola. It is an outstanding addition to the general jollity.

·DIRTY DICK'S·

202 Bishopsgate, EC2 **283 5888**

'Farewell dirty days'

Open
Sun–Fri
Hours
11.00–23.00
(12.00–15.00 Sun)
Closed Bank Holidays
Credit Cards
All major cards accepted
Food Available
Bar 11.00–23.00
Restaurant
11.30–15.00
Special Features
Wheelchair Access
2 Private Rooms each seating up to 10
Beers Available
Young's Bitter, Young's Special, Tetley, London Lager, Castlemaine, Beamish, Red Stripe
Nearest Tube Station
Liverpool Street

Dirty Dick's is one of London's top tourist pubs. It is full of character and has an interesting story to tell, but I'm sorry to say that nowadays tourists are often disappointed. It is not nearly dirty enough for them. It is, in fact, not dirty at all. It used to be but these are the hygienic 1990s. The original Dirty Dick's would have been in deep trouble. As for Dirty Nat...

Dirty Nathaniel Bentley, an 18th-century dirty person, had a hardware shop in Leadenhall Street. The story goes that his bride-to-be died on their wedding day. Rather put out he locked the room in which the wedding breakfast was set, swore it would never be re-opened and thereafter neither changed his clothes nor washed.

He became quite a celebrity. People flocked to his shop, which daily grew dirtier, and when his landlord eventually got him out Ye Olde Port Wine House in Bishopsgate bought the entire contents, rotting wedding breakfast, dead cats and all and displayed them in its cellar bar. Ye Olde Port Wine House became Dirty Dick's.

Poor dirty Nat died broke but Dirty Dick's prospered, and when it was rebuilt in 1870 all the grisly artefacts were stored and then carefully put back in their place. There they stayed until just ten years ago, and a ghastly sight the old bar was with mummified dead cats and other frightful things hanging from the black rafters. Finches had it at the time and eventually decided on a clean-up. Out went poor Nathaniel's vile household goods and a cleaner was taken on. Farewell dirty days.

Young's has Dirty Dick's now and it remains a very successful pub. The main bar with its wooden floor, old beams and copper counter is crowded and notably cheerful, the first-floor restaurant has just been enlarged and done over – you have to book these days – and the candle-lit cellar bar seems roomier since the clean-up and some may think a great deal more congenial.

· THE DOG AND FOX ·

24 Wimbledon High Street, SW19   **0181-946 6565**

'You can be too big, that seems clear'

The Victorians were used to these things but even they must have been impressed by the Dog and Fox. Such a display of turrets, decorated gables and pillared porticos and the like, and its size! It occupies an enormous site, dominating its bit of the High Street.

Young's, whose pub it is, points out that the actual pub bit isn't all that big considering. It is just that it is backed up by what seems an acre or two of terrace between pub and High Street, also by a whole Chinese restaurant, specializing in Peking and Szechuan food, and a ballroom, not used for balls much these days but essential for conferences, weddings, annual dinner dances and the like.

It comes as a shock to hear that it used to be even bigger, that it once had eight public rooms, two butteries, two barns and several hundred acres of land. But you can be too big, that seems clear, and Young's must be relieved that with good Queen Victoria on the throne it was rebuilt in its present modest proportions and set back a bit so that the High Street could be widened.

It wasn't exactly poky even then. It still included gardens, coach houses, a bowling green and a paddock but they are now absorbed into Wimbledon Village, a lovely place on its hill top. Some stables have survived. The young of Wimbledon learn to ride at the end of the adjoining alley, but there is no sign of the bowling green or paddock.

As for the bar, it would be considered a good size in a pub of more usual dimensions and it has just been totally refurbished in the modern Victorian style that Young's and its customers like so much.

Open
All Week

Hours
11.00–23.00
(12.00–22.30 Sun)

Credit Cards
All major cards accepted

Bar Food Available
12.00–15.00 and
18.00–21.00

Special Features
Wheelchair Access
Tables outside seat 70
Private Room seats 160

Beers Available
All Young's bitters, Tennent's, Red Stripe, Premium, London Lager, Castlemaine

Nearest Tube Station
Wimbledon

· DOGGETTS COAT AND BADGE ·

1 Blackfriars Bridge, SE1   **633 9057**

'As in life the higher you go the better the view'

A modern pub on the river hard by Blackfriars Bridge, custom-built for Allied Lyons in 1976.

A wine bar on the ground floor spills out onto the Embankment in the summer with picnic tables and a riverboat view of the bridge. The main bar is on the floor above, there's a brasserie on the floor above that and a conference centre, board room and terrace at the top. There is a lift. Not many pubs have lifts. As in life the higher you go the better the view.

Open
Mon–Fri

Hours
11.00–23.00
Closed Bank Holidays

Credit Cards
All major cards accepted

Food Available
Bar 11.00–15.00
Restaurant
12.00–15.00

Special Features
Wheelchair Access
(but not lavatory)
Gardens outside
seat 200

Beers Available
Tetley, Adnams,
Wadworth 6X,
Carlsberg,
Castlemaine, Tuborg,
Guinness

Nearest Tube Stations
Blackfriars, Waterloo

Open
All Week

Hours
11.00–23.00
(12.00–22.30 Sun)

Credit Cards
All major cards accepted

Bar Food Available
12.00–15.00 and
18.00–22.00 Sun–Thur;
12.00–17.00 Fri–Sat

Special Features
Wheelchair Access
(but not lavatory)
Tables outside seat 50

Beers Available
London Pride, ESB,
Grolsch, Heineken,
Guinness

Nearest Tube Station
Hammersmith

The name refers to Doggett's Coat and Badge Race, rowed by young watermen every July between London Bridge and Chelsea. This has been going on since 1715, which makes it the oldest single sculls race in the world. There were only four competitors this year. Watermen on the Thames grow fewer.

·THE DOVE·

19 Upper Mall, W6   0181-748 5405

'I bet they all loved it, these famous faces'

A roll call of just some of the people who have visited the Dove hangs over the fireplace in the bar. It is a remarkable list, a Who's Who of the theatre and cinema, life and letters, and I bet they all loved it, all these famous faces. This is, after all, the Pigeons of *The Water Gypsies*, the perfect riverside pub.

It has always attracted artists and writers. William Morris lived next door; James Thomson, in an on-rush of patriotism, wrote 'Rule Britannia' upstairs; Ernest Hemingway drank here; and so did Graham Greene.

This, then, is the calibre of person you must expect to find as you step inside from the narrow alleyway, but first look in the room immediately on your right. If you can squeeze in you will be in what the *Guinness Book of Records* says is the smallest bar in the UK, 4'2" by 7'10", big enough for four medium-sized drinkers, two of them sitting on stools at the bar.

You will have to back out again into the dark, low-ceilinged, oak-beamed saloon bar, all black panelling, cushioned wall settles and copper-topped tables, and you may well decide to stay right there, particularly in winter when the fire is on.

Up those steps, though, are rooms serving food and rooms for eating in – Thai food in the evening – and past them is the Dove of summertime, a verandah shaded by an old vine, a terrace overlooking the river, another terrace reached by a spiral staircase, sunny places and shady places.

Brian Lovrey has the tenancy and guards the old pub's character. No music. No gaming machines. The river is never as threatening as in the days before the Thames Barrier, and the London Pride, the ESB and the two draught lagers stay dry and cool in the old tavern's cellars. The Dove has been a Fuller's house since 1796.

· THE DRAYTON ARMS ·

153 Old Brompton Road, SW5   **373 0385**

'Buff terracotta and purple brick'

For grandeur and self-confidence it is hard to beat the Drayton Arms. It is high Victoriana, all buff terracotta and purple brick. You may feel impelled to give it a round of applause as you pass.

The interior is almost as grand as the exterior with beautiful art nouveau lanterns and a wonderful mahogany bar with wrought-iron flourishes and marble columns. There is a much less attractive back room, but that's back rooms for you. It is in all other regards a most distinguished pub and I congratulate the Day family, who own it, on their choice of forebears.

The Days do not intervene in the running of the pub, the manager has not met any of them, but Days have owned the land on which a lot of Old Brompton Road stands for more than 200 years. They remain the pub's freeholders.

The first pub on the site went up in 1847 and contained the largest single household in the area – the publican, his wife, their seven children and five servants. It was demolished in 1891 and up went this one, far bigger, infinitely grander, and thankfully it has survived the thousand natural shocks that pubs are heir to.

It is a listed building now but it still likes to let its hair down sometimes and at 9.00 pm every Friday and Saturday it becomes a lively venue for folk, jazz and assorted entertainers. An Elvis impersonator is a great favourite.

It does well with an all-day menu called Goodbye Mr Chips – no chips – and there is a loyal following for the Caffrey's Irish Ale, brewed in Belfast. This takes four minutes to settle.

The Webber-Douglas Academy has a small theatre for its student productions on the first floor – capacity houses every time, I'm told. It seats 33.

Open
All Week

Hours
11.00–23.00
(12.00–22.30 Sun)

Credit Cards
All major cards except AmEx

Bar Food Available
11.00–23.00

Special Features
Wheelchair Access
(but not lavatory)
Tables outside seat 48

Beers Available
Caffrey's, Bass, Worthington, Grolsch, Carling Black Label, Tennent's Extra, Guinness

Nearest Tube Stations
Gloucester Road, South Kensington

· THE DUBLIN CASTLE ·

94 Parkway, NW1   **485 1773**

'Rap, ska, R & B and every customer a critic'

Open
All Week

Hours
12.00–24.00
(12.00–22.30 Sun)
Closed Christmas Day

Credit Cards
None

Special Features
Wheelchair Access
(but not lavatory)
Tables outside seat 12
Private Room seats 70

Beers Available
John Smith's,
Webster's, Budweiser,
Sol, Molsen Dry,
Holsten, Foster's,
Carlsberg, Guinness
Cider: Strongbow

Nearest Tube Station
Camden Town

A small Victorian local in Camden Town making its way in a competitive new world with a music room behind the bar. It's rap, ska, R & B, and every customer a critic at the Dublin Castle nowadays.

From Parkway this report: 'Long established on the rock scene. Madness got their first break here. Smallish venue means you're close to the band so ennui if band not up to much. Different bands on pub circuit seven days a week, some MoR. So pick your night.'

MoR: derog. middle of the road.

· THE DUKE OF CUMBERLAND ·

235 New King's Road, SW6   **736 2777**

'A man of broad and varied interests...'

Open
All Week

Hours
11.00–23.00
(12.00–22.30 Sun)

Credit Cards
None

Bar Food Available
12.00–15.00 (hot) and
18.00–21.00 (cold)

Special Features
Wheelchair Access
Tables outside seat 20

Beers Available
All Young's bitters,
Tennent's, Castlemaine,
Premium Lager, London
Lager, Beamish,
Guinness, Oatmeal
Stout

Nearest Tube Station
Parson's Green

There was a tremendous pub boom in the 1890s. Potential profits seemed limitless and old pubs were being bought, sold and extravagantly remodelled all over London. As prices spiralled heavenwards, Young's rebuilt its comparatively modest Duke's Head in the splendid style of the times.

This is the pub we now know as the Duke of Cumberland, the big, swanky four-storey pub looking across New King's Road to Parson's Green, balusters, arched windows and soaring chimneys, superbly fitted inside.

The pub kept its original name until 1971 when it was thoroughly renovated. It reopened as the Duke of Cumberland and won the *Evening Standard* Pub of the Year Competition the same year. It has had two more refurbishments since then.

It is a fine, upstanding public house, proud of the character and achievements of the man whose name it now bears. A large board, prominently displayed in the well-groomed and spacious saloon bar, recalls that he murdered his valet, committed adultery, sodomy and incest, blackmailed his brother, indecently assaulted the wife of the Lord Chamberlain and plotted the assassination of his niece, the future Queen Victoria. A man, in short, of broad and varied interests, most suited to the role of King of Hanover, which is what he became.

· THE DUKE OF WELLINGTON ·

179 Portobello Road, W11   **727 6727**

'Customers forbidden to take their bar stools with them'

Stallholders in the Portobello Road still call the Duke of Wellington Finches, which would have pleased the late Mr H H Finch who owned so many pubs in central London and unofficially lent his name to them all.

It is a busy pub with a lot remaining of the great gin palace it must have been – the ornate mahogany of the island bar, the brass candelabra and etched-glass windows. Low partitions form booths for drinkers around the walls, and in the summer customers spill out onto the pavement with their drinks and are forbidden to take their bar stools with them. Summer or winter, the world's best-known antique market guarantees hectic Saturdays.

The Duke, in his Goya mode, looking just like Michael Wilding, looks haughtily down from the inn sign, and the windows on the side seem permanently open at the bottom. Note to burglars. Don't bother. They are trompe l'oeil, just painted on.

Open
All Week

Hours
11.00–15.30 and
17.30–23.00
11.00–23.00 Sat
(12.00–22.30 Sun)

Credit Cards
None

Bar Food Available
12.00–15.00

Special Features
Wheelchair Access
Benches outside
seat 18

Beers Available
Young's Special,
Young's Bitter, London
Lager, Oatmeal Stout,
Tennent's, Castlemaine,
Guinness, Becks, Stein

Nearest Tube Station
Notting Hill Gate

· THE DUKE'S HEAD ·

8 Lower Richmond Road, SW15   **0181-788 2552**

'20 barmen, 16,000 pints'

The 1995 University Boat Race beat at least one record for the umpteenth time. The 20 barmen assembled for the day by the Duke's Head in Putney sold 16,000 pints of beer. That was 1,000 pints more than they sold in 1994 and THAT was the all-time record. The Boat Race gets bigger all the time.

If you stand on Putney Bridge and look up river, the first pub on the left is the massive Star and Garter, which also had a gala boat race day. The Duke's Head is the next pub along, an elegant Georgian building painted cream. After that it's all rowing-club boathouses.

The Duke's Head has always been deeply involved in rowing. At one time a boat-builder built boats on the top floor, lowering the finished ones down on the hoist that is still there. For years Putney Town Boat Club used the front part of the pub's cellars as its boathouse, and rowing men and women still drink in the Duke's Head as a matter of course.

It is a good-looking pub, well preserved, lots of carved mahogany and fine etched glass. Some of this was lost in the war. A bomb in Fulham put a lot of windows out but they have all been carefully and expensively replaced.

Open
All Week

Hours
11.30–15.00 and
19.00–23.00 Mon–Fri;
11.00–23.00 Sat
(12.00–22.30 Sun)

Credit Cards
None

**Bar and Restaurant
Food Available**
12.00–14.30

Special Features
Wheelchair Access

Beers Available
Young's Special, Dirty
Dick's, Castlemaine,
Red Stripe, Tennent's
Extra, Stella, Oatmeal,
Beamish, Guinness

Nearest Tube Station
Putney Bridge

It is a peaceable place. Norman Golding, the landlord, is very much in control. There are no children or dogs, no pool tables or juke boxes. Plastic glasses only if you take your drink outside. They get through a lot of plastic glasses at the Duke's Head on a sunny day – 16,000 on boat race day in 1995.

· THE EAGLE ·

159 Farringdon Road, EC1 **837 1353**

'A foodie revolution'

Open
Mon–Fri

Hours
12.00–23.00
Closed Bank Holidays

Credit Cards
None

Restaurant Food Available
12.30–14.30 and 18.30–22.30

Special Features
Wheelchair Access
Tables outside seat 15

Beers Available
Eagle IPA, Bombardier Best Bitter, Carlsberg, Kronenbourg, Holsten, Gambrinus

Nearest Tube Station
Farringdon

There has been a foodie revolution in pubs. One pub after another is now doing the sort of food that you used to get only in Mediterranean bistros and the Eagle is where it started.

The Eagle is basically a robust local boozer. When Michael Belben and David Eyre took it they gave over half the bar counter to an open kitchen and started cooking the kind of things that people had on their hols. Fay Maschler put it in her London Restaurant Guide and Egon Ronay gave it a star.

So you might suppose that this was more a restaurant than a pub. Not at all, say Belben and Eyre, it is still every inch a good pub. Why shouldn't a pub have good food? Why not indeed, and now quite a lot do and the style that is most widely adopted is that of the Eagle's. Pleb Med is what *Harpers* called it.

There's no booking at the Eagle, no quiet little table anywhere. The menu is chalked up and changes often. You see and smell what is being cooked, order your food from the bar and have a drink at your table.

All these people tucking into the crostini, the fresh tuna, the grilled squid and the lovely pasta are *Guardian* journos, fashion people, advertising people and they are in and out in no time, a drink, a shared bottle of wine, lots of chat and just one course, hardly anyone has more than one course. There's not much call for puddings at the Eagle but there are Spanish cheeses and excellent coffee and then it's back to the office, darkroom or studio, so you'll get a seat before long and this is food worth waiting for.

Nothing matches at the Eagle, it is all odd chairs and strange tables, nothing smart, nothing designed. They do good cask beers and get through a lot of wine, and in the afternoon when it empties you can see what a nice old pub it is. It opens at midday and stays open until 11.00 pm, and on Saturdays and Sundays they close it and recover from the week.

· THE EAGLE TAVERN ·

2 Shepherdess Walk, N1 **253 4715**

'Up and down the City Road, in and out the Eagle...'

The words of the song that still makes this pub a household name are high on the side wall so that all who turn into Shepherdess Walk from the City Road can read them.

Up and down the City Road
In and out the Eagle
That's the way the money goes
Pop goes the weasel!

The Eagle of the song was actually the Royal Eagle Music Hall, which stood on this site. Marie Lloyd first appeared there at the age of 15. It had pleasure grounds with fountains, gas devices, illuminations, cosmoramas, magic mirrors and the famous Grecian Saloon. It became so notorious that General Booth of the Salvation Army took it over to close it down. The whole lot was demolished in 1901 and this pub went up instead.

It is looking very well just now, confident Edwardian frontage all spruced up, handsome eagle on the cupola brightly gilded, big saloon bar with its pictures of music hall stars, public bar with its pool table and TV sport and the big beer garden at the back. You have to get there early on summer lunchtimes or you don't get a table.

The Eagle is part of local life, of course, and there is always the Pop Goes the Weasel bonus. It brings in the most unexpected people. The Brits know all the words, of course. We learned this song about pawning our tailor's iron or whatever at our mother's knee. Weird, really. It doesn't even rhyme.

Half a pound of twopenny rice
Half a pound of treacle
That's the way the money goes
Pop goes the weasel!

Open
Sun–Fri
Hours
11.00–23.00 Mon–Fri
(12.00–22.30 Sun)
Closed 23–26
December
Credit Cards
Access, Visa
Bar Food Available
12.00–15.00 and
18.00–22.00
Special Features
Wheelchair Access
(but not lavatory)
Beer Garden seats 100
Beers Available
Bass, Carling Black
Label, Carling Premier,
Grolsch, Caffrey's
Guinness,
Nearest Tube Station
Old Street

· EARLS ·

180 Earls Court Road, SW5 **835 1826**

'A new profession and quite well paid, they say'

If a chap runs across a cricket pitch with nothing on he is a streaker. If he does the same in the local park he is a flasher. If he undresses on a platform in a pub he is a stripper, a new profession and quite well paid they say.

It is a job that involves a lot of racing round. Male strippers may have three or four bookings in an evening and they all do their stuff from time to time in Earls. This Earls Court

Open
All Week
Hours
16.00–24.00
(12.00–24.00 Sun)
Bar Food Available
All opening hours

Beers Available
Worthington Best,
Carling Black Label,
Tennent's Pilsner,
Grolsch, Staropramen,
Guinness
Cider: Red Rock

Nearest Tube Station
Earls Court

gay pub is known for its strippers. On Sunday there's one on every two hours. In the middle of the week there are amateur nights when half a dozen may have a go.

Earls has had a chequered career. It used to be an Earls Court local, its name no one can recall. Since then it has been Harpos and then Banana Max. In a competitive world like this you have to keep moving.

·THE EDGAR WALLACE·

40 Essex Street, WC2   353 3120

'The Edgar who?'

Open
Mon–Sat

Hours
11.00–23.00;
11.00–15.00 Sat
Closed Christmas Day

Bar and Restaurant Food Available
11.00–14.30 (no food Sat)

Special Features
Wheelchair Access
(but not lavatory)
Private Room seats 40

Beers Available
Boddingtons, London Pride, Brakspear, Old Hazy, Castle Eden, Heineken, Stella Artois, Murphy's,
5 guest ales

Nearest Tube Station
Temple

In 1975 the Essex Arms, a small pub in a little street off Fleet Street, was renovated and given a new name. Whitbreads decreed that to mark the 100th anniversary of the birth of Edgar Wallace it would henceforth be called the Edgar Wallace.

The great man's daughter Penny loaned the pub a collection of memorabilia, handsomely framed. It was distributed over the walls of the saloon bar – photographs, letters, newspaper cuttings, playbills, interesting stuff. The Edgar Wallace society descended on the pub's first-floor restaurant, once for lunch, once for dinner. Miss Wallace went too.

This pleasing custom has continued every year since and the pub has had another going-over. It is now one of Whitbread's real-ale pubs, a Hogshead, home-made food and ten real ales on the handpumps. It remains the Edgar Wallace.

Did I hear the dread words Edgar who? Edgar Wallace was a great journalist. He wrote more than 170 novels and plays and films, *The Four Just Men*, *Sanders of the River*, *The Ringer*, and when he died in Hollywood in 1932 they brought his body home on the *Berengaria*. He was a household word. Now he's on an inn sign, smoking a cigarette.

It was time we had a pub named after a journalist.

· The Elephant and Castle ·

Newington Causeway, SE1   **357 9134**

'Seriously famous'

A number of Elephant and Castles have flourished in London and one became seriously famous. It gave its name to a road junction, a tube station, a bus route and a vast pink shopping centre and it stood more or less where this one does.

The original Elephant and Castle was an 18th-century tavern that had the sense to pick a site where five major roads met. When it became a stop on the Northern Line and the south London terminus of the Bakerloo, well, you can't get more famous than that.

Planners promised to replace this famous old pub when they redeveloped the Elephant and Castle after the war and in the early 1960s the work began – a vast new traffic system, a gargantuan shopping centre of hideous aspect, Erno Goldfinger's Alexander Fleming House. The new pub had not been forgotten. Alexander Fleming House appeared to have pupped. A smaller version stood in the lee of the big one and a peculiarly uninteresting public house occupied the ground floor. It was called, of course, the Elephant and Castle. Goldfinger's building stands empty and dire, its unhappy occupant, the Department of the Environment, having fled. It has supporters. Some want it to be listed – 'unhinged,' breathed Brian Sewell when he heard – but there seems little chance of that now. Eventual demolition seems certain.

All this is hard lines on the poor pub. Its fate seems bound to that of the hulk behind it, but it got good news recently. A refurbishment is planned, its immediate future seems assured. So it soldiers on. It has a pool table, a darts board, a darts team. It sells elephant and castle lighters for £1 each and has a clear view of the Elephant and Castle electricity substation and of the horrendous shopping centre, now painted pink.

Quiz programmes like to ask why Elephant and Castle and you are meant to say that it was really the Infanta of Castile but the Brits got it wrong. The boring answer has to do with the sign of the Cutlers' Company and, alas, this is probably it.

Open
All Week

Hours
11.00–23.00
(12.00–22.30 Sun)

Credit Cards
None

Bar Food Available
12.00–21.00

Special Features
Wheelchair Access
Tables outside seat 30

Beers Available
Ruddles, Kronenbourg, Budweiser, Foster's, Carlsberg

Nearest Tube Station
Elephant and Castle

· THE ENGINEER ·

65 Gloucester Avenue, NW1 **722 0950**

'Distinctly classy'

Open
All Week

Hours
12.00–11.00 Mon–Sat
(12.00–22.30 Sun)

Credit Cards
Switch, Mastercard,
Access, Visa

Restaurant Food Available
12.00–15.00 and
18.30–22.30
(Mon–Sun)

Special Features
Tables outside
seat 100

Beers Available
Adnams, Caffreys,
Tennent's, Grolsch,
Guinness, London
Pride, Michelob, Sol
Cider: Red Rock

Nearest Tube Stations
Chalk Farm, Camden Town

When Tamsin Olivier, daughter of Lord Olivier and Joan Plowright, married her long-time friend Simon Dutton, star of The Saint series and much besides, she had the reception in a pub. Her pub actually.

Tamsin is, of course, an actress but this pub, the Engineer, has rather taken over. It is so all-absorbing, so much work, that she has put her acting career on hold. Later perhaps. Meanwhile, if the West End doesn't mind she has a pub to run.

This unexpected chapter in her life started in the summer of 1994. Tamsin and the artist Abigail Osborne were thinking of opening a restaurant, looked at Primrose Hill and came across the Engineer, very handsome, early Victorian, built in 1841 and named after Isambard Kingdom Brunel. He is the man in the tall top hat on the pub sign, and Tamsin says he might well have designed the Engineer himself.

By the time Tamsin and Abigail came into its life it was not looking its best. They loved the building, though, bought the lease and set about it. They were paying rent, they couldn't hang about, and in five and a half weeks it was looking lovely. The saloon bar gleamed, restaurant tables lined the old public bar and filled the one-time snug, there was an entirely new kitchen, Tamsin had postponed her wedding, and people were beating a path to the door.

The food, distinctly classy and not cheap, is a big draw at the Engineer. If you want a table in the restaurant it is best to book, particularly in the evening. You can eat in the bar if you like, though it does get very crowded, and in the summer there's the big flagged garden.

It is a different sort of pub altogether now and Tamsin and Abigail are both in the thick of it, taking orders, serving, doing their stuff. They have never been so busy. Nor, in all its days, has the Engineer.

·THE ENTERPRISE·

35 Walton Street, SW3　　　　　　　　**584 3148**

'So up-market that it is hardly recognizably a pub at all'

Something very remarkable has happened to the Enterprise. Four years ago it was a slightly gloomy local doing its best but look at it now! Gone the shades of nicotine brown, instead pale walls, great looped tapestried curtains, blue jugs of fresh flowers, designer baskets of lemons and lots of white tablecloths. Gone the venerable row of handpumps, in their place magnums of champagne gathering casually on the bar counter.

The result, of course, has been a total change in the cast list. You will know what I mean when I tell you that Nigel Havers and Tom Conti drop in and that the Princess of Wales herself has been seen having lunch with her chums. You can see why she would like it. The atmosphere is fizzy but not Hooray noisy, the food is very classy indeed with delicious wafts of garlic, rosemary, and thyme from passing dishes, and the personable young manager is greeted with mwah-mwah kisses from elegant regulars.

The Enterprise has indeed become so up-market that it is hardly recognizably a pub at all. A pub, though, it remains. It has a pub licence. It has pub hours and one or two residual pub ways. You can look in at noon, have a drink and go your way. Pubs come in many forms. This is one of them.

Open
All Week

Hours
12.00–15.30 and
17.30–23.00
(12.00–22.30 Sun)
Closed Christmas Day,
Boxing Day, Easter Sunday

Credit Cards
All major cards except Diner's Club

Restaurant Food Available
12.30–14.30 and
19.30–22.30

Special Features
Wheelchair Access
Tables outside seat 10

Beers Available
Rolling Rock, Sol,
Becks, Budweiser

Nearest Tube Stations
South Kensington,
Knightsbridge

·THE FALCON·

33 Bedford Road, SW4　　　　　　　　**274 2428**

'Rough local boozer makes good'

One pub at a time, you might think, but here are Ann and Tom Halpin with three, all of them in Clapham. This is one of them, an unusual place given its unpromising location. Coming in off the street you don't expect this cool open room, pink and blue with large wooden settles and sculptures dotted around.

There's jazz every Sunday and a barbecue in the garden at weekends. There are two pool tables. What used to be a rough local boozer has been transformed into a pleasant modern pub with a young local clientele.

Open
All Week

Hours
12.00–23.00
(12.00–22.30 Sun)
Closed Christmas Day,
Boxing Day

Credit Cards
None

Food Available
Bar food all day;
Barbecue Fri & Sat

Special Features
Wheelchair Access
(but not lavatory)
Tables outside seat 75

Beers Available
Fuller's London Pride,
Bass, Guinness,
Caffrey's Irish Ale,
Grolsch, Newcastle
Brown, Becks

Nearest Tube Station
Clapham North

· THE FALCON ·

234 Royal College Street, NW1   **485 3834**

'The newest, the hottest and the brightest'

Open
All Week

Hours
11.00–23.00
(12.00–22.30 Sun)

Credit Cards
None

Bar Food Available
All day, snacks and sandwiches only

Beers Available
Boddingtons, Becks, Lowenbrau, Stella, Heineken, Castlemaine, Murphy's, Guinness

Nearest Tube Station
Camden Town

The Falcon, once a local boozer, then a Bohemian joint with a fringe theatre at the back, has become the place to catch the newest, hottest and brightest of the young rock bands.

Bands being bands, the newest and hottest are certain to be the loudest and loud means trouble from the neighbours. Never mind, soft words and sound proofing, that is the answer, and all is well again in Royal College Street.

From Camden this front-line report: 'Guitar-led indie-rock bands play six nights a week under different banners. Sometimes it is Club Foot at the Falcon, sometimes the Starfish Club. They get good bands. Dodgy has been playing there lately and The Rockingbirds.

'The music room is not over-large. I have seen bigger living rooms. It is furnished with a park bench and a table, otherwise everything – walls, floor, stage, ceiling – is painted black for the nihilistic ambience so loved by indie connoisseurs. Go dressed in black and you may disappear from view altogether.'

· FERRET AND FIRKIN ·

114 Lots Road, SW10   **352 6645**

'Grand new neighbours'

Open
All Week

Hours
11.00–23.00
(12.00–22.30 Sun; restaurant licence in afternoon)

Credit Cards
All major cards accepted

Bar Food Available
12.00–14.30

Special Features
Wheelchair Access

Beers Available
Ferret Ale, Dogbolter, Balloonastic, Golden Glory, Castlemaine, Carlsberg

Nearest Tube Station
Fullham Broadway

This semi-circular old pub is on the semi-circular corner where Lots Road heading for the river turns left and heads for Cheyne Walk. It now has the towers of the new Chelsea Harbour against the skyline. That's Michael Caine's penthouse up there.

These grand new neighbours suit the Ferret and Firkin well. It is distinctly up-market and would be obliged if you would give it its full name, which is the Ferret and Firkin in the Balloon up the Creek. This is the longest pub name in London. The ferret and the balloon appear on the pub sign, a rather cliquey set of regulars call themselves the Balloonatics, and the brewhouse in the cellar produces copious quantities of a bitter called Balloonastic. The best bitter is Ferret ale.

The Ferret shows how well the classic Firkin style wears. The brass chandeliers, the ceiling fans, the wooden floor, the church pews, they will last, you feel, for ever. The pews are unexpectedly roomy and comfortable. They come from a firm in the Midlands called Pew Corner.

All Firkins have music, usually several times a week. There is in fact a Firkin circuit of entertainers. Some appear at a different Firkin every night. The star of the circuit is still Jamie Borer, known just as Jamie, sometimes as Jamie and his Organ. He arrives with his electronic keyboard and is a success everywhere, but he is a sensation at the Ferret. On Fridays, his night at the Ferret, you can hardly move.

· FINCH'S ·

190 Fulham Road, SW10　　　　　　　　　　　351 5043
'A large feisty-looking finch'

The public houses of Mr Henry Hobson Finch all had proper names of their own but almost all of them were known as Finch's. This one, the Finch's in Chelsea, was really called the King's Arms. The name appears, rather small but very permanently in wrought iron, above the entrance but it has been Finch's to anyone who ever drank there since, oh, probably 1897, which is when Mr Finch bought it.

Young's bought all the Finches in 1991 and in this case at least it has accepted the reality of the situation. This Finch's really is Finch's now. FINCH'S declares the fascia, and a new pub sign has gone up. On it is a large feisty-looking finch. Old Mr Finch would surely be pleased. He would be pleased, too, to see that his handsome Victorian pub, once considered so Bohemian, has kept so much of its splendid mahogany and brass, so many of its decorated mirrors and etched-glass screens and that it remains as popular as ever.

Open
All Week

Hours
11.00–23.00
(12.00–22.30 Sun)

Credit Cards
None

Bar Food Available
All open hours

Special Features
Wheelchair Access

Beers Available
Young's Ordinary, Young's Special, Oatmeal Stout, Castlemaine, London Lager, Tennent's Extra, Red Stripe, Guinness, Beamish

Nearest Tube Station
South Kensington

· THE FITZROY TAVERN ·

16 Charlotte Street, W1　　　　　　　　　　　580 3714
'Those were the days'

This famous Bohemian pub seems to have settled down to a respectable middle age now, looking nostalgically back at scandalous days gone by.

Those were the days – the 1930s when free spirits gathered round Augustus John and Nina Hamnet in the boozy, high-spirited saloon bar; the war years when the Fitzroy Tavern adopted HMS *Fitzroy* and wore a banner saying 'We're Here for the Duration We Hope'; the 1950s with an all-star cast as the photographs on every wall show, George Orwell, Dylan and Caitlan Thomas, Tommy Cooper, Michael Bentine, a very pretty Barbara Castle, a very young Richard Attenborough...

Open
All Week

Hours
11.00–23.00
(12.00–22.30 Sun)
Closed Christmas Day

Credit Cards
Visa

Bar Food Available
11.00–22.30

Special Features
Wheelchair Access
(but not lavatory)
Private Room
seats 30

Beers Available
Samuel Smith variants, Museum Ale, Old Brewery

Nearest Tube Stations
Goodge Street, Tottenham Court Raod

The regulars today are every bit as sparky, of course, who can doubt it? Their time will come to be photographed, glass in hand, and hung on the wall. Meanwhile the Fitzroy has been greatly smartened up by the new owners, Sam Smith – a smart new carpet and modern wallpaper, swagged curtains, new comfortably upholstered seats.

What would Augustus John have made of the piped music and the gaming machines? Well, he could always have gone downstairs to the panelled Writers and Artists Bar. No music or machines in there. This is where local writers' groups and historical societies meet. I think he would have been back in the saloon bar quite soon, though. It is still where the action is.

· THE FLASK ·

14 Flask Walk, NW3   **435 4580**

'Idleness, dissipation and frivolity'

Open
All Week

Hours
11.00–23.00
(12.00–22.30 Sun)

Credit Cards
None

Bar Food Available
12.00–15.00 and 18.00–22.00 Mon–Fri;
11.00–23.00 Sat
(12.00–15.30 Sun)

Special Features
Wheelchair Access (disabled lavatory)
Tables outside seat 25
Private Room seats 30
Live Music occasionally

Beers Available
Young's Bitter, Young's Special, Young's Oatmeal Stout, Young's Premium Lager, Young's London Lager, Tennent's Extra, Red Stripe, Castlemaine

Nearest Tube Station
Hampstead

The current passion for bottled water is not new. It was a hot item in the 18th century too, much to the advantage of Hampstead where medicinal springs were found that cured idleness, dissipation and frivolity.

These rather glum waters were bottled in the Thatched House and sold to the public for 3d a flask. The Thatched House became the Lower Flask to distinguish itself from the Upper Flask, which was much grander, and both got a place in Eng. Lit. In his novel *Clarissa*, Samuel Richardson let his heroine take tea in the Upper Flask. He described the Lower Flask, though, as a place where second-rate characters were to be found in swinish conditions.

Never mind, the Lower Flask did well with its flasks of water, delivered by cart to pubs and coffee houses all over London, and in 1874 the old thatched building was replaced by the tiled and distinctly unswinish one we see today. It has been the Flask ever since. Nothing is now heard of Hampstead's spring, and idleness, dissipation and frivolity flourish.

The Flask, made of Hampstead's nice yellow brick with big gas lanterns to guide you to the door, has always been a popular local. It has kept its separate public and saloon bars and they are divided by a fine listed Victorian screen. A big conservatory was recently added at the back and is used for food, music hall nights, live jazz and whatever else comes to mind. It sells Young's ale and was CAMRA's pub of the year in 1993.

· THE FLASK ·

77 Highgate West Hill, N6   **0181-340 7260**

'You then get the freedom of Highgate and kiss the prettiest girl in the room'

The Flask in Highgate is one of London's best-loved pubs. People like it for its age, for its character, for where it is. This is a lovely bit of London with its old churches, trees, and comely houses. John Betjeman was born up the road. 'Deeply I loved you, 31 West Hill!' he wrote in *Summoned by Bells*.

The Flask, the archetypal village pub, was built in 1663, rebuilt in 1767, done over in 1910 and again three years ago, a thorough renovation that closed the pub for three months. People who had feared the worst were relieved by what they found when it re-opened. The Flask now had the plumbing and the kitchens of a three-year-old, but it wandered along as always, up steps here, down steps there, ceilings still low, oak panelling and floorboards, doors and windows as they were.

It got its name from the flask it sold to be filled with water from Hampstead's mineral springs, but it was its strong ale that attracted the villagers, Hogarth among them. He is glimpsed down the years sketching in the bar after a particularly nasty brawl. Brawls are out at the Flask now but other old customs survive. There is, for instance, the annual Swearing on the Horns. This is one of those Merrie England things like morris dancing and involves an ancient set of antlers and strange oaths. You then get the freedom of Highgate and can kiss the prettiest girl in the room.

They serve food all day at the Flask. They serve up to 1500 meals a week and in high summer half of Highgate seems to want to eat there. The forecourt has beautiful white wisteria and lots of picnic tables, which fill with people at the first glimpse of the sun. These tables are still largely occupied in the depths of winter, actually. The British, a hardy island race, sit snugly in their overcoats, warmed by the ingenious outdoor heaters. These are a long-felt want, some think. May they soon catch on.

Open
All Week

Hours
11.00–23.00
(12.00–22.30 Sun)

Credit Cards
Access, Visa, AmEx, Mastercard, Eurocard

Bar Food Available
12.00–23.00 Mon–Sat
(12.00–15.00 and
19.00–21.00 Sun)

Special Features
Beer Garden seats 150

Beers Available
Tetley, Burton, Young's IPA, Young's Special, Winter Warmer

Nearest Tube Station
Highgate

· FLOWER AND FIRKIN ·

Kew Gardens Station **0181-332 1162**

'Pick up a picnic'

A sight as welcome as flowers that bloom in the spring, tra la, a Firkin on the District Line, a pub where once the British Railways buffet was. It does very well in the spring and summer with thousands taking the tube to Kew to see the botanical gardens and stopping off for a drink and a snack. It stays open all Sunday afternoon, does good salads, and on sunny days you can pick up a picnic there and have it on the grass.

It is proud of its conservatory but in this department I rather think Kew Gardens has the edge.

Open
All Week
Hours
11.00–23.00
(12.00–22.30 Sun)
Closed Christmas Day
Credit Cards
All major cards accepted
Bar Food Available
12.00–20.00
Special Features
Wheelchair Access (but not lavatory)
Tables outside seat 30
Beers Available
Cactus Ale, Rail Ale, Dogbolter, Murphy's, Guinness, Lowenbrau, Castlemaine, Carlsberg
Nearest Tube Station
Kew Gardens

· FLYMAN AND FIRKIN ·

166–170 Shaftesbury Avenue, WC2 **240 7109**

'Shaftesbury Avenue, albeit the wrong end'

Not a lot happens in this distant stretch of Shaftesbury Avenue. It is not the most obvious place for a new pub, but the Flyman and Firkin opened here at the end of 1994 to almost instant success. It is now one of the two most profitable pubs in the whole Firkin chain.

With its wooden floors, its settles and tables and old yellow brick walls it looks as if it had been a pub for ever, but it was a hair care clinic and warehouse when the Firkin people took it over. Into the skips went the hair care clinic. Goodbye floors, ceilings, walls. Down they came leaving a great open space for a vast bar and the latest thing in brewhouses.

This being Shaftesbury Avenue, albeit the wrong end, the flyman in the title is the chap who swings scenery about in the space above the stage. So the Flyman and Firkin has ropes and pulleys and lots of theatrical geegaws. That wooden thing next to the Firkin piano is a rain machine in good working order.

But the main thing is the Firkin food, baps and butties, pies and vegetable pot, and the Firkin ales brewed on site, Flyman bitter, the best seller, Critics Ale, a bit lighter, and, of course, the strong dark Dogbolter.

This is a worthy addition to the Firkin family, which expands as you look. There are at least 25 Firkins in London now, 60 more in other parts.

Open
Mon–Sat
Hours
12.00–23.00
Credit Cards
All major cards accepted and Switch
Food Available
12.00–23.00
Special Features
No-smoking Area
Wheelchair Access
Live Music Saturday nights, guitar duo
Beers Available
All ales brewed on the premises in highly visible brewery. Flyman Bitter, Critics Ale, Dogbolter, plus cask-conditioned guest ales from other London Firkin pubs, large range of bottled lagers and wines
Nearest Tube Stations
Covent Garden, Piccadilly Circus, Leicester Square

·The Founders Arms·

52 Hopton Street, Bankside, off Southwark Street, SE1   **928 1899**

'The Dean of St Paul's managed all right'

This fine modern pub stands boldly on the river bank on the south side of Blackfriars Bridge. It is hard to find the first time but it's worth the effort. The Dean of St Paul's managed all right. He formally opened it in 1979.

When you get there you have Young's beer, a glass-walled bar, a pleasant restaurant and a big riverside terrace, wonderful on a sunny day. Bar and terrace give you a fine view of the river and one of the great views of St Paul's.

Open
All Week

Hours
11.00–23.00
(11.00–15.00 and
19.00–22.30 Sun)

Credit Cards
AmEx, Visa, Access,
Mastercard

Food Available
Bar 11.00–21.30
Restaurant
12.00–14.30 and
18.30–21.30

Special Features
Wheelchair Access
Beer Garden seats 80

Beers Available
All Young's variants

Nearest Tube Station
Blackfriars

·The Fox and Anchor·

115 Charterhouse Street, EC1   **253 4838**

'Few white coats, none blood-stained'

After a night's work in Smithfield market, blood-spattered bummarees streamed into the Fox and Anchor on the dot of 6.00 am for a pint of porter and a hearty breakfast. They had spent the night manhandling dripping carcasses.

There is no such work for them in Smithfield now. Historic and fiercely-defended old practices have been swept away by EU hygiene regulations. Today Smithfield is a place of stainless steel counters, electronic trolleys and robotic doors. Refrigerated lorries now deliver carcasses without any human contact at all.

Remarkably, though, the Fox and Anchor is as busy as ever. It still has its all-day licence and at 7.00 am, an hour later than in the old days, in come the new customers. There are few white coats among them, none bloodstained. Instead there are men in suits on their way to the office, business-women having business breakfasts, and they come in such numbers that they have to book the day before. It is nothing for the Fox and Anchor to have 90 for breakfast and to turn another 20 away.

Such a breakfast it is – sausages, bacon, black pudding, fried egg, fried bread, baked beans, tomatoes, toast – you can't see the plate. It is known as the English breakfast and it costs £6.50. With it they drink pints of Guinness, pints of Tetley. A pint of champagne is not unknown. There's not much call for the coffee.

Open
Mon–Sat

Hours
7.00–22.00;
8.00–12.00 Sat
Closed Bank Holidays

Credit Cards
All major cards
accepted

Bar Food Available
7.00–10.30 and
12.00–14.30

Special Features
Private Room seats 20

Beers Available
Wadsworth 6X, Tetley,
Nicholson's, Carlsberg,
Castlemaine, Guinness

Nearest Tube Stations
Farringdon, Barbican

The Fox and Anchor has been serving this breakfast virtually unchanged since 1898. Its lunches are pretty hearty too, the steak and kidney pie is recommended. The pub itself does not seem to have changed much. It was decorated quite recently but you would hardly know. Look at the old snugs at the back. Surely they have always been here? They are, in fact, just three years old. They replaced the loos, now upstairs.

· THE FOX AND GRAPES ·

Camp Road, SW19 **0181-946 5599**

'Dogs, unusually, are welcome. Children too'

Open
All Week

Hours
11.00–23.00
(12.00–22.30 Sun)

Credit Cards
AmEx, Mastercard, Visa

Restaurant Food Available
12.00–22.00
(12.00–15.00 and 19.00–21.30 Sun)

Special Features
Wheelchair Access (but not lavatory)

Beers Available
Wadworth, Courage Directors, Courage Best, Webster's London Pride, Kronenbourg, Foster's, Miller

Nearest Tube Station
Wimbledon

Camp Road potters along on the west side of Wimbledon Common where the golf courses are, and an attractive low black and white pub overflows onto the narrow pavement. This is the Fox and Grapes, which has been there, part of it anyway, since 1787.

It was a tea and gin shop then. Now the tea and gin bit is a cosy, comfortable bar with a low wooden ceiling supported by huge oak pillars – Caesar's Bar they call it after a J Caesar who built the Roman fort up the road.

It is not known if Jules called in on some distant forebear of the Fox and Grapes before marching on London, or if Dick Turpin really stabled Black Bess here, but people like to think so. The stables now form the lounge bar, a large, high room with a gas log-fire, wood panelling and a beamed and raftered roof. An old wooden propeller adorns one wall. This may or again may not be connected with the World War II bomber pilot who, having just crashed on the common, staggered in for a little something to steady the nerves.

The Fox and Grapes is renowned for its home-cooked food, served all day. At busy times people will perch their plates on any available surface – radiators, the floor, cars parked outside. Special occasions such as Burns Night and St Patrick's Day are huge thrashes, when all the tables and chairs are cleared out of the lounge to make room.

The Fox and Grapes is popular with most ages, shapes and sizes. Plastic glasses are provided for younger drinkers heading for the common; golfers stock up here after their morning rounds; and dog-walkers particularly like to pop in. Dogs, unusually, are welcome. Children too.

·THE FOX AND HOUNDS·

29 Passmore Street, SW1   **730 6367**

'Safer than gin for the working man'

The Fox and Hounds is sorry but you can't have a gin and something or a whisky and anything. They are, they will explain for the millionth time, only licensed to sell beer or wine. No spirits.

There used to be lots of pubs like this, beer houses, a Victorian notion. Beer, thought the licensing authorities of the time, was safer than gin for the working man. The Fox and Hounds may be the only one left, and Diane Harvey, the licensee, doesn't mind at all.

The Fox and Hound started out in the 1860s, the archetypal beer house. The street door opened onto a small room with a wooden floor, settles round the walls and a couple of tables. The landlady would hand you your beer through a flap in her living-room door. Things hardly changed for 100 years. One room for the pub, three for the licensees and their children. Family and customers shared one outside loo.

The outside lav stayed right up to 1980 by which time the whole character of the district had changed. What had been terraces of working men's cottages had become fashionable and expensive. In Passmore Street today the modish new shop on the corner is Lord Linley's, and if one of the small houses comes up for sale nowadays they ask around £400,000 for perhaps a 50-year lease.

The pub has changed too, of course, but thankfully it has not been spoiled. It is actually quite nice to have inside loos, a bar counter and more room, and it remains a period piece with nice Mrs Harvey still running the show in the old way.

She has been at the Fox and Hounds for 27 years, has survived successive attempts to pull it down, endured building work that closed the pub altogether for five months. Her customers have an agreeable diversity. It is not unusual on a Sunday night to see a white-cassocked priest having a beer with acolytes and members of the choir. They are regulars from St Mary's, Bourne Street, and the pub is regularly discovered by successive casts of the Royal Court, hence the occasional presence of Peter O'Toole, Harrison Ford, Richard Harris and Pierce Brosnan.

Open
All Week
Hours
11.00–15.00 and
17.30–23.00 Mon–Fri;
11.00–15.30 and
18.00–23.00 Sat
(12.00–14.00 and
19.00–22.30 Sun)
Closed Christmas Day
Credit Cards
None
Bar Food Available
11.00–15.00
Special Features
Wheelchair Access
(but not lavatory)
Beers Available
Real ales
Nearest Tube Station
Sloane Square

· THE FOX AND PHEASANT ·

1 Billing Road, SW10 **352 2943**

'Chelsea fans can be Fox and Pheasant fans too'

Open
All Week
Hours
12.00–15.00 and
17.30–23.00
(12.00–22.30 Sun)
Closed Christmas Day,
New Year's Day
Credit Cards
None
Food Available
Basket meals
12.00–15.00 and
19.00–21.30
Special Features
Beer Garden seats 30
Beers Available
Greene King IPA, Rayments Special, Abbott Ale, Carling Black Label, Kronenbourg, Harp, Guinness, Brewers Bitter, Steinlager, Budweiser, Becks, Pale Ale, Gold Label
Nearest Tube Station
Fulham Broadway

There is a smart little enclave off Fulham Road known to estate agents as The Billings. This is where the Fox and Pheasant is. It is worth seeking out. It is a little country pub created 200 years ago by knocking two small houses into one, and it cheers you up just to look at it. It is extraordinarily pretty now with its hanging baskets and antique lanterns.

Inside, it is quite unmodernized, with exposed beams, leaded windows, basic hardwood tables and chairs and a big log fireplace. The two rooms are separated by a central bar and both have lots of sporting prints. Foxes feature. Also pheasants.

There is an excellent walled beer garden at the back, very popular in the summer. They have taken to doing basket meals at lunch and in the evenings for £2 to £3 – chicken nuggets and chips, that sort of thing.

A minor drawback, you may think, is its nearness to Chelsea Football Ground. You can hear them score. Chelsea fans can be Fox and Pheasant fans too. Best keep away on match days.

· THE FREEMASONS ARMS ·

32 Downshire Hill, NW3 **435 4498**

'This game, known as London skittles, was once played in pubs all over the south of England'

Open
All Week
Hours
11.00–23.00
(12.00–22.30 Sun)
Credit Cards
Visa, Mastercard
Bar Food Available
12.00–22.00
Special Features
No-smoking Area
Wheelchair Access
Beer Garden seats 200
Private Room seats 50
Beers Available
Adnams, Bass, London Pride, Carlings Black Label, Tennent's Pilsner, Tennent's Extra, Grolsch
Nearest Tube Station
Hampstead

What's with these Freemasons Arms? Do Freemasons meet in them, exchanging coded handshakes and doing good works? Apparently they used to but that was in the 18th century when lots of lodges met in pubs. They have other meeting places now.

London has at least four Freemasons Arms. There's one in Long Acre, others in Stepney and Wood Green and this one in Hampstead near the Heath. It is a big, prosperous modern pub, built in 1932 to replace an earlier Freemasons Arms that was having trouble standing up.

There can be few bigger pubs in North London. The garden is vast, full of roses and picnic tables. It also has a sunken courtyard with a fountain and more tables and a flagged terrace overlooking the fountain with yet more tables.

Inside the pub a well turned-out saloon bar merges with the public bar, which has a pool table and a darts board. There is another sitting room and a large comfortable dining room and down a flight of stairs you are in a skittle alley, a 21-ft pitch with big hornbeam skittles set in a diamond formation awaiting Tuesday, Thursday and Saturday nights when the skittles club arrives and tries to knock them over. They do this by throwing massive cheeses made from lignum vitae at them. They can weigh up to 12lb, these cheeses, and take some throwing.

This game, known as London skittles, was once played in pubs all over the south of England. It is an endangered species now but it is alive and well in the Freemasons Arms.

·THE FRENCH HOUSE·

49 Dean Street, W1   **437 2799**

'Vive la French pub'

Ah the French pub, still a favourite watering hole of the chattering classes. It is officially the French House now. It used to be officially the York Minister but no one ever called it that either. The French pub is what it is.

Its Frenchness began with the splendidly moustachioed Victor Berlemont who bought the pub just before the First World War and through the 1920s and 1930s filled it with singers and actors and boxers. Maurice Chevalier came. So did Georges Carpentier. Then the war and the Free French took it over and General de Gaulle was writing his historic declaration of defiance to the Nazis in the room above the bar.

The war over, Victor's son, Gaston, took charge. He had the stylish moustaches and strong personality of his father and life at the French pub got more bohemian than ever. Dylan Thomas left the only manuscript of *Under Milk Wood* there, Brendan Behan sang and danced in the bar, Francis Bacon, Lucien Freud, Dan Farson *et al* got agreeably tanked up, and Gaston opened yet another crate of champagne.

He retired on Bastille Day, 1989, and, happily, ideal new owners were at hand. Noel Botham and Lesley Lewis had been drinking in the French pub for years and, apart from reopening the restaurant, which Gaston had closed, they changed nothing that mattered.

The restaurant – the French House Dining Room – has proved an outstanding success and the pub remains uniquely itself, tricolours flying, photographs of regulars, famous and not, plastering the walls. The regulars chat in carrying tones, newcomers feel a bit out of it but it was ever thus.

The French pub still sells more champagne across the bar than the Savoy Grill, is still the country's largest single retail outlet of Ricard.

Open
All Week

Hours
12.00–23.00
(12.00–22.30 Sun)

Credit Cards
All major cards accepted

Food Available
Bar 12.30–15.00 and 18.00–22.00
Restaurant 12.30–23.15

Special Features
Wheelchair Access to pub (but not to lavatory or restaurant)
Private Room seats 35

Beers Available
John Smith's Extra Smooth, Carlsberg, Beamish, Guinness

Nearest Tube Station
Leicester Square

·Friar and Firkin·

120 Euston Road, NW1   387 2419

'Impeccably Ferkinized'

Open
All Week

Hours
11.00–23.00
Mon–Wed;
11.00–24.00
Thur–Sat
(12.00–22.30 Sun)
Closed Christmas Day

Credit Cards
None

Bar Food Available
12.00–19.30

Special Features
No-smoking Area
Wheelchair Access
(but not lavatory)
Tables outside seat 16

Beers Available
Dogbolter, Friar Ale,
Confession Ale,
Firkin Full Mash Mild,
Tetley, Carlsberg,
Castlemaine,
Budweiser Budvar,
Lowenbrau, Rolling
Rock, Oranjeboom,
Newcastle Brown Ale
Cider: Weston's
Scrumpy

**Nearest Tube
Stations**
Euston, King's Cross

David Bruce, founder of the Firkins, sold his idiosyncratic chain of pubs in 1978 and was soon regretting it. He tried to get them back when they came on the market again, but by December 1991 they were firmly in the hands of Allied Lyons.

People got quite nervous when the new owners started adding new Firkins. This was the first of them, The Rising Sun, a Victorian pub no one had given a second glance for years. It closed and four weeks later re-opened as the Friar and Firkin. Firkin fans breathed again. It had been impeccably Ferkinized.

At this stage it was a long, wandering pub with all the well-tried Firkin features, the bare floorboards, the pews, the barrel tables, the Firkin food and Firkin notices – 'The Firkin Loos', 'Mind the Firkin Step'. It was soon so popular you could hardly move. It badly needed more space.

Luckily for the pub, the brewers owned the freehold of the shop next door. Inevitably this has become part of the booming Friar and Firkin, almost doubling its floorspace. It is surely big enough now, but I don't know; it still gets pretty crowded, particularly on Thursday and Friday nights when it has a late-music licence. Lots of bands – soul, r and b, trad English blues, that sort of thing.

The five-barrel brewhouse in the cellar works to capacity to keep up with the demand for the four house ales – Confession Ale, Friar Ale, Firkin Full Mash Mild and the redoubtable Dogbolter. A carefully placed mirror gives you a glimpse of the brewhouse, while outside a friar stands astride a barrel on the new pub sign, beaming sunnily down on the impassable traffic of the Euston Road.

·The Front Page·

35 Old Church Street, SW3   352 2908

'The old Bohemian quarter'

Open
All Week

Hours
11.00–15.00 and
17.30–23.00;
12.00–15.00 and
18.00–23.00 Sat
(12.00–22.30 Sun)
Closed Christmas Day

Credit Cards
Visa, Mastercard,
Eurocard, but not AmEx

Some say that this is now *the* Chelsea pub. It's the social mix. The Front Page reflects the old bohemian quarter as no other does just now. Its patrons include the local vicar and the rag-and-bone man, the dustmen on collection days and several peers, writers and celebrated thespians rehearsing at the parish hall down the street. After 9.00 pm crowds of young Chelsea arrive.

The Front Page used to be the Black Lion but when the

present owners took it over in 1986 they changed the name. There had been a Black Lion on the site for at least 300 years so not everyone was pleased. But theirs has been a popular regime. The Front Page is a plain pub without piped music, fruit machines or fitted carpets, its big windows make it light and airy and the food is original and substantial.

The locals go for lunch; audiences of the Cannon cinema up the street go for pre- or post-movie supper; there is a private dining room upstairs. The staff is young and cheerful, the regulars are all ages and cheerful and everyone gets on well.

Bar Food Available
12.00–14.30 and
19.00–22.00
(12.00–14.30 and
19.00–21.30 Sun)

Special Features
Wheelchair Access
Private Room seats 22

Beers Available
Boddingtons,
Webster's, Ruddles
County, Foster's,
Holsten, Kronenbourg,
Beamish

Nearest Tube Station
Sloane Square

BUILT JUST AFTER THE BATTLE OF TRAFALGAR THE LOCALS RE-ENACT THE FIGHT EVERY SATURDAY NIGHT...

· FULMAR AND FIRKIN ·

51 Parker Street, WC2   **405 0590**

'Four, five, even six alternative comedians'

Here we have a Firkin, class of '93, just off the Kingsway, formerly, indeed, the Kingsway Tavern and much bigger than it looks. It is popular with students and tutors from various local groves of academe, including the LSE and the St Martin's School of Art, who can make Friday evenings very far out indeed.

In its previous life the pub was so quiet on Saturday night that it stopped opening. The Fulmar has found the answer. Every Saturday it now has free alternative comedy, four, five, even six alternative comedians one after the other, and it is packed. The Fulmar is considered a good audience. This means it does not actually throw things. Exhausted, it closes on Sundays.

Fulmars are large handsome sea birds. Three of them, stuffed, are in evidence, one in a tie, one in dark glasses, one sitting on eggs. Others appear on T-shirts, and one soars high on the inn sign. No one knows why the pub was named after them. Alliteration, of course. Firkins running out of Fs, probably.

Bitters to ask for at the Fulmar: a Firkin Fulmar, a Firkin Wingspan, a Dogbolter.

Open
Mon–Sat

Hours
11.00–23.00
Closed Bank Holidays

Credit Cards
All major cards
accepted

Bar Food Available
11.30–18.00

Special Features
Wheelchair Access
(but not lavatory)

Beers Available
Dogbolter, Fulmar,
Wingspan, Golden
Glory, Firkin Mild,
Castlemaine,
Lowenbrau,
Carlsberg Export

Nearest Tube Station
Holborn

·FUSILIER AND FIRKIN·

7–8 Chalk Farm Road, NW1   **485 7858**

'Dragging in the crowds by their ears'

Open
All Week

Hours
12.00–23.00 Mon–Thur;
12.00–24.00 Fri;
11.00–24.00 Sat
(12.00–22.30 Sun)
Closed Christmas Day

Credit Cards
All major cards accepted

Bar Food Available
12.00–16.00;
12.00–17.30 in winter
(11.00–14.30 Sat
(12.00–18.00 Sun)

Special Features
Wheelchair Access
(but not lavatory)

Beers Available
The Firkin brews, Lowenbrau, Carlsberg, Castlemaine, Guinness, Mersey's, Scrumpy, Old English

Nearest Tube Station
Camden Town

A rather drunken-looking redcoat on the new pub sign welcomes you to another of the Firkin class of '92, the one-time Carnarvon Castle with a new name and a whole new personality. This cavernous old pub stands directly opposite Camden Market, which is thick with people every week from Thursday onwards, and, big as it is, gets packed. Stall holders, bargain hunters, tourists, they all crowd in.

It has a little platform and piano as all Firkins do, but alone among them it has live music every Saturday afternoon, dragging in the crowds by their ears. There's live music on Friday evenings too.

In its Carnarvon Castle days it had pool tables at the back. Now there is bar billiards pleasantly lit by the bell vault, a superior skylight they discovered behind the old false ceiling.

The Fusilier does big business with ozzie steak baps – hot steak in a bap with a fried egg added or mushrooms or cheese or whatever. The espresso coffee machine is in demand and the Firkin phonograph much used.

·THE GALLERY·

1 Lupus Street, SW1   **821 7573**

'The yobs departed'

Open
All Week

Hours
11.00–23.00;
12.00–15.00 Sat
(12.00–15.00 and
19.00–22.30 Sun)

Credit Cards
None

Bar Food Available
12.00–14.30
(12.00–15.00 and
19.00–21.30 Sat–Sun)

Special Features
Wheelchair Access
(but not lavatory)

Beers Available
Webster's, Yorkshire Bitter, Marston's Pedigree, John Smith's, Thomas Hardy Country Bitter, Wadworth, Moorlands Old Speckled Hen

Nearest Tube Station
Pimlico

It is surprising how often pubs change their names. This one, for instance, originally the Queen of Denmark, became the Perseverance, went back to the Queen of Denmark, then became the Perseverance again. What about the Dither?

It was having its second go at the Perseverance when Edward and Patricia Burke saw it two years ago. They already had a pub in Chelmsford and another in Ashford, Middlesex, but two isn't many. Bass has 7,190. A third would be nice, thought Mr and Mrs Burke, and the Perseverance, very run down, Christmas decorations still up in March, did seem in need of a little TLC. So they bought it, refurbished it from top to bottom, changed its name for the fifth time and put their nephew Paul Corcoran in to manage it. It was now the Gallery.

Lupus Street is well-behaved Pimlico. The Tate is near – hence the Gallery – and Dolphin Square is nearer still, so young Mr Corcoran was surprised to find it so, well, rough. 'Unbelievable,' he says. So his first job was to lose some very regular customers. They bowled into the newly furbished pub, prints of famous paintings all round the walls, and resumed the yobbish tenor of their ways.

Confrontation. Verbals. Threats. A full can of lager through one of the costly etched windows. New manager stands ground. Mona Lisa, tight-lipped in lobby, makes *her* position plain. 'After five or six weeks they got the message that they weren't welcome and weren't going to get a drink,' says Corcoran. A further discouragement. He closed on Saturday nights. The yobs departed – an even better name for the pub.

It is pleasant and peaceful now and I wouldn't be surprised if the Burkes were not looking for a fourth pub. They seem to have the bit between their teeth.

·THE GATEHOUSE·

North Road, Highgate   **0181-340 8054**
'Consternation in the well-established old pubs round about'

In Elizabethan times the Bishop of London built a toll house on the top of the hill, a high gate spanning the road. It gave the place its name, Highgate. There was an old tavern up there too and when they pulled the toll gate down it stayed put.

Its successor is the Gatehouse, still there after many ups and downs. It was on a major down in 1993, standing empty and disconsolate. Then Wetherspoons took it over and it seems to be enjoying life again.

There it is on its hilltop, glossily repainted from top to toe and totally changed inside. It has no music, gives non-smokers a big non-smoking bit, serves good quick food all day and its cask ales include the great Wetherspoon bargain, a pint of Youngers Scotch Bitter for only 99p. This caused consternation in the well-established old pubs round about.

Traffic grinds past, bumper to bumper. That Bishop of London who put the toll house up had his head screwed on. Get stuck on the other side of the road and it might take you half an hour to reach the refurbed bar.

Open
All Week

Hours
11.00–23.00 Mon–Thur;
11.00–24.00 Fri–Sat
(12.00–22.30 Sun)

Credit Cards
Access, Visa, Delta,
Switch, AmEx

Bar Food Available
11.00–22.00

Special Features
No-smoking Area
Wheelchair Access
Beer Garden seats 30

Beers Available
Theakston Best,
Theakston XB,
Youngers Scotch Bitter,
Courage Directors,
Marston's Pedigree,
Becks, Foster's,
McEwans

Nearest Tube Station
Highgate

·THE GAZEBO·

Kings Passage, Kingston upon Thames   **0181-546 4495**

'Twin wooden gazebos, steps down to moorings'

The Gazebo is currently the extreme tip of Sam Smith's southern colonization, which started a few miles down river at the Rose of York at Richmond and proceeds apace.

It is an attractive modern pub less than ten years old in a lovely spot on the Thames, right next door to Young's Bishop out of Residence. Twin wooden gazebos flank the frontage, and steps lead down to moorings for customers who have come by boat. Downstairs the public bar, wooden floors, a pinball machine and a pool table; upstairs the saloon bar with a big verandah overlooking the river and the green vistas beyond. On the river bank new picnic benches.

Very impressive choice of salads, a carvery on Sundays, a children's menus and some good old-fashioned puds.

Open
All Week

Hours
11.00–23.00
(12.00–22.30 Sun)
Closed Christmas Day

Credit Cards
All major cards accepted

Bar Food Available
All opening hours

Special Features
Wheelchair Access
Tables outside seat 65
Private Room seats 180

Beers Available
Samuel Smith Old Brewery Ale, Museum Ale, Ayingerbrau, Pils, Prinz, Samuel Smith's Extra Stout
Cider: Samuel Smith Cider Reserve

Nearest BR Station
Kingston

·G E ALDWINKLES·

154 Fleet Road, NW3   **485 2112**

'Let's see what old G E Aldwinkles can do'

G E Aldwinkles? Who he? The truth must out. He was made up. Still, so was Mr Pickwick whom he much resembles, and the new owners thought a change might perk this old Hampstead pub up a bit. It had been the White Horse for its first 100 years or so and it certainly needed something. Let's see what old G E Aldwinkles can do, thought Regent Inns.

Regent Inns is emerging as an interesting contender in the highly competitive pub business. The driving force is David Franks, who bought his first pub in 1977, soon had a couple of dozen, went public in 1993 and expects a turnover of well over £20 million this year.

G E Aldwinkles has certainly smartened up the old White Horse, uncovering its original floor tiles, restoring its enamel plate ceiling and its nice horseshoe bar, replacing gloomy windows with clear glass, improving the food. The cellar bar had become a tremendous dump. Now people book it for parties and it is becoming known as a comedy venue.

In the old days the White Horse did bed and breakfast in its upstairs rooms. The staffs of several company pubs lodge in them now.

Open
All Week

Hours
11.00–23.00 Mon–Sat
(11.00–22.30 Sun)

Credit Cards
All major credit cards accepted

Bar Food Available
12.00–14.30 and
18.30–21.30 Mon–Sun

Special Features
Tables outside seat 25,
Function Room seats 60

Beers Available
Foster's, Holsten Export, Kronenbourg, Wadworths 6X, Courage Directors, Courage Best, Youngs Special, Beamish, Brakspears,
Cider: Dry Blackthorn, Cidermaster

Nearest Tube Station
Belsize Park

· THE GEORGE IV ·

185 High Road, Chiswick   **0181-994 4624**

'What better way to become a household name?'

Kindly persons have been brewing beer on the same site in Chiswick for well over 300 years. The old brewery got into a spot of bother in 1829 and Fuller, a Wiltshire grandee, rode to the rescue. Smith and Turner were not far behind and it has been Fuller, Smith and Turner ever since. What better way to become a household name?

The company has more than 200 pubs and this is one of the eight it has in Chiswick encircling the brewery. There's the Mawson Arms on the corner of the brewery itself, the Bell and Crown and the Dove on the river, the Cross Keys, the Duke of York, the George and Devonshire, and the two in the High Street, the Old Packhorse and the George IV. They are all historic old pubs. The George IV has always been rather grand, genuine Georgian outside, mock Tudor inside. Well you have to keep up and mock Tudor was the height of fashion for years. It is no longer though and Fuller's has just spent more than £460,000 bringing it bang up-to-date.

Some of the changes belong entirely to this end of the 20th century, the new lavatories and kitchens, the air conditioning, the computer monitors operated by a touch on the screen and recording every aspect of every sale, a concealed big television screen for major sporting events.

Nothing remotely Tudor remains, leaded lights, olde black panelling, copper counter top that absorbed tons of Brasso over the years, gone all gone, also the old separate public bar. Instead there is a single, open bar, low timber ceilings, bare floorboards, tongue-and-groove panelling, mahogany stairs leading to a gallery, drinking booths with old church pews, a cobbled yard with a fountain. It is, in short, an old English ale and pie house, Fuller's seventh, and in a matter of weeks trade doubled. It is a comfortable style. The original John Fuller, Henry Smith and John Turner would, you feel, have felt entirely at home.

Open All Week

Hours 11.30–23.00 (12.00–22.30 Sun)

Credit Cards All major cards accepted

Bar Food Available All day

Special Features Wheelchair Access (with lavatory) Beer Garden seats 40 Private Room seats 35

Beers Available London Pride, ESB, Chiswick Bitter, Batcombe Bitter, Grolsch, Tennent's Extra, Carling Black Label, Heineken, Murphy, Guinness Cider: Scrumpy Jack, Strongbow

Nearest Tube Station Turnham Green

· THE GEORGE INN ·

77 Borough High Street, SE1   **407 2056**

'The all-time coaching inn'

The George Inn at Southwark is perhaps the most famous pub in London. To come across it for the first time is to meet an old friend. You feel you know it already from Christmas cards, Dickens, and old movies. It is the all-time coaching inn, you should really arrive in a stage coach.

Open All Week

Hours 11.00–23.00 (12.00–22.30 Sun)

Credit Cards Access, Visa, AmEx, Diner's Club

Food Available
Bar 12.00–14.30
Restaurant
18.00–21.30 Wed–Fri
Special Features
Courtyard seats 80
Private Room seats 60
Beers Available
Abbot Ale,
Boddingtons, London
Pride, Castle Eden,
Flowers IPA, Gale's
Pompey Royal
Cider: Inch's Harvest
Nearest Tube Station
London Bridge

Instead you park where you can and walk through the wrought-iron gateway on Borough High Street and there it is, the cobbled yard, the overhanging galleries, the south front, all still in daily use. It is a moving sight.

We know a lot about the George. We know it was going strong in 1542, the year Henry VIII executed his fifth wife, we know it was rebuilt three times, emerging splendidly intact into the railway age, the same three-sided galleried building as before with one big courtyard and a smaller one beyond it surrounded by stables.

Then, humiliatingly, the George became a depot of the Great Northern Railway, which pulled down two of the fronts and built warehousing in their place. Luckily the south front survived and the warehouses did not. They were bombed in the war and what replaces them is pretty awful, two dreadful modern blocks, but you can keep your back to them as you sit at one of the picnic tables in the courtyard. With only the George in view you are in another age.

The old floorboards creak loudly as you pass from bar to bar in the old inn, twice as loudly as you go upstairs to the dark panelled restaurant and various function rooms. These upper storeys, of course, were bedchambers in the George's great days. You can't find a bed there now but the food is good, the ale is better, old settles and chimney corners beckon and in the summer there's the courtyard where Shakespeare, they say, once performed. It is a romantic place. The George Inn, safely in the hands of the National Trust, does not disappoint you.

It is, of course, an *Evening Standard* pub of the year.

·THE GIPSY MOTH·

Open
All Week
Hours
11.00–23.00
(12.00–22.30 Sun)
Credit Cards
All major cards
accepted
Bar Food Available
11.30–20.00
Special Features
Wheelchair Access
Beer Garden seats 150

60 Greenwich Church Street, SE10   **0181-858 0786**
'It is hard work looking at famous ships'

The magnificent Cutty Sark and the gallant little Gipsy Moth, both enjoying new careers as tourist attractions at Greenwich, get perhaps 300,000 visitors every year. It is hard work looking at famous ships and after seeing two of them the whole family needs a drink and a snack and a loo. This large efficient pub is right on the spot. A bit of luck all round.

It used to be, unmemorably, the Wheatsheaf but changed its name to the Gipsy Moth when Sir Francis Chichester's little boat, having gone round the world with only him on board, settled on its doorstep. So now every summer tourists arrive in a never-ending stream, have a meal and a drink, go to the loo and move on, letting someone else have the table.

A diplomatic new manager has established an *entente* reasonably *cordiale* with the neighbours who didn't care for jollity in the pub's big garden at the back. He has abandoned proposals for a barbecue and live music and in return his customers are allowed to drink in the garden. There are seats for 150 at a time.

· THE GLASSBLOWER ·

Glasshouse Street, W1   734 8547

'Blokish'

An everyday sort of pub five minutes from Piccadilly Circus. Gaming machines, juke box, Sky TV. Blokish is the word that comes to mind,

It used to be the Bodega. It was sort of Spanish in those days. Then Youngers got it and called it the Kilt and Celt and it became Celtic. Sort of. Now Scottish and Newcastle has gone for the Glassblower. Still that's easier to say after a few pints than Kilt and Celt.

They recently spent £120,000 on doing it up a bit and they have beefed up the air conditioning. It remains an everyday sort of pub.

> WHEN THEY UNCOVERED THE INGLENOOK FIREPLACE THE BUILDERS DISCOVERED THE REMAINS OF AN ELIZABETHAN AFTER — HOURS DRINKING CLUB...

· THE GLOUCESTER ·

187 Sloane Street, SW1   235 0298

'A famous victory'

The Battle of Alexandria, 1801, is celebrated on the sign outside the Gloucester, a famous victory against Napoleon that earned the Gloucestershire Regiment the unique distinction of being permitted to wear a badge at the back of their headdress as well as the front.

The Gloucester has been loyally marking this noted feat of arms ever since it was built 150 years ago and the Gloucestershire Vets still meet in the back room there on the first Friday of the month.

Beers Available
Tetley, Burton Ale, Young's Special, Adnams, Lowenbrau, Carlsberg, Castlemaine, Double Diamond, Guinness

Nearest BR Station
Greenwich

Open
All Week

Hours
11.00–23.00
(12.00–22.30 Sun)

Credit Cards
All major cards accepted

Food Available
Bar 12.00–15.00 and 18.00–21.00
Restaurant 11.30–21.00 Mon–Thurs;
11.30–17.00 Fri–Sat
(12.00–21.00 Sun)

Special Features
Wheelchair Access (but not lavatory)
Private Room seats 60

Beers Available
Theakston Best, Theakston XB, Theakston Old Peculier, Courage Best, Courage Directors, Foster's, Kronenbourg, Gillespie's, Guinness

Nearest Tube Station
Piccadilly Circus

Open
All Week

Hours
11.00–23.00
(12.00–22.30 Sun)
Closed Christmas Day

Credit Cards
All major cards accepted

Food Available
Bar 11.00–23.00
Restaurant 9.00–21.00

Special Features
Wheelchair Access
(but not lavatory)
Private Room seats 25
Beers Available
Courage, Theakston,
Molsen, Grolsch,
Budweiser, Becks,
Holsten Pils, Foster's,
Coors
Nearest Tube Station
Knightsbridge

Open
All Week
Hours
11.00–23.00
(12.00–22.30 Sun)
Closed Christmas Day
Credit Cards
None
Bar Food Available
12.00–15.00 and
18.00–21.00
Special Features
Wheelchair Access
(but not lavatory)
Private Room seats 15
Beers Available
Theakston Best,
Theakston XB,
McEwans, Coors Extra
Gold, Becks, Guinness
Nearest Tube Station
Piccadilly Circus

Open
Mon–Sat
Hours
11.00–23.00;
12.00–16.00 Sat
Closed Bank Holidays
Credit Cards
Visa, Mastercard,
AmEx
Bar Food Available
12.00–14.30
Special Features
Private Room seats 40
Beers Available
Nicholson's Best,
Tetley, Greene King
IPA, Brakspear
Nearest Tube Station
Green Park

It is a small, comfortable pub which opens at 9.00 am for breakfast – the full fandango for £5.50. Food is then served all day until 9.00 in the evening, traditional English food, steak and kidney pies, chicken pies, things like that.

·THE GOLDEN LION·

51 Dean Street, W1 **434 0661**

'Female friendly'

For years the Golden Lion in Dean Street was one of London's best-known gay pubs, packed with solitary and, if they were wise, watchful drinkers. It was one of the haunts of Dennis Nilsen, the serial killer.

Nilsen would find it harder to find victims there now. New managers and a new bar policy have wrought radical change. 'Female friendly' is the declared aim. The bar has gaming machines, satellite TV and a juke box. There is traditional bar food upstairs.

·THE GOLDEN LION·

25 King Street, W1 **930 7227**

'Feeling better'

The Golden Lion, or Golden Lyon Tavern as it was in 1732, is a striking sight in this rather uneventful street. Five storeys and a roof garret of imitation Jacobean baroque, black marble columns, projecting windows and stucco balustrade, hemmed in by flat modern office buildings, you certainly can't miss it.

Something is missing, though. The lovely old St James's Theatre, its old friend that stood next to it for more than 100 years, was pulled down by developers in 1959. There were furious objections. Sir Laurence Olivier and Vivienne Leigh actually led demonstrations, but the demolition men went in anyway. One of those office blocks replaced it. The one on the right...

Theatre and pub were unusually close. A door led directly from the circle to the Golden Lion's upstairs bar, which became the official theatre bar with warning bells for the start of performances and ordered drinks waiting at the interval. Playgoers came and went and generations of actors too, so it was a body blow for the Golden Lion when the theatre was demolished. It went into rather a depression for a while, actually, but it has now had a necessary face-lift and seems to be feeling a lot better.

Did I mention that Nell Gwyn was often here when she wasn't at the Red Lion round the corner? And that in 1822 one of the customers murdered the landlady?

· GOOSE AND FIRKIN ·

47–48 Borough Road, SE1 **403 3590**

'The first-ever Firkin'

The first-ever Firkin, 16 going on 17, is still as wholesome and welcome as home-made brown bread. David Bruce and his wife started the Firkin chain with this old Southwark pub, then the Duke of York, in 1979. What they did here set the pattern for all the Firkins to come – plain wooden furniture, bare floorboards, one bar, a little stage with a piano, home-made food and, above all, a brewhouse in the cellar.

This bold revival of an ancient tradition is still the heart of the Firkin philosophy, though the brewing technique has been improved. So, sadly, the Goose and Firkin's original brewhouse has been mothballed. The equipment may be replaced, but this is one of the smaller Firkins so it may not. Meanwhile it takes its beer from the big brewhouse in the Falcon and Firkin at Hackney, which delivers regular supplies of Firkin Borough, Firkin Goose and Dogbolter.

All Firkins have Dogbolter, all Firkins have live music sometime in the week – at the Goose it is every Wednesday and Saturday. This is much enjoyed, it is thought, by the perky goose flying overhead in scuba gear, though perhaps less by the rather regal one behind the bar. It presides over the happy hours on Mondays, Tuesdays and Thursdays from 4.00 to 7.00 pm, during which you get Firkin Borough for a guinea a pint.

Very little changes at Firkin pubs, though the Goose and Firkin did have a bit of a face-lift recently. A new bar counter was being installed and the pub was astonished to hear that the producers of the television programme EastEnders wanted to buy the old one. They had a starring role for it, they said, and indeed they did. When the Victoria, the famous pub in Albert Square, caught fire it was the old bar from the Goose and Firkin that blazed on the nation's television screens.

Open
All Week

Hours
12.00–23.00
(12.00–15.00 and 19.00–23.00 Sat;
12.00–15.00 and 19.00–22.30 Sun)
Closed Good Friday, Easter Sunday, Christmas Day, Boxing Day

Bar Food Available
12.00–19.00 Mon–Fri;
12.00–15.00 Sat

Special Features
Wheelchair Access (but not lavatory)
Tables outside seat 18

Beers Available
Goose, Borough Bitter, Dogbolter, Winter Warmer, Firkin's Golden Glory, Castlemaine, Lowenbrau, Carlsberg

Nearest Tube Stations
Elephant and Castle, Borough

· GRAFTONS ·

2 Strutton Ground, SW1   **222 7310**

'People still go to Graftons to ask about the Goons'

Open
Mon–Sat

Hours
11.00–23.00
(12.00–15.00 Sat)

Credit Cards
Mastercard, Visa, Access

Bar Food Available
11.00–21.00

Special Features
Wheelchair Access

Beers Available
John Smith's, Theakston Best, Wadworth 6X, Foster's, Carlsberg, Holsten, Guinness, Beamish

Nearest Tube Station
St James's Park

Graftons is famous for the Goons. They started there upstairs in the front room, Harry Secombe, Spike Milligan, Peter Sellers and Michael Bentine, young comic hopefuls brought together by aspiring script writer Jimmy Grafton, son of the house, and whoosh, up, up and away they went, all of them but Jimmy. That was getting on for 50 years ago and people still go to Graftons to ask about the Goons.

The pub stands at the Victoria Street end of Strutton Ground where there has been a daily market since 1718. Its panelled wooden front at street level is painted a pleasing red, there are fine latticed windows, three gas lamps and above them the name spelled out in gold: Graftons.

The thick brick pillar in the long saloon bar has been getting in the way of generations of drinkers making their way to the fireplace at the back, some noticeably sporting size 11 footwear. This is one of New Scotland Yard's locals. It is also the regular meeting place of the Goons' appreciation society and a place of pilgrimage for other fans from all over.

Alcoves facing the bar display Goons memorabilia, which they like, but the fans are not invited upstairs. What might have been a hallowed temple is now the living room of manager Paddy Rice and his wife, Joanna, who had not heard of the Goons before they took over at Graftons. It's their young age, you see.

Still, they have heard of them now all right, and give out leaflets at the bar telling more of the story.

· THE GRAPES ·

76 Narrow Street, E14   **987 4396**

'Press gangs and dark doings'

Open
All Week

Hours
11.00–15.00 and
17.30–23.00;
12.00–15.00 and
19.00–23.00 Sat
(phone pub for Sunday opening hours)
Closed Boxing Day,
New Year's Day

Credit Cards
All major cards accepted

'The Six Jolly Fellowship-Porters, a tavern of a dropsical appearance, had long settled down into a state of hale infirmity,' wrote Charles Dickens in *Our Mutual Friend*. 'In its whole constitution it had not a straight floor and hardly a straight line…'

The real name of the Six Jolly Fellowship-Porters was, and is, the Grapes. Dickens knew it well, described it perfectly, and it is still there on the river at Limehouse. It hasn't changed all that much.

It was old when Dickens knew it, with a history of press gangs and dark doings. It is 100 years older now and, not surprisingly, there is still not a straight floor, hardly a straight line. The bar and tap of Dickens' day have somehow come together, and it is up a shallow step to what used to be the parlour and cosy where old bottles apparently long-forgotten sleep on a high shelf.

It has recently had a thorough propping-up. It cost more than £200,000. Happily not a lot of it shows, but the ancient deck that recently hung over the river in the old dropsical way has been replaced with a robust new one, and a flight of new teak steps leads to a smaller deck outside the little first-floor dining room where fresh fish is served every day.

The Grapes now has a lively and charismatic licensee in Barbara Haig, a one-time Playboy bunny who has set her heart on becoming Master Cellarman of the Year. She may well do it. Her Dickensian cellar may be just 4' 3" high but the beer, she says, is superb.

Food Available
Bar 12.00–14.00 Mon–Fri;
19.00–22.00 Tues–Sat
Restaurant
12.00–13.45 Mon–Fri;
19.00–21.30 Tue–Sat

Special Features
Wheelchair Access
(but not lavatory)
Private Room seats 28

Beers Available
Burton, Tetley, Friary Meux, Guinness, Becks, Castlemaine, Carlsberg

Nearest Tube Station
Mile End

Docklands Light Railway
Westferry

· YE GRAPES ·

16 Shepherd Market, W1   **499 1563**

'Ye quiet background music'

Shepherd Market is not what it was. It used to have girls smiling at you from every doorway and when Ye Grapes was built in 1882 one of its five bars was called the cow shed because it was exclusively used by the ladies of the night, not to mention the afternoon.

Today the girls rely on tasteful advertisements and you could take your maiden aunt to Ye Grapes provided she doesn't mind a crush. It is a popular pub on the corner of the market square and you will find that it gets very crowded on occasion.

Ye Grapes is a privately owned pub, a true free house, and there are not too many of them around. The owner is Anthony Wigram who has a lot of property, property being his thing. He is said to enjoy owning a pub, as who would not, and pops in from time to time. He has a tenant, Eric Lewis, who runs it.

It is hard to see the walls of Ye Grapes for the profusion of objects. You might suppose that the contents of a grand country house attic had been scattered on it, the heads of horned beasts, a pair of oars, a pair of guns, fish in glass cases, birds in glass cases.

There is a restaurant upstairs and snacks in the bar and seven real ales on offer. Two gambling machines are tucked away at the back. There used to be a juke box but this has now been exiled. It is ye quiet background music at Ye Grapes now.

Open
All Week

Hours
11.00–23.00
(12.00–22.30 Sun)
Closed Christmas Day

Credit Cards
None

Restaurant Food Available
12.00–22.30

Special Features
Wheelchair Access
(but not lavatory)

Beers Available
Boddingtons, Wadworth, Old Speckled Hen, Flowers Original, Marston's Pedigree, Tetley, Caffrey's, Brakspear, Murphy's, Guinness, Heineken, Stella Artois
Cider: Scrumpy Jack, Old Hazy

Nearest Tube Station
Green Park

·THE GREEN MAN·

Putney Heath, SW15   0181-788 8096

'Highwaymen lurked and footpads abounded'

Open
All Week

Hours
11.00–23.00
(12.00–22.30 Sun)

Credit Cards
None

Bar Food Available
12.00–14.30 and
19.00–21.30
(12.00–21.30 Sun)

Special Features
Beer Garden seats 100

Beers Available
Young's Bitter, Young's Premium, London Lager, Castlemaine, Stella Artois, Red Stripe, Oatmeal Stout, Guinness

Nearest Tube/BR Stations
Putney Bridge/Putney

In May 1798, the Prime Minister, William Pitt, rather fell out with the MP for Southwark, so they rode to Putney Heath and fought a duel. Each fired twice, missed, agreed that honour was satisfied and rode home again. It was the talk of the Green Man that day, I can tell.

The Green Man was then a remote country inn on the edge of a notoriously dangerous bit of London – two cottages, really, back to back. Putney had become a fashionable suburb but the heath was not a place to walk at night. Highwaymen lurked, footpads abounded and rough justice was dispensed. Dick Turpin hid his guns in the Green Man and lived to rob another day, but Jerry Abbershaw, who used it as his base, was hanged on a gibbet outside it.

Putney spread and prospered and respectable Victorians enjoyed a walk to the Green Man. Algernon Charles Swinburne, living with his friend Theodore Watts-Dunton at The Pines, 11 Putney Hill, always called in for a drink on his way to the Rose and Crown in Wimbledon Village. It was a warren of private bars and snugs then, but Swinburne would still know the pub today. It is still really two cottages back to back, two bars now, the public bar on the right, the saloon bar on the left, linked by the counter. They are light and cheerful on summer days, snug and cosy after dark.

Outside, the old pub is flanked by two pretty courtyards with tables and benches, and a big garden at the back has just been newly landscaped to its great advantage. The fine old brick wall was surely there in Pitt's day, and Swinburne would have known the towering horse chestnut. As generations pass, the Green Man remains one of London's favourite pubs.

·THE GRENADIER·

Old Barrack Yard, Wilton Row, SW1   235 3074

'The most patriotic of pubs'

Open
All Week

Hours
12.00–15.00 and
17.00–23.00
(12.00–15.00 and
19.00–22.30 Sun)
Closed Christmas Day, Boxing Day, New Year's Day

Credit Cards
All major cards accepted

A smart little pub, a well-bred little pub, tucked away in a quiet Knightsbridge mews and keeping up its standards. 'It is house policy,' says the notice on the door, 'that customers should be suitably dressed…' 'Gentlemen, 'tis my desire that everyone should see the fire' begins a poem over the fireplace. Mine too.

The Duke of Wellington is the presiding spirit in the Grenadier. His officers used it as their mess, he is said to have played cards here himself, his mounting block is outside and his patrician features look scornfully down at you from the walls.

Did I mention it was small? The bar is tiny, but happily customers can spill out into the mews if it is fine and there always seems to be room. The little restaurant at the back, candlelit at night, crisp white linen cloths, crystal glassware and Beef Wellington on the menu, can't seat more than 28. It is best to book.

It is the most patriotic of pubs, red, white and blue outside, with a sentry box, pillarbox red, by the steps to the front door. The pewter bar counter has been scrubbed and polished daily since 1827 when the pub was built, and military memorabilia has steadily accumulated. They used to send a man from Wellington Barracks every week to groom the Guardsman's bearskin in the bar. It is made from the pelt of a female Canadian bear, which, they say, like fingernails, goes on growing.

A Sunday morning Bloody Mary bar is a tradition at the Grenadier. The Bloody Marys are made from a recipe passed from licensee to licensee and the long-standing record for a single session is 276. Paul Gibb, who runs the pub now, says his customers have run it pretty close.

The Grenadier is said to have a ghost who haunts only in September. The pub has been investigated by mediums and visited by priests and the ghost seems to be lying low for the moment.

Bar and Restaurant Food Available
12.00–14.30 and
18.00–22.00
(19.00–22.00 Sun)

Special Features
Wheelchair Access

Beers Available
Courage Best, Young's Special, Theakston Best, Theakston XB, Foster's, Guinness, Kronenbourg, Budweiser

Nearest Tube Station
Hyde Park Corner

· 49 GRESHAM STREET ·

49 Gresham Street, EC2   **606 0399**

'Observe the name and address. The same. Will this work?'

A brand-new pub in the City, a very smart pub at that and a great relief to people who had started to think that no one would ever do anything with this prime corner site. It had been an empty concrete shell for years and now look at it, a most superior Fuller's pub with a wine bar underneath.

Is this a sign of better times? It certainly is and, should you wish to celebrate, the landlord, Mark Noble-Campbell, can offer you a choice of five cask ales and 24 wines including a house champagne that started at £17.99 a bottle and has now gone down to £17.85. Is this another sign of better times?

Observe the name and the address. The same. Will this work? My bet is that 49 Gresham Street will be known as Fuller's, prominently placarded on the canopy. Note: it keeps City hours. That is to say it closes at 9.30 on weekdays and doesn't open at all at weekends.

Open
Mon–Fri

Hours
11.00–21.30
(11.00–22.30 Fri)
Closed Bank Holidays

Credit Cards
All major cards accepted

Bar Food Available
12.00–15.00

Special Features
Wheelchair Access (disabled lavatory)
Private Room seats 60

Beers Available
Chiswick Bitter, London Pride, ESB, Lummer Ale, Guinness

Nearest Tube Stations
St Paul's, Bank

· THE GREYHOUND ·

1 Kensington Square, W8   **937 7140**

'The Greyhound Mark III'

Open
All Week

Hours
11.00–23.00
(12.00–22.30 Sun)

Credit Cards
All major cards accepted

Bar Food Available
12.00–21.00

Special Features
Tables outside seat 8

Beers Available
Theakston Best, Theakston XB, Courage Best, Courage Directors, Foster's, Carlsberg, Holsten Export, Kronenbourg, Guinness

Nearest Tube Station
High Street Kensington

Thackeray lived opposite the Greyhound. He mentioned it in his novel Henry Esmond. His elegant regency house is still there with one of the early LCC brown plaques and the Greyhound is still there too. Or rather a Greyhound is.

The Greyhound Thackeray knew was the Greyhound Mark I but this did not survive him long. In 1899 it was replaced by the Greyhound Mark II, much smarter. The Evening Standard thought a lot of it, particularly admiring its glass-fronted billiard room, which had two full-size billiard tables and took up a lot of the bar. Most leading players played there, Joe Davis often.

In 1975 we made it *Evening Standard* Pub of the Year and in 1979 it blew up.

It was a gas leak and the explosion it caused was quite spectacular in its way. It took the pub out as in a surgical strike. There was hardly anything left. Luckily it was at night, the landlord and his wife were on holiday and the relief managers weren't in either.

There was a neat gap in the row of offices and shops and houses for a time, then they built the Greyhound Mark III. That is the one there now and it looked the same from the outside. The pub itself though...

Never mind. Scottish and Newcastle has just given it a major going over. The pub was closed for weeks and covered in scaffolding, there were builders everywhere, also carpenters, plumbers, painters, decorators, carpet layers, upholsterers... It looks much better now.

· THE GRID INN ·

22 Replingham Road, SW18   **0181-874 8460**

'The day the heavens did not fall'

Open
All Week

Hours
11.00–23.00 Mon–Sat
(12.00–22.30 Sun)

Credit Cards
Access, Visa, AmEx, Delta, Switch

Bar Food Available
11.00–22.00 Mon–Sat
(12.00–14.30 and
19.00–21.30 Sun)

Special Features
No smoking Area, Wheelchair Access

Southfields is where you get off the tube if you're going to the tennis at Wimbledon. It is a place that owes everything to the railway, which arrived in 1889, planting a pretty little terracotta-red brick station among the fields, and by 1907 a pleasant village-like community was comfortably established.

There was a network of terraced streets known as the Southfields Grid. In time there were parades of shops, a church, a school and a stripped-pine merchant, but as the years went by you could hardly fail to notice that something was missing. Southfields didn't have a pub.

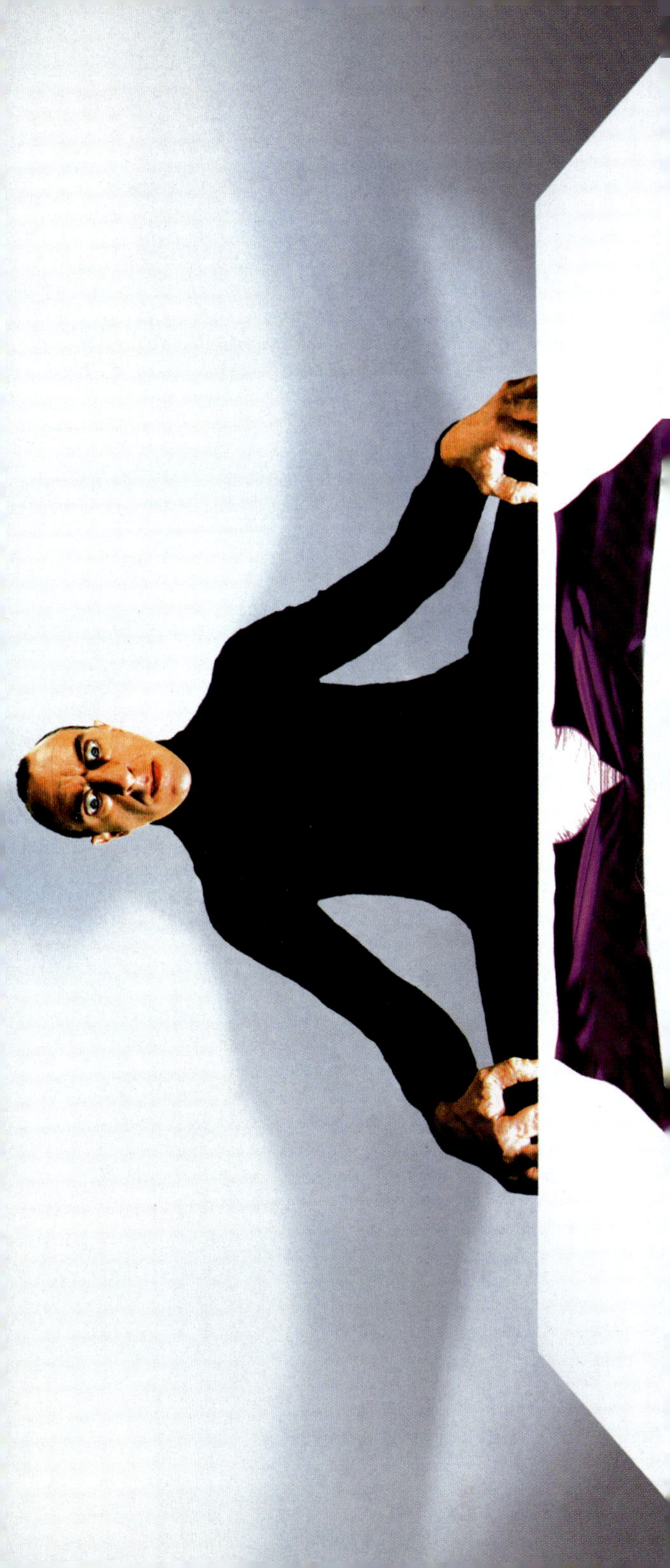

SMOKING WHEN PREGNANT HARMS YOUR BABY

Chief Medical Officers' Warning
5 mg Tar 0.5 mg Nicotine

Newcomers to Southfields were always given the same explanation. There was, said Southfields folk, a covenant. Some said the church, others the Spencer family, but someone had attached this covenant to the deeds of the land when selling it. No pub could ever be built there.

The local council is puzzled by this. It can find no evidence for any covenant. Indeed they have come to believe it to be a phantom covenant, a myth, a mere rumour. Southfields, in short, has been publess for 100 years for no good reason.

No longer, though. On 6 October 1994, Southfields got a pub at last, the Grid Inn, a pleasant pub owned by J D Wetherspoon. It was a restaurant when Wetherspoons found it but it is unmistakably a pub today, an agreeably pubby pub with a splendid panelled bar. This being Wetherspoons there is no music or games machines. This being Wetherspoons there is a large no-smoking area and a 99p pint.

A lot of local history is framed on the walls, pictures of local landmarks and local notables. George Eliot was both, really. She lived a secret life up the road. I only hope *someone* with a camera was around that October day in 1994 to catch the moment when a pub opened in Southfields and the heavens did not fall.

Beers Available
Youngers Scotch Bitter, Theakston Best, Theakston XB, Courage Directors, Marston's Pedigree, plus guest beers available daily

Nearest Tube Station
Southfields

· THE GROUND FLOOR BAR ·

186 Portobello Road, W11   **243 8701**

'A new chapter'

No one ever voted the Colville Arms the Pub Most Likely to Succeed. It was the one opposite the Electric Cinema in the busiest bit of Portobello Road. It started rough and got rougher. Why did Inspector Knacker and his men look in so often? Could they have heard whispers of exotic substances? Perish the thought.

The Colville Arms closed down, changed hands, reopened as the Colville Rose, changed hands and became the Colville Arms again. Then a new chapter…

The first floor became the First Floor, a most respectable and respected restaurant, visited and approvingly reviewed by Fay Maschler no less. The ground floor struck out anew as the Ground Floor Bar, walls black, ceilings black, and now it's jazz and Latino to get you through the day, blues, soul, rap at night, DJ Rose on Friday and Saturday, new manager, Aggy Khan, and King, the security ace, keeping the place in perfect order.

High bar counter, towering barstools, great parties, VERY big at Carnival. Cool man.

Open
All Week

Hours
12.00–23.00 Mon–Fri;
11.00–23.00 Sat
(12.00–22.30 Sun)
Closed Christmas Day

Credit Cards
All major cards accepted

Food Available
Bar 17.00–22.00
Sun–Thur
Restaurant
10.00–22.30 Mon–Sat
(12.00–22.00 Sun)

Special Features
Wheelchair Access
Private Room seats 40

Beers Available
Flowers IPA, Becks, Holsten, Stella Artois, Sol, Guinness

Nearest Tube Station
Ladbroke Grove

· THE GUINEA ·

Open
Mon–Sat
Hours
11.00–23.00
Closed Bank Holidays
Credit Cards
All major cards accepted
Food Available
Bar 11.30–14.30
Restaurant
12.30–14.30 Mon–Fri
and 18.30–23.00
Mon–Sat
Special Features
No-smoking Area
Wheelchair Access (but not lavatory)
Private Room seats 30
Beers Available
Young's Ordinary, Young's Special, Oatmeal Stout, Beamish, London Lager, Tennent's Extra, Castlemaine
Nearest Tube Stations
Green Park, Bond Street

30 Bruton Place, W1   **409 1728**

'Jack Nicklaus...Sylvester Stallone...King Hussein...'

This exclusive little pub tucked down a Mayfair mews is of astonishing antiquity. It goes back to 1423 when the infant king Henry VI had just had his first birthday and all round here was fields.

The bar is small and dark and richly accoutred and gets packed at lunchtimes. Well, the beer is Young's and the bar food is so good. Its steak, kidney and mushroom pie keeps winning the national championship – a key ingredient is Young's bitter – and even the sandwiches get national prizes.

It was not the sandwiches, I think, that brought Princess Margaret here, or Richard Burton and Elizabeth Taylor or Frank Sinatra. They came for the restaurant, one of the classiest pub restaurants in town, known for its grills. Its steaks are aristos, certified as genuine Aberdeen Angus by the Aberdeen Angus Society, laid out raw for you to select and then grilled before your eyes. This is serious steak fancying.

They do a two-course set lunch at the Guinea for £16.50, which includes a rump steak if you like. Stray to the à la carte side of the menu, though, and the price rises like a soufflé. It was ever thus.

· THE HALF MOON ·

Open
All Week
Hours
11.00–23.00
(12.00–22.30 Sun)
Credit Cards
None
Bar Food Available
Sandwiches only
Special Features
Seats outside for 50
Music Room seats 50
Beers Available
Young's Bitter, Young's Special, Dirty Dicks', Stella, Tennent's, Castlemaine
Nearest Tube Station
Putney Bridge

93 Lower Richmond Road, SW15   **0181-780 9383**

'It is as if punk had never happened'

A long-established music venue. From Lower Richmond Road comes this report:

'Conventional, unspectacular public and saloon bars and an outdoor patio hide a spacious back room dedicated to music seven nights a week. The Half Moon is a leading venue on the rhythm and blues and folk scene and has been for years. Big names like Roy Harper, Lindisfarne, Fairport Convention, John Martin and the Blues Band play here. Consequently the crowd is largely made up of 30 and 40 somethings who like their music delivered by proper musicians. It is as if punk had never happened.

'You pay anything from £2 to £8 to squeeze into the back room to hear the band. One night you will find a bluesy laid-back mood with candles on the tables and somewhere to sit. Or you may find more uptempo acts and the audience dancing. Really mellow music will find people at the front sitting on the floor so everyone can see. A pub floor so clean that punters will SIT on it? Only at the Putney Half Moon...'

· HAMILTON HALL ·

Liverpool Street Station, EC2   **247 3579**
'Expecting the king to call?'

In 1901, the year Edward VII at last became king, the new Great Eastern Hotel built itself a ballroom. Perhaps it was expecting the king to call. It set out to impress and impress it did. From floor to ceiling it was three storeys high with sumptuous decorations based on an apartment in the Palais Soubise in Paris. Nymphs, garlands and cornucopias, marble fireplaces, soaring mirrors, fine paintings... It was lit, of course, by chandeliers.

Who could have foreseen that this extravagant *folie de grandeur* would end up a pub? A pub it has become, though, an extraordinary pub, possibly the most successful pub in the country. It is now known as Hamilton Hall and it sometimes seems that everyone heading for Liverpool Street Station is having a drink there first.

In its ballroom days life was a lot less exciting. Finding occasions grand enough for it must always have been a problem and when war broke out in 1939 it was closed. It stayed closed until the recent renovation of Liverpool Street Station when J D Wetherspoon won the contract to take it over. The priceless fittings and decorations were found in a storeroom and Hamilton Hall started a new life. It was a pub now and it astonished everyone all over again.

Wetherspoons had to make one major alteration. A pub needs kitchens, lavatories and space to store beer, so a utilities block was built in the far corner of the ballroom and its flat roof became a mezzanine bar bigger than some pubs. This is now a no-smoking area and does well, but lean over the parapet and look down. Sometimes you can't see an inch of carpet, such is the crush.

If Hamilton Hall is a phenomenon so is Wetherspoons. Tim Martin, the founder, has now built up a chain of 120 pubs and the number keeps on growing. These pubs have some things in common. No music. Big no-smoking areas. Cut-price beer. A 99p pint. Hamilton Hall has these too. It is a remarkable pub.

Open
All Week
Hours
11.00–23.00
(12.00–22.30 Sun)
Credit Cards
Access, Visa, AmEx, Delta, Switch
Bar Food Available
11.00–22.00
(12.00–21.30 Sun)
Special Features
No-smoking Area
Wheelchair Access
(disabled lavatory)
Tables outside seat 60
Beers Available
Theakston Best, Theakston XB, Younger Scotch Bitter, Courage Directors, Marston's Pedigree, Greene King IPA, Abbott Ale, Becks, Foster's, McEwans
Nearest Tube Station
Liverpool Street

· THE HAND AND SHEARS ·

1 Middle Street, EC1 **600 0257**

'A man may nod off over his pint in the afternoon'

How nice to see this seemly old pub enjoying the autumn of its days in its placid little backwater off Smithfield.

John Betjeman, who lived along the way in Cloth Fair, used to pop in sometimes, and overworked doctors and nurses from nearby Barts like it. There is no music or machines. It has kept its snug, the fire burns at the far end, the service is friendly, you can get doorstep sandwiches at the bar and a pubby lunch upstairs quite cheaply. It gets quite busy at lunchtime but a man may nod off there over his Directors' bitter in the afternoon. It closes altogether at weekends.

In the Middle Ages, though, it was absolutely buzzing. The Lord Mayor proclaimed Bartholomew Fair open from the inn doorway every year and the court of Pie Poudre (Pieds Poudres, dusty feet) met in the room above the bar to grant licences, test weights and measures, redress grievances and pursue fraud.

Open
Mon–Fri
Hours
11.00–23.00
Closed Bank Holidays
Credit Cards
All major cards except AmEx
Restaurant Food Available
12.00–15.00
Special Features
Wheelchair Access
Private Room seats 36
Beers Available
Courage Best, Courage Directors, Theakston, Foster's, Kronenbourg, Holsten
Nearest Tube Station
Barbican

· THE HAND IN HAND ·

6 Crooked Billet, SW19 **0181-946 5720**

'A lovely village pub'

A few doors along from the Crooked Billet, facing the same small green where customers from both pubs lounge on the grass on long summer evenings, is the Hand in Hand, the *Evening Standard* Pub of the Year in 1982. We said then that it was a lovely village pub. It still is.

What you see is four cottages run together with a pretty south-facing courtyard in front. There is a prize-winning riot of hanging-baskets and window-boxes, a horse-chestnut gives shade to the tables, a vine crawls over one wall, and a wooden porch leads into the pub itself.

You find yourself in a popular, busy inn, plainly decorated and simply furnished with carved wooden benches, simple stools and solid old tables. There is a smoke-free family room for children, games machines and darts, and people are very keen on the home-made pasta, the pizzas and the burgers, but the Hand in Hand's great achievement is having kept the atmosphere of the simple beer house it was for a hundred years before Young's took it over in 1974.

There have been changes but most are hard to spot. The general feeling is that this exceptionally nice cottagey pub is much as it always has been.

Open
All Week
Hours
11.00–23.00
(12.00–22.30 Sun)
Credit Cards
Visa, Mastercard, Access, Switch
Bar Food Available
12.00–14.30 and 19.00–22.00
Special Features
No-smoking Area
Wheelchair Access
(but not lavatory)
Beer Garden seats 30
Private Room seats 20
Beers Available
Young's IPA, Young's Special, Young's Winter warmer, Red Stripe, Castlemaine, Young's London Lager, Stella Artois
Nearest Tube Station
Wimbledon

· The Hare and Hounds ·

216 Upper Richmond Road West, SW14　　**0181-876 4304**

'The finest pub in East Sheen'

The Hare and Hounds is a fine Georgian house of red brick on the Upper Richmond Road in East Sheen. My East Sheen correspondent says quite flatly that this is the finest pub in East Sheen and makes the following observation: 'Sadly the pub's faded, rather dingy charm has been swept away in a major renovation just completed. The pub is now lighter, sprucer, more comfortable, more intimate and consequently much busier. Some good bits remain, the old bar, the panelling, the huge garden with its vast lawn and, most important, the Hare and Hounds' most distinguished feature, the full-sized snooker table.'

Others file good reports on the barbecue and the live music in the public bar on Sunday nights – '50s, '60s, jazz and folk.

Open
All Week

Hours
11.00–23.00
(12.00–22.30 Sun)

Credit Cards
All major cards accepted

Bar Food Available
12.00–21.30

Special Features
No-smoking Area
Wheelchair Access
Beer Garden seats 100

Beers Available
All Young's variants, Tennent's Extra, Castlemaine, Young's Victory Ale

Nearest BR Station
Mortlake

· Harvey Floorbangers ·

1 Hammersmith Road, W14　　**371 4105**

'A big exhibition can double its trade'

Should any of the several Harvey Floorbangers remind you in any way of the Slug and Lettuces this is because they were started by one of the Slug and Lettuce founders. He sold this one to Regent Inns and very handsome it is, a substantial Victorian public house on the busy road opposite Olympia, the even more substantial Victorian exhibition hall.

The pub used to be the Hand and Flower and all its days has found Olympia a most useful neighbour. A big exhibition there can double its trade. It has a particularly fine function room upstairs, a huge room with nine long windows filling two of the walls and above that are ten rooms to let, all, as they say, en suite. A single room is £35, a double £45 with TV and a continental breakfast. For Olympia's exhibitors what could be handier?

THEY SAY ON MOONLIGHT NIGHTS THE GHOST STAGGERS THROUGH THAT WALL AND TUMBLES DOWN THE STAIRS...

Open
All Week

Hours
11.00–23.00 Mon–Sat
(12.00–22.30 Sun)
Closed Christmas Day

Credit Cards
All major cards except Diner's Club

Bar Food Available
12.00–14.30 and
18.00–21.30

Special Features
Wheelchair Access
(but not lavatory)
Function Room
seats 150

Beers Available
Boddingtons, 6X, Brakspear, Theakstons, Caffrey's, Guinness, Carling, Holsten Export, Fosters, Kronenbourg 1664
Cider: Dry Blackthorn

Nearest Tube Stations
Olympia, Kensington High Street, Hammersmith

·HEATHROW AIRPORT·

'Friends in need'

Open
All Week

Hours
Landside pubs;
11.00–23.00 Mon–Sat
(12.00–22.30 Sun)
Airside pubs;
From the first flight of the day to the last

If there's a place where you really need a drink it is surely an international airport. Happily, Heathrow does us pretty well with big bars, umpteen licensed restaurants and no fewer than nine pubs. They are friends in need.

Terminal 1 has a Tap and Spile on both sides of passport control, known as landside and airside. Terminal 2 has a Shakespeare Alehouse on this side and the John Bull on that. Terminal 3 has a Shakespeare Alehouse on each side of the great divide, with an extra pub, the Cask and Glass, on the landside. J D Wetherspoon has two pubs in Terminal 4. Wetherspoon is on the landside and J J Moon's is on the airside, a comfortable, reassuring little pub with the usual Wetherspoon no-smoking bit.

The landside pubs operate ordinary pub hours and they are all staying open on Sunday afternoons. The four airside pubs, on the other hand, are allowed to open from the first flight of the day to the last and they usually do. This can mean staying open from 6.00 am to midnight.

Still, these four pubs are your last chance to get a pint of British beer for, oh, perhaps days. Nervous flyers and serious drinkers leave them only when they must.

·THE HENRY ADDINGTON·

22–28 Mackenzie Walk, E14 **512 9022**

'Bass spent £1 million on it'

Open
All Week

Hours
11.00–23.00 Mon–Fri;
11.00–18.00 Sat–Sun

Credit Cards
All major cards accepted

Food Available
Bar all day
Restaurant
12.00–15.00

Special Features
Wheelchair Access
Beer Garden seats 40
Private Area seats 50

Two contrasting new water-holes have been provided for the hard-pressed toilers on Canary Wharf. This is the light and airy one. 'It is like being on the deck of a luxury liner,' say the Henry Addington licensees, Colin and Phyl Romney-Swallow, in lyrical mood.

Bass spent £1 million on it at the start and, not wishing to appear niggardly, gave it a £250,000 refurbishment in 1995. It seems a lot but, as it points out, it is aiming for environmental friendliness. This is daily reflected in the demeanour of journalists plotting and financiers computing. Its bar is 100-ft long – Europe's longest, claims the extrovert landlord, who has just won the National Innkeeper of the Year award. 'The Oscar of the industry,' he says modestly.

The Romney-Swallows have been in the business for 30 years and pride themselves on their real-ale weeks, also on their food that includes justly famed salt-beef sandwiches and home-made pickled onions, a specialité of the maison.

Henry Addington, as of course you know, was Prime

Minister from 1801 to 1804. In course of time he became Viscount Sidmouth and gave the go-ahead for a wharf to be built on the Isle of Dogs to receive goodies from the Canary Isles. Hence Canary Wharf. Canning wrote of him 'Pitt is to Addington as London is to Paddington'. Jolly rude, really.

Beers Available
Bass, London Pride, Stones, Old Speckled Hen, Boddingtons, Brew 11, Exmoor Beast, Young's, Tennent's Extra, Tennent's Pilsner, Grolsch, Carling Black Label, Carling Premier, Caffrey's, Staropramen

Nearest Docklands Station
Canary Wharf

· THE HENRY HOLLAND ·

39 Duke Street, W1　　　　　　　　　　　**629 4426**

'This Henry Holland was quite a goer'

This pleasant old pub is sometimes taken for a mirage by persons shopping till they drop in Oxford Street. There it is down a side street with a good-looking bar downstairs and a fine panelled dining room upstairs and a general air of having actually been built by the great 18th-century architect Henry Holland. Actually it was built, or anyway rebuilt, by Whitbreads in 1956. It was called the Red Lion before that.

This Henry Holland was quite a goer. He had his setbacks. His new Drury Lane Theatre incorporated all the latest safety devices but burned down all the same. By then, though, he had designed the first version of the Brighton Pavilion, quite a lot of Knightsbridge and, rather a stroke of luck, Southill Park in Beds for Mr Samuel Whitbread, the brewer. The present Samuel Whitbread, great-great-great-great-grandson of the founder, lives there still. Furthermore Henry Holland designed Brooks's, Mr Whitbread's club.

So now his name is on a Whitbread pub whether he built it or not. Quite right.

Open
All Week

Hours
11.00–23.00
(12.00–22.30 Sun)
Closed Christmas Day, Boxing Day

Credit Cards
Mastercard, Visa, Switch

Bar Food Available
12.00–15.00

Special Features
Wheelchair Access (but not lavatory)
Tables outside seat 24
Private Room seats 75

Beers Available
Flowers Original, Wadworth, Marston's Pedigree, Brakspear, Boddingtons, Heineken, Stella Artois

Nearest Tube Stations
Marble Arch, Bond Street

· HENRY J BEANS ·

195 King's Road, SW3　　　　　　　　　　**352 9255**

'An American vision of a London pub'

In the swinging sixties this was the swinging Six Bells. It has certainly swung some since then.

Henry J Beans is an American vision of a London pub. About an acre of floor space. High pedestal tables with swivel-top stools. Wallfuls of enamelled ads. A vast paved garden with rows of picnic tables and benches. Jokey young barmen, their names pinned to their chests, wall-to-wall music, a high-speed kitchen producing burgers, hot-dogs, deli sandwiches and Tex-Mex specials. Big demand for French fries.

Open
All Week

Hours
11.45–23.00
(12.00–22.30 Sun)
Closed Christmas Day, Boxing Day

Credit Cards
All major cards except Diner's Club

Bar Food Available
11.45–22.45
(12.00–15.00 and 19.00–22.15 Sun)

Special Features
Beer Garden seats 300

Beers Available
Webster's, Foster's, large range of bottled lagers

Nearest Tube Stations
Sloane Square, South Kensington

Lots of bottle beers at the bar and many a cocktail. New ones include Sea Breeze (vodka and cranberry) and Sex on the Beach (peach schnapps, vodka, cranberry and orange). They still charge £2.40 for a pint of Webster's.

The King's Road brat pack loves it – doesn't drink bitter anyway and keeps the place buzzing. It may not sound like a pub but the hours at least are familiar.

· THE HERCULES TAVERN ·

2 Kennington Road, SE1 **928 6816**

'As good as a Dublin pub now, says the manager'

Open
All Week

Hours
11.00–23.00
(12.00–22.30 Sun)

Credit Cards
None

Bar Food Available
12.00–15.00

Special Features
Wheelchair Access
Tables outside seat 36

Beers Available
Boddingtons, Flowers, Courage Directors, Marston's Pedigree, Foster's, Carlsberg, Kronenbourg 1664

Nearest Tube Station
Lambeth North

On the wall of this much-improved Lambeth pub is a picture of two chaps of a certain age chatting. One is Frank Sinatra. The other is Paddy Maddigan.

Paddy Maddigan is a household name in Dublin. His family firm, Maddigan's, owns some of the best-known pubs there. It has two pubs in London too, and this is one of them.

It used to have more. Maddigan's started buying pubs in London in the 1980s when pubs were doing well and had 14 when the recession started biting. One by one they went and now there's only the Hercules and the Pineapple down the road left.

Never mind, they are looking very spry and Maddigan's has certainly made a difference here, reshaping the bar entirely, pushing the counter right back, recarpeting, recovering the banquettes, bringing an artist over from Ireland to paint Hercules murals.

It is as good as a Dublin pub now, says the manager.

· THE HEREFORD ARMS ·

127 Gloucester Road, SW7 **370 4988**

'Miss Haversham comes to mind'

Open
All Week

Hours
12.00–23.00
(12.00–15.00 and 19.00–23.00 Sat; 12.00–22.30 Sun)
Closed Christmas Day

Credit Cards
AmEx, Mastercard, Visa

Bar Food Available
12.00–14.00 and 17.00–21.00
(12.00–22.30 Sun)

The Hereford Arms is extremely smart outside, a low William and Mary building, painted black with gold lettering. Inside it is, well, dark – dark panelled walls, dark beams, dark pillars and a low dark ceiling made lower and darker with sagging dark rope netting containing hops. Miss Haversham comes to mind.

I think I know why it is so dark. Not much light gets in, that may be it. There is a sweep of windows the full length of the bar but most of the small square panes are tinted yellow and putting the lights on doesn't seem to make much difference.

The effect is deliberate and comparatively recent and seems to work. The barmen are friendly and uniformed, white shirts, dark trousers, the music quiet, the food traditional and filling. One part is reserved for waitress service, though you can eat anywhere, and there are half a dozen picnic tables outside. This is a very popular up-market pub. Did Jack the Ripper really drink here? They say so.

Special Features
Wheelchair Access
Bear Garden seats 30

Beers Available
Wadworth 6X,
Theakston Old Peculier,
Courage Best,
Brakspear, Holsten Pils,
Budweiser, Foster's,
Newcastle Brown Ale,
Molsen, Becks
Cider: Scrumpy Jack

Nearest Tube Station
Gloucester Road

· THE HILLGATE ARMS ·

24 Hillgate Street, W8   **727 8543**

'A quiet backwater off Notting Hill Gate'

This is a very pleasant upmarket pub in a quiet back-water off Notting Hill. There is just room for tables and small benches along one outside wall and they bask in whatever sun there is, but I won't mention this. It is hard enough getting a seat there in summer as it is. There are luxuriant window boxes, hanging baskets and tubs. Estate agents are calling this Hillgate Village now.

Open
All Week

Hours
11.00–23.00
(12.00–22.30 Sun)

Credit Cards
All major cards accepted

Food Available
Bar 12.00–21.30
Restaurant 12.00–14.45

Special Features
Wheelchair Access
(disabled lavatory)
Beer Garden seats 70

Beers Available
Ruddles County,
London Pride,
Webster's Yorkshire,
Wadworth 6X,
Carlsberg, Foster's,
Holsten, Budweiser

Nearest Tube Station
Notting Hill Gate

· THE HOBGOBLIN ·

95 Effra Road, SW2   **501 9671**

'Funky Saturday nights'

A hobgoblin has been busy in Brixton's Effra Road. The last time we looked there was substantial old pub called the George Canning here and now look. It has been translated into one called the Hobgoblin. What would the serious-minded Mr Canning have made of that?

In its later days the George Canning had become known for its country and western, its line dancing and its funky Saturday nights, an unexpected fate for a pub named after a Prime Minister so sound on the corn laws, but would he have liked it any more now? The airy bar with its big windows is looking a lot better, but what would he have

Open
All Week

Hours
11.00–23.00
(12.00–22.30 Sun)

Food Available
Hot food and bar snacks 11.00–18.00

Special Features
Tables outside seat 100
Private Room seats 180

Beers Available
Wychwood Best, Shires Bitter, Dr Thirsty's, Dog's Bollocks, Hobgoblin Original, Courage Directors, Foster's, Budweiser, Holsten Export, Kronenbourg, Guinness
Ciders: Scrumpy Jack, Strongbow

Nearest Tube Station
Brixton

Open
All Week
Hours
11.00–23.00
(12.00–15.00 and
19.00–22.30 Sun)
Closed Christmas Day
Credit Cards
None
Bar and Restaurant Food Available
12.00–14.30
Special Features
Wheelchair Access
(but not lavatory)
Private Room seats 20
Beers Available
Boddingtons, Flowers IPA, Old Speckled Hen, London Pride, Summer Lightening, Bombadier, Heineken, Stella Artois, Guinness
Cider: Scrumpy Jack

Nearest Tube Stations
Bond Street, Oxford Circus

Open
All Week
Hours
12.00–15.00 and
17.30–23.00
(12.00–15.00 and
19.00–22.30 Sun)

made of the list of real ales below? The new owners, the Wychwood Brewery people, are strong on real ales. The rock bands still take over on Friday and Saturday and there is stand-up comedy on Thursdays now. Prime Ministers rarely like stand-up comedy.

When the pub was the George Canning it had a large car park. The Hogboblin has replaced the cars with tables. They were much used in the recent long hot summer.

·THE HOGSHEAD IN ST JAMES·
11 Dering Street, W1   **629 0531**
'You could be in an 18th-century taproom'

This used to be a little Victorian pub called the Bunch of Grapes. 'A pretty wooden-fronted building,' reported a Nicholson guide. 'Olde worlde red and gold interior...' It's nothing like that now.

Outside it has a smart glossy black and gold new frontage and inside it seems to have moved back a further 100 years. You could be in an 18th-century country taproom, plain and spare, wooden floors, timber bar fittings, next to no furniture. Furthermore it has a new name and a new role.

It has become one of Whitbread's specialized real-ale pubs, the Hogsheads. There are 70 of them now, 14 in London. There will be 120 nationally before long, all going in for real ale in a big way. This one, for instance, manages to offer eight cask ales, quite a trick when you have such small cellars. Three of them come direct from ten-gallon barrels in full view behind the bar. They sit there in a chilling unit enjoying the limelight.

A little dining room upstairs sits 20 people and has busy lunchtimes. People take it for parties and meetings in the evening. There is no charge for this. You pay to get in on Saturday nights, though, if there's alternative comedy. While stand-up comics try to bring the house down, a single slender iron pillar tries to keep it up.

·THE HOLLY BUSH·
22 Holly Mount, NW3   **435 2892**
'Dr Johnson and Boswell must have caused a stir'

A long flight of steps up the hill from Heath Street and you reach one of Hampstead's oldest and most picturesque pubs. When it was built in 1643 it stood high and proud on its hill with wonderful views. Now the houses and cottages of old Hampstead crowd round it, no bad thing for a village pub like this one.

Apart from that it has changed less that anyone could have expected. Well it had seven bars in Victorian times but they must have been exceptionally small. There are four now, including one that used to be the landlord's living room. But the general look of the place can't have been much different in the days when they hung a green branch over the door to announce that the beer was ready, the bare boards, the wood and plaster walls, the old wooden furniture, everything dark brown and nicotine. This is the effect that modern pub designers go for. The Holly Bush has always been like that.

Dr Johnson and Boswell both drank here they say. They must have caused a stir but nothing to the one made by Romney. In 1796 he gave up his grand house in Cavendish Square and bought a house behind the pub. He pulled down the stables, built a gallery for his pictures, enclosed half the garden for a riding house, got very miserable and went back to his wife in Kendal. Peace returned to the Holly Bush.

Bar Food Available
All opening hours

Special Features
Wheelchair Access
Private Room seats 30

Beers Available
Benskins, Tetley,
Burton Ale, Lowenbrau,
Castlemaine

Nearest Tube Station
Hampstead

· HOLLYWOOD ARMS ·

Hollywood Road, SW10   **351 1031**

'Hot-air balloons and Hollywood Outings

There must have been times in the past hundred years when this high-Victorian local would have exchanged its neo-Gothic arched windows for a little more passing trade. Life is not always easy so far from the Fulham Road. Happily, good little restaurants have opened on every side and the Hollywood Arms has now become a popular meeting place for young Chelsea.

The Hollywood Arms has a favourite historical figure, not one you may have come across – Jean-Pierre Blanchard, balloonist. In 1784 he took off from the field where the pub now stands and became the first man to cross the English Channel by air. So he and his balloon are on the pub sign and there are lots of pictures of hot-air balloons inside.

The pub used to have day trips known as Hollywood Outings but they have not survived the years. Possibly the name led to disappointments. Spoof has not survived here either. It was once so popular that regulars founded an International Spoof Club. It is a good old pub game, spoof.

There's a nice beer garden at the back with wooden picnic tables, much enjoyed by parents and children in the summer. Children are allowed, indeed encouraged, until 7.00 pm.

Open
All Week

Hours
11.00–23.00
(12.00–22.30 Sun)

Credit Cards
None

Bar Food Available
12.00–14.30 Mon–Sat

Special Features
Wheelchair Access
Tables outside
seat 100
Private Room seats 80

Beers Available
Theakston XB,
Theakston Bitter,
Courage Directors,
Kronenbourg

Nearest Tube Stations
Fulham Broadway,
West Brompton

· The Hoop and Grapes ·

Open
Sun–Fri
Hours
11.00–22.00
(11.00–23.00 Thur–Fri;
12.00–15.00 Sun)
Closed Bank Holidays
Credit Cards
All major cards accepted
Bar Food Available
All opening hours
Special Features
Wheelchair Access
(but not lavatory)
Tables outside seat 12
Beers Available
Hancock's HB, London Pride, Wadworth 6X, Bass, Carlsberg, Black Label, Budweiser, Becks
Nearest Tube Station
Aldgate

47 Aldgate High Street, EC3 **480 5739**

'It looks very old. Well it is very old'

A remarkable thing happened to the Hoop and Grapes in 1666. It was NOT burned down in the Great Fire of London. It escaped by 50 yards and there it still is, the only surviving 17th-century timber-framed building in the City of London. Everyone used brick after the fire.

Until quite recently the Hoop and Grapes was as you might expect so old a pub to be. It leaned, it creaked, its floors sloped to the east. Everyone liked it but it was getting a bit alarming, and in the early 1980s Bass Charrington called in experts and spent £1.2 million on it.

They stripped the building back to its original softwood frame, replaced timbers when necessary and rebuilt it, keeping as closely as they could to the original design. The Hoop and Grapes is now totally underpinned, the old frame is supported by steel. It is good for another 300 years.

The two courtyards of its coaching inn days are gone, I'm afraid. These are now part of the main bar, which is huge, all exposed timbers and brick and changing levels, bare floorboards here, flagstones there, a long bar counter, a busy servery, eating areas, drinking areas, standing-room-only chatting areas. It looks very old. Well it is very old and it has never been so popular. It is shoulder-to-shoulder time in all parts every lunchtime.

Petticoat Lane is just across the road so the Hoop and Grapes opens on Sundays from 12.00 to 3.00. This is a classic City pub so it closes, of course, on Saturdays.

· The Hope ·

Open
All Week
Hours
11.00–23.00
(12.00–22.30 Sun)
Credit Cards
Access, Visa
Bar Food Available
12.00–14.30 Mon–Fri
Special Features
Wheelchair Access
(but not lavatory)
Tables outside seat 16
Private Room seats 22

15 Tottenham Street, W1 **637 0896**

'A sausage and ale house'

Big notices outside and in this busy little Whitbread pub announce that this is a Sausage and Ale House. The sausages certainly rule okay every lunchtime, a choice of 15 very different bangers supplied by the ingenious Simply Sausages.

There's the Kentish hop sausage, for instance, made with pork, fuggles hops and porter; John Nott's sausage made from a 1720 recipe involving spinach, a beef and Guinness sausage; a Creole sausage from the States; and four for vegetarians. Glamorgan sausage turns out to be made of Caerphilly and leeks. These, dished up with mash and baked beans fill the little dining room upstairs from noon to 2.30

and in the evening it returns to its role as second bar and function room.

The Hope has a very lively landlord in Roger Fonseca from Portugal. The sausages were his idea. He thinks highly of this British delicacy. 'They are cheap and they fill you up,' he says. As for the ale, you get a choice of ten, eight on the handpumps and two served direct from barrels behind the bar. When I was last there these were the Welsh bitter Double Dragon and Bunces Pigswill, which rather defies you to drink it.

Beers Available
Boddington, Flowers Original, Wadworth 6X, Old Speckled Hen, Castle Eden, London Pride, Stella, Heineken, Guinness, Murphy's Cider: Strongbow

Nearest Tube Station
Goodge Street

· HORNIMAN AT HAY'S ·

Hay's Galleria, Tooley Street, SE1 **407 3611**

'The style beer drinkers prefer above all others'

Hay's Galleria with its soaring atrium, its shops and galleries and cafes is a great place for a pub. HMS *Belfast* lies romantically offshore, Tower Bridge with its extraordinary power to cheer you up is just down river, and if you have been doing the riverbank walk you will be in need of a drink at just this point.

You will be pleased, then, to find Horniman at Hay's waiting, expansive, confident and glossy, the long polished mahogany counter with its choice of five real ales, not to mention all the lagers, turning into a tea bar that also sells coffee and chilled milk. Then there's the big wide-open cafe, good fast food, with children welcome, special portions, special prices. There is a carvery upstairs and a no-smoking bit somewhere.

The Horniman in question was Mr F J Horniman, the Victorian tea importer, and this used to be the wharf where his tea was landed. He seems to have been a charismatic character, a great traveller and collector.

You can see his collections at the Horniman Museum in Forest Hill where he lived, and now there is this pub on his quay with lots of reminders of his life's work and the set of clocks from his office showing the time in foreign parts.

The pub is just nine years old, the style Victorian. This is the style, we are told, that beer drinkers prefer above all others.

Open
All Week

Hours
10.00–23.00
(10.00–16.00
Sat;10.00–15.00 Sun)
Closed Christmas Day, Boxing Day, New Year's Day

Credit Cards
Visa, Mastercard, AmEx

Restaurant Food Available
12.00–15.00 and
18.00–22.00

Special Features
No-smoking Area
Private Room seats 60

Beers Available
Tetley, Burton, Wadworth 6X, Timothy Taylor, Adnams Broadside, Brakspear

Nearest Tube Station
London Bridge

·THE HORSE AND GROOM·

68 Heath Street, NW3   435 3140

'The height of late Victorian taste'

Open
All Week

Hours
12.00–23.00 Mon–Fri;
11.00–23.00 Sat;
12.00–22.30 Sun
Closed Christmas Day

Credit Cards
None

Bar and Restaurant Food Available
12.00–15.00
(12.00–16.00 Sun)

Special Features
Wheelchair Access
(but not lavatory)
Private Room seats 70

Beers Available
Young's Bitter, Young's Special, Young's Oatmeal Stout, Young's Premium Lager, Young's London Lager, Tennent's Extra, Red Stripe, Castlemaine, Dirty Dick's Real Ale

Nearest Tube Station
Hampstead

The original Horse and Groom seems to have been just the sort of old pub we now most admire. It was an 18th-century tavern, all beams and low ceilings, the kind of old inn we put on Christmas cards, but it must have seemed very rural to the newly fashionable Hampstead. So in 1899 Young's replaced it with something bang up to date.

This was it, an imposing five-storey public house with a modish striped brick and stone façade and a high decorated gable, the height of late Victorian taste. It was then the tallest building in Heath Street. It still is.

The rich Victorian interior has been largely dismantled over the years but bits of it remain. Today there is one long open room. The front half is where the counter is, the back half where most of the tables are.

It is a friendly local with pleasant girls who bring your lunch to your table and chat to regulars spending happy, ruminative afternoons on their bar stools.

Convincing replicas of Charles I's death warrant and the Act of Union, 1707, are to be found tucked behind a gaming machine.

·THE HOUSE THEY LEFT BEHIND·

27 Ropemaker's Fields, E14   538 5102

'Its new name perfectly describes its curious situation'

Open
All Week

Hours
11.00–23.00
(12.00–15.00 Sun)
Closed Christmas Day,
Boxing Day

Credit Cards
All major cards accepted

Food Available
Bar and Restaurant
11.00–21.45

Special Features
Wheelchair Access
(but not lavatory)
Tables outside seat 25

Looking at Limehouse now it is hard to imagine it as it used to be, the busy boatyards, the boisterous docks, the maze of tenements. One day in 1871 Alexander II, Tsar of Russia, visited a ropeworks here. Could this have been in Ropemaker's Fields where, at number 27, the Black Horse stood?

The Black Horse was a small, busy inner-city pub built in 1856, part of a terrace in the heart of this teeming bit of the East End. Today it is the only house left in Ropemaker's Fields. All the others have gone, and it is no longer called the Black Horse. Its new name perfectly describes its curious situation. It is now called The House They Left Behind.

For years now public work has gone on week after week, month after month, all round the solitary House They Left Behind, a long trial by noise, mess and dust, but the crystal starts to clear.

The dump at one side is a park now, and the empty space at the front door is recognizably the piazza the pub was promised. There are benches, young trees, a sculpture of a seagull on a coil of real rope and, most important of all, a development of 11 new flats has brought new neighbours at last.

Things have moved on and there have been changes to the pub itself. There are now new owners and there are also new managers. The decorators have been in and an electric organ has arrived, bringing the Sunday night sing-alongs with it.

In one of the tall terrace houses of Narrow Street beyond the new piazza, David Owen is famously in residence. He hasn't been spotted at a sing-along yet.

Beers Available
Courage Directors, Ruddles, Webster's, John Smith's Extra Smooth Bitter, Carlsberg, Kronenbourg, Foster's, Guinness
Cider: Red Rock Draught

Nearest Tube Station
Mile End

·THE INTREPID FOX·

99 Wardour Street, W1

'The new intrepid foxes'

Like Soho itself the Intrepid Fox is old and battered and has seen a thing or two. In its young days its passion was politics, the Whig leader Charles James Fox its hero. It is he who is the Intrepid Fox, he the stout party in the beaver hat on the pub sign. In the 1784 election there was free beer for anyone who would vote for him, and a bas-relief on the outside wall showing Fox waving a banner saying Champion of the People is still there.

The old pub has hit some rough patches along the way since then, but it has new heroes today. It is now a leading rock, punk, neo-technic and trash pub, so popular that you sometimes have to queue to get in. It is black leather jackets, pony tails and half-shaved heads in the big downstairs bar these days and the walls are covered with icons of the new intrepid foxes – Jimi Hendrix, the Rolling Stones, the Who, David Bowie, Freddie Mercury, the Stranglers...

Their music and that of their successors is the current passion of the Intrepid Fox. It plays all day.

Open
All Week

Hours
12.00–23.00
(15.00–22.30 Sun)
Closed Christmas Day

Credit Cards
None

Bar Food Available
12.00–23.00
(19.00–22.30 Sun)
sandwiches only

Special Features
Wheelchair Access
Private Room seats 80

Beers Available
Castlemaine, Lowenbrau, Carlsberg, Tetley, Burtons, Guinness

Nearest Tube Station
Piccadilly Circus

·THE ISLAND QUEEN·

87 Noel Road, N1   **359 4037**

'Agreeably eccentric'

Wooden puppets of life-sized pirates hang from the ceiling over the horseshoe bar in this agreeably eccentric Islington local. One climbs a net, two fight, one lights a cannon. Bare floorboards, ceiling-high Victorian mirrors, a small pool room at the back – people who drink there on a regular basis like it just as it is.

Open
All Week

Hours
12.00–15.00 and
17.30–23.00
Mon–Thur;
11.00–23.00 Fri;
12.00–23.00 Sat
(12.00–22.30 Sun)
Closed Christmas Day

Credit Cards
None

Food Available
Bar 12.00–14.30
Restaurant
18.00–21.00 Fri–Sat;
(12.00–15.00) Sun
Set-price lunch and dinner £15.95

Beers Available
London Pride, Caffey's, Bass, Grolsch, Carling Black Label

Nearest Tube Station
Angel

Open
Mon–Sat

Hours
11.00–23.00
Closed Sundays and Bank Holidays

Credit Cards
Visa, Master, All Mastercards

Food Available
11.00–21.00

Special Features
Wheelchair Access
Tables outside seat 48

Beers Available
Fuller's real ales, London Pride, ESB, Chiswick, Hock Summer Ale, Indian Pale Ale, Mr Harry, Fuller guest beers

Nearest Tube Station
Tottenham Court Road

Open
All Week

Hours
11.00–23.00
(12.00–22.30 Sun)

Credit Cards
All major cards accepted

Food Available
Bar 12.00–21.00
Restaurant
12.00–15.00 and
18.00–22.00
(all day Sun)

Special Features
Wheelchair Access
(lift to restaurant)
Beer Garden seats 70
Private Room seats 50

For years one of the original juke boxes played the magic music of the Sixties, thus ensuring a clientele of discrimination and allure. Alas it became unwell and was pronounced beyond repair. A modern all-singing CD version took its place, brash, some thought. It has kept true to the music, though. There is a nice restaurant upstairs.

· JACK HORNER ·

Tottenham Court Road, W1   **636 2868**
'What a good boy am I'

Fuller's press on with their admirable campaign to change all of London's banks into pubs. In the living memory of anyone born in 1994 this was a branch of Martins. It is now a useful new pub called the Jack Horner, named after Little Jack Horner, one of the great heroes of English Literature.

Jack Horner's is a moving story. He was sitting in his corner eating his Christmas pie when, in a dramatic scene, he stuck in his thumb and pulled out a plum. 'What a good boy am I!' he said. I see Robbie Coltraine in the part.

You get a very nice pie in the Jack Horner, this being one of Fuller's Ale and Pie Pubs, but it does get very busy. I put this down to the choice of opener, me actually. I made a speech, pulled the first pint and haven't been able to reach the bar since.

· JACK STRAW'S CASTLE ·

North End Way, NW3   **435 8885**
'Georgian Gothic said the architect.
Grounded Mississippi showboat said the Evening Standard'

This famous old coaching inn has a swashbuckling past and quite a showy present. Its past first though…

Jack Straw was Wat Tyler's right-hand man, a fiery leader of the Peasants' Revolt. He burned down the priory in Clerkenwell, addressed the assembled peasants from a hay waggon on Hampstead Heath and hid in the inn. He was caught there and executed outside the front door.

The old inn was known as Jack Straw's Castle after that and kept the name when it was replaced by a coaching inn in 1721, after which it was all coaches arriving and coaches leaving and horses to water and travellers to feed and bustle and drama and ruffians lying in wait. Meanwhile Hampstead grew and got fashionable and Jack Straw's Castle was discovered by literary London. Wilkie Collins started riding over, and Thackeray and Dickens (of course), after which nothing much happened until the Second World War when it was banged about by a landmine.

It was rebuilt in the early 1960s. A leading architect, Raymond C Erith, was engaged and London got a spectacular new pub. Georgian-Gothic said Mr Erith. Grounded Mississippi showboat said the *Evening Standard*. It was three storeys high with a long weatherboard frontage, a parade of bay windows, arched Gothic windows from end to end and battlements on top.

It got another major going-over in 1993. Just painting the weatherboarding cream and white took three men six weeks, but it is looking very spruce now, as do the refurbished bars, function rooms and à la carte restaurant.

There's lots going on. The big L-shaped bar on the ground floor is a home-from-home for Hampstead's rugby, cricket and football clubs. There's a barbecue most summer evenings in the big courtyard at the back, a pleasant place with brick paving and cobbles, a tree with a tree seat and lots of wooden tables and benches The first floor is receptions and private parties and the top floor is the restaurant.

Jack Straw's Castle occupies one of the highest points in London and the restaurant has panoramic views over the heath. If he had got a good table Jack Straw would have seen them coming.

Beers Available
London Pride, Bass, Hancock's, Carling Black Label, Tennent's, Grolsch, Guinness, Caffrey's

Nearest Tube Station
Hampstead

· THE KING OF BOHEMIA ·

10 Hampstead High Street, NW3 **435 6513**

'Just the thing for a neo-king'

The young Elector Palatine should have left well alone but no, he would become King of Bohemia. You could see what was going to happen – he lost both Bohemia and his Palatinate and Europe got the Thirty Years' War.

What Hampstead got was this pub on the High Street. Not this one exactly, you understand, but one on the same site, built in 1613, the year the would-be King of Bohemia married James I's daughter. This is more or less the one that replaced it in 1935, bow-fronted, neo-Georgian, just the thing for a neo-king.

It has had a thorough going-over and is now very smart and glossy, with glass doors that open the whole frontage to the street in fine weather. New parquet flooring links a series of bars to the distant black wall. It has a games corner, lots of bric-à-brac, a most efficient food operation and no original features. The music gets going in the evening.

Open
All Week

Hours
11.00–23.00
(12.00–22.30 Sun)
Closed Christmas Day

Credit Cards
None

Bar Food Available
12.00–14.30

Special Features
Wheelchair Access (but not lavatory)
Tables outside seat 12

Beers Available
Boddingtons, Pedigree, Becks, Budweiser, Stella Artois, Grolsch; Cider: Old Hazy

Nearest Tube Station
Hampstead

· The King and Queen ·

1 Foley Street, W1 **636 5619**

'Every known Irish whiskey'

Open
All Week

Hours
11.00–23.00 Mon–Fri
11.00–15.00 Sat
(12.00–15.00 Sun)

Credit Cards
None

Bar Food Available
11.00–21.00

Special Features
Wheelchair Access
(but not lavatory)
Tables outside seat 24
Private Room seats 96

Beers Available
Ruddles, Adnams, John Smith, Holstein, Foster, Kronenbourg 1664, Carlsberg
Cider: Strongbow

Nearest Tube Stations
Goodge Street, Warren Street, Great Portland Street

This unpretentious local is directly opposite the casualty department of the Middlesex Hospital, so naturally it fills up with nurses, porters, brain surgeons and the like. Patients too, I shouldn't wonder.

Pictures of various kings and queens decorate the bar, also one of William Lee who has the lease and, he says, the most expensive range of spirits in London – amazing vodkas, exotic tinctures from the East and every known Irish whiskey.

William Lee has three other pubs. One, the Royal Military in Aldershot, is a resort of the Parachute Regiment. It is known locally as the Rat Pit.

EVERY TIME WE STEP INTO A PUB I'M FILLED WITH A DREADFUL FOREBODING...

· The King's Head ·

4 Fulham High Street, SW6 **736 1413**

'No 1 for secret gigs'

Open
All Week

Hours
11.00–23.00 Mon–Tue;
11.00–24.00 Wed–Sat;
(12.00–15.00 and
19.00–22.30 Sun)

Credit Cards
None

Bar Food Available
12.00–15.00 Mon–Fri

Special Features
Wheelchair Access
Beer Garden seats 200
Private Room seats 150

Beers Available
Budweiser, Sol, Rolling Rock, Molsen, Holsten Pils, Caffrey's, Carling, Tennent's Pilsner, Tennent's Extra, Guinness,
Cider: Red Rock, Dry Blackthorn

Nearest Tube Station
Putney Bridge

Drive the full length of the New King's Road in a car without brakes without turning right or left and this is what you would eventually hit. It is an enormous five-storey Edwardian pub with a fairytale tower in the middle and a banner with a bold claim: 'London's Premier Live Music Venue' it says.

There may be something in that. A new stage and lighting system recently installed have taken it a long way. Bands of many sorts play seven nights of the week and it is now, says the manager, No 1 for secret gigs. Recent acts include Robert Plant, Nigel Kennedy, Little Angels and Paul Young. Regular record launches and album previews are held there. It has made a place for itself in the scheme of things.

Discovering a secret gig is not hard. You leave your name, address and telephone number in the book at the door and you will be told about it. At secret gigs, as at any other sort, they need an audience. The admission price varies but starts around £3.

The place itself remains as uncheery as before. A large black room with a bar leads to a smaller black room with a stage and sophisticated equipment.

This is punk and skinhead territory sometimes, sometimes various kinds of rock, sometimes middle-of-the-road pop, with different audiences for each but they are all tolerant of strangers wearing the wrong clothes. If this is not your scene you can go through the unlabelled connecting door, past the ladies and into the comparatively bright lights of the public bar.

This has its own customers. You will find them drinking at a massive U-shaped bar, playing pool, feeding coins into machines, watching television and listening to a major juke box in constant use. The bar has its own entrance from the street and one to the beer garden where on sunny days 200 people can and do find a seat.

·THE KING'S HEAD·

115 Upper Street, N1 **226 1916**

'Brilliant casts and national reviews'

There are now at least a dozen theatre pubs in London. This was the first – the first, that is, since Shakespeare's day, or so says Dan Crawford, the licensee of this big Islington pub. It was Crawford who turned the big room behind his bar into a theatre in 1970. In spite of regular crises it has been an extraordinary success. Its productions get brilliant casts and national reviews. Many have transferred to the West End. One transferred to Broadway and won four Tony awards.

The pub itself is a substantial Victorian pile with a busy and in some ways eccentric life of its own. When the nation went decimal in 1971 Dan Crawford was reluctant to replace his noble Victorian till so he didn't. The King's Head, he decreed, would continue with the old currency and it still does. A pint of Guinness costs two guineas; a bottled beer £1 16s; a cup of coffee 12s. Good Lord! A cup of coffee used to cost 6d.

The theatre is at the back. It has seats from the Scala Theatre, Marylebone, burgundy velvet curtains from the Theatre Royal, Haymarket, and ancient theatre lanterns from the Lyric, Shaftesbury Avenue. There is a fair-sized apron stage and a decent view from just about anywhere.

Supper is served at tables in the theatre before the performance – you don't have to eat there but most people do and there is something very companionable about it. A three-course meal costs £8 10s and you stay on at your table

Open
All Week
Hours
11.00–24.00 Mon–Thur;
11.00–1.00 Fri and Sat
(12.00–24.00 Sun)
Closed Christmas Day
Credit Cards
None
Special Features
Wheelchair Access
Private Room seats 125
Beers Available
Benskins, Adnams,
Burton Ale,
Castlemaine,
Lowenbrau, Guinness,
Nearest Tube Stations
Highbury & Islington,
Angel

to watch the play. Tickets for this cost £9 during the week and £10 on a Saturday. The capacity is 125 with 90 able to eat.

Meanwhile the pub will have been filling up and, the play over, departing theatre-goers have to squeeze through a crowded bar to reach the street. Some stay on for the Adnams and the music that follows the show – there is folk, rock or jazz until midnight.

Some good bands have played here, Dire Straits among them, but that's the King's Head. Both halves crackle with energy and talent.

THE KING'S HEAD AND ·EIGHT BELLS·

50 Cheyne Walk, SW3   727 6648

'A wealth of modern period features'

Open
All Week

Hours
11.00–23.00
(12.00–22.30 Sun)

Credit Cards
Visa, Mastercard,

Bar Food Available
12.00–15.00 and
19.00–22.30

Special Features
Wheelchair Access
(but not lavatory)

Beers Available
Boddingtons, Fuggle's, Flowers IPA, Courage, Heineken, Guinness

Nearest Tube Station
Sloane Square

For years this much-loved pub was the heart of bohemian Chelsea. Generations of painters, craftsmen and writers drank there – Whistler, Turner, Walter Greaves, Augustus John... It is still a pleasant, good-looking pub and while successive modern improvements have lessened its old romantic appeal they have certainly increased its turnover.

The King's Head and Eight Bells had modest beginnings, starting life as two small 15th-century seamen's pubs side-by-side on the riverbank. The King's Head was for officers, the Eight Bells for the crews. Eight bells were rung to summon the men back to their ships.

The two pubs merged in 1580 and it became the local river boatmen's pub, then the artists made it their own and by the 1960s the old stucco building, much changed, had become a tourist attraction. Yet more changes lay ahead.

Tourists come in greater numbers than ever. What they see may not be the pub that Whistler knew, but it is comfortable and goodness knows well-appointed with its big bar at the front opening up to a busy restaurant at the back, both with a wealth of modern period features.

It is sad but no one's fault that it is no longer on the river bank. The original riverside Cheyne Walk still passes the door but Chelsea Embankment long since came between river and pub. The embankment gardens have also intervened. Today, customers of the King's Head and Eight Bells must be content with a glimpse of distant ships and pleasureboats as they slide by above the river wall at high tide while the traffic of modern London thunders past in between.

· THE LADBROKE ARMS ·

54 Ladbroke Road, W11   **727 6648**

'A shining light'

Egon Ronay's inspector inspected this pub and wrote thus: 'On the corner of Ladbroke Road and the charming Willby Mews, the Ladbroke Arms is a shining light, hopefully leading other pubs where many fear to tread.'

Mr Ronay's inspector is right in every particular. The Ladbroke Arms is indeed a shining light, which will surprise those who remember it as it used to be. It was a pedestrian sort of pub, noticeably unshining until Ian MacKenzie took it over. He had already shown what he could do. He had been part of the successful team that launched the Slug and Lettuce on an alarmed world in the early Eighties. First there was one Slug and Lettuce, then another and another. When there were nine MacKenzie and his partners sold them and went their several ways.

MacKenzie started his new venture with the Ladbroke Arms. It was built in 1843 and had always been a nice-looking pub. The original mahogany fittings just needed a good polish and the rest of it some papering and carpeting. What needed changing most was the character of the place.

The key to its renaissance has been the bright, friendly new staff and the change in the food. This was dramatic. The Ladbroke Arms, bastion of traditional pub grub, now has an adventurous menu that changes daily. The house dressing for the salads is basil and honey. How many pubs have a house dressing?

As for the beer, well, see left, and the wine list isn't bad either. Classical music or light jazz plays quietly in the background and the raised terrace outside is famously crowded all summer.

Open
All Week

Hours
11.00–23.00
(12.00–22.30 Sun)

Credit Cards
Access, Visa, Switch, Delta

Bar Food Available
12.00–14.30 and
19.00–21.30

Special Features
Wheelchair Access

Beers Available
Webster's Yorkshire, Wadworth 6X, Courage Best, Courage Directors, Elridge Pope, Royal Oak

Nearest Tube Station
Holland Park

· THE LAMB ·

94 Lamb's Conduit Street, WC1   **405 0713**

'Brilliant-cut hinged snob screens, the very latest thing in 1894'

The Lamb has long been one of the most admired pubs in London. People like it because, they say, it has not been spoiled, which is true. It has been altered quite bit, all the same.

It was built in the 1720s and twice improved almost beyond recognition by the Victorians who despised the 18th century. There were alterations in our own time too, but thankfully the 1959 restorers left the handsome façade and the etched windows and the splendid U-shaped bar counter

Open
All Week

Hours
11.00–23.00
(12.00–22.30 Sun)

Credit Cards
Visa, Access, Mastercard, Diner's Club,

Bar Food Available
12.00–14.30

Special Features
No-smoking Area
Wheelchair Access
(but not lavatory)
Beer Garden seats 30

Beers Available
Young's IPA Bitter,
Special, Porter, Winter
Warmer, London Lager,
Premium, Castlemaine,
Tennent's Extra

Nearest Tube Stations
Russell Square,
Holborn

ringed by brilliant-cut hinged snob screens. These were the very latest thing in 1894. Open them and you are face to face with the barman. Good heavens! Close them and your drink will slide discreetly towards you under the screens.

It is all convincingly Victorian, the Spy cartoons, the musical comedy stars, the leather sofas and the splendid Polyphone, great grandfather of the CD player with discs going back to 1830. It belongs to John Young, chairman of the brewers, and is quite a celeb, making movies and starring in the Antiques Roadshow. Put £1 in the charity box and the staff will wind it up and let it play.

There is a little patio at the back but, whenever they can, regulars at the Lamb like to drink outside in Lamb's Conduit Street where, in 1577, a conduit was laid to bring water to the houses. It was designed and paid for as an act of charity by William Lamb, an Elizabethan engineer with a good heart who also provided 120 pails for poor women to carry the water in. The name of the pub and the name of the street ensure that this good deed is still remembered 400 years later.

· THE LAMB AND FLAG ·

33 Rose Street, WC2　　　　　　　　　　　　**497 9504**

'Proud of its hairy youth'

Open
All Week

Hours
11.00–23.00
(12.00–22.30 Sun)
Closed Christmas Day,
Boxing Day

Credit Cards
None

Bar Food Available
12.00–17.00 Mon–Sat

Beers Available
Courage Best, Courage
Directors, John Smith's,
Wadworth 6X, Old
Speckled Hen, Foster's,
Kronenbourg, Guinness,
Beamish

Nearest Tube Station
Covent Garden

This small, charming, much-loved pub is tucked away up an alley between Garrick Street and Floral Street. Half Covent Garden seems to go there for a drink after work. If they can't get in they drink on the pavement. In the summer when everyone drinks outside you can hardly see the pub for the people.

It is easily the oldest pub in Covent Garden and it is proud of its hairy youth. The back room was called the Bucket of Blood after the bare-knuckle fights held there and John Dryden was badly beaten up in the alley in 1679. Serve him right for being satirical. They call the upstairs room the Dryden Room now. You get a good straightforward lunch up there and Dixieland jazz on Sunday nights.

There is a newish tradition of screwing brass tags onto the bar counter with the names of favoured regulars. Two American girls sent their own for consideration having spent 12 of the 14 days of their London holiday in the Lamb.

·The Lamb Tavern·

Leadenhall Market, EC3 **626 2454**

'One of London's stateliest pubs'

Sir Horace Jones, the Victorian architect, gave London three magnificent markets – Smithfield, Billingsgate and Leadenhall. The grandest of these was Leadenhall, the game, fish and poultry market in the heart of the City. It is still a fine sight with its great stone arches, lofty arcades and stunning cast-iron work and it includes one of London's stateliest pubs, the Lamb Tavern.

Every weekday the Lamb fills up with energetic, talkative men in suits. Many work at Lloyd's and seem to take every opportunity to get out of their spectacular new building and into the pubs and wine bars of Sir Horace's market.

I can tell you something about those who pick the Lamb Tavern. In good times and in bad they are great drinkers of draught bitter. This understandable enthusiasm has meant that the recession was not felt at all at the Lamb. Indeed, in recent years the Lamb, always thought rather on the large side with its three floors, all high ceilings and high principles, began to seem a little cramped and Young's slotted in a new mezzanine floor and a spiral staircase into the once soaring saloon bar.

So there are now four floors for these new market traders to populate. They cheerfully do so, arriving around lunchtime, and the Lamb is then busy until about nine in the evening when the last City gent makes for home and a dried-up dinner in the oven.

Now that the marble pillars disappear into a ceiling of modest height, the main bar is nowhere near as impressive as it was, but the cavernous smoking room in the basement keeps its old style and so does the top floor with its tall windows and fine view of the market. This is a no-smoking bar. It was the City's first and has proved very popular. Each level of the Lamb serves food but this high, elegant room is the place to eat.

At weekends the highly photogenic market closes and quite often film crews move in. John Wayne spent days at the Lamb when scenes for *Brannigan* were being shot there. Robert Mitchum was there for *The Winds of War* and Tom Selleck for *Magnum*. The BBC shot some of *Bleak House* in the Lamb and the landlord's children both got parts.

Open
Mon–Fri
Hours
11.00–21.00
Credit Cards
All major cards accepted
Bar Food Available
11.00–14.30
Special Features
No-smoking Area
Private Room seats 50
Beers Available
Young's Bitter, Young's Special, Dirty Dick's, Oatmeal, Beamish, London Lager, Stella, Castlemaine.
Nearest Tube Station
Bank

· THE LATCHMERE ·

Open
All Week

Hours
11.00–23.00
(12.00–22.30 Sun)
Closed Christmas Day

Credit Cards
Visa, Access

Food Available
12.00–22.00 (full meals)

Special Features
Wheelchair Access
Tables outside seat 60
Theatre Bar for hire during the day
Live Music occasionally

Beers Available
Courage Directors, Courage Best, Greene King, John Smith's, Foster's, Kronenbourg, Miller Pilsner, Guinness, plus cider

Nearest BR Station
Clapham Junction

503 Battersea Park Road, SW11   **223 3549**

'Goodbye to the kicked-in counter'

The most imposing Victorian pubs can have their ups and their downs. I have to report that the Latchmere, always a powerful presence, is having an up. The big shabby bar has been thoroughly refurbished. The battered kicked-in counter has been replaced by a smart new one, and the walled garden, not long ago a dump, is lovely, its picnic tables encircled by climbing roses, vines and ivy.

Well, it has an energetic and ambitious lessee now, the one-time paratrooper Alan Grace. It was Grace who started the Canal Café Theatre in a Little Venice pub called the Bridge House. Taking over the Latchmere meant he had one of London's leading pub theatres on his first floor.

It had a high reputation then and it still has. It seats 90 and has a new production every month, good modern plays as a rule with excellent casts. Susannah York was playing there recently, as well as Kate O'Mara and Dermot Walsh. Familiar television faces appear in productions there all the time.

It is called the Grace Theatre at the Latchmere now after Alan Grace, not the present Alan Grace but his father. He was a rising young actor at the beginning of a promising career when the war broke out.

· LEGLESS LADDER ·

Open
All Week

Hours
12.00–15.00 and
17.15–23.00 Mon–Fri;
12.00–23.00 Sat;
(12.00–22.30 Sun)

Credit Cards
All major cards accepted

Bar Food Available
12.00–14.30 and
19.00–22.00 Mon–Sat;
(12.00–21.30 Sun)

Special Features
Wheelchair Access
(but not lavatory)
Beer Garden seats 20

Beers Available
Brakspear, John Smith's, Courage Directors

Nearest BR Station
Battersea Park

339 Battersea Park Road, SW11   **622 2112**

'The Prince himself was often legless'

The Prince of Wales in Battersea Park Road, having got tired and dusty, closed for good and Jeremy Hampton bought the lease. He turned the three Victorian bars into one big open-plan space, scrapping the massive old bar counter in the middle and bringing in lots of big old pine tables with numbered pews. All that remains of the old Prince of Wales is a tiled portrait of the good 'ol boy, soon to become Edward VII. He himself was often legless.

The new Legless Ladder has become a popular drinking hole for young and sporty Battersea settlers who go for the big helpings of hearty British food and pints of lager, also for big matches featured on screens installed for the occasion. Major rugby internationals pack the place with cheering fans.

Having got a taste for it Hampton has now opened another Legless Ladder, this one in Harwood Terrace in Fulham.

·THE LEINSTER ARMS·

17 Leinster Terrace, W2   **723 5757**
'The Grand Master Cellarman'

The Leinster Arms is the home of a Burton Ale Grand Master Cellarman, a notable personage so watch it, that's all. Her name is Olive McCarthy and she is the first woman Grand Master Cellarman ever.

Mrs McCarthy, disconcertingly youthful-looking mother of two sons both at college, has run the Leinster Arms herself since her husband left. She took over from him as manager and she has been a conspicuous success. The pub has blossomed and she has been heaped with prizes. Every year it seems there is a new trophy for being puller of the perfect pint.

This has always been an attractive pub. It is an old coaching house in Bayswater with a big, cheerful, comfortable bar, good plain food served all day, Olive herself behind the bar and, you will not be surprised to hear, cask ales that rise from an immaculate cellar in perfect condition.

Open
All Week
Hours
11.00–23.00
(12.00–22.30 Sun)
Credit Cards
All major cards accepted
Bar Food Available
11.00–20.30
(12.00–22.30 Sun)
Special Features
Wheelchair Access
Tables outside seat 30
Beers Available
Tetley, Nicholson's, Lowenbrau, Castlemaine, Carlsberg, Burton Ale
Nearest Tube Stations
Queensway, Lancaster Gate

·THE LORD MOON OF THE MALL·

16–18 Whitehall, SW1   **839 7701**
'The Queen's local?'

The imposing Victorian building next to the Whitehall Theatre was built in 1872 by a favourite pupil of Sir Gilbert Scott to house one of London's grandest banks. Cocks, Biddulph and Co were bankers not just to Prime Ministers and Lord Chancellors but also to Thomas Chippendale and John Constable. Edward VII had an account there from the age of three. Much later it became the most prestigious branch of Martins Bank and then of Barclays.

Barclays moved out in 1992 and in came J D Wetherspoon with a million pounds to spend on one of the most distinguished buildings on the market. What had been a most superior bank became a most superior public house. Early customers lowered their voices as they entered. The building is used to that sort of thing.

It is much jollier than it used to be, of course. Widely spaced tables occupy the one-time banking hall with its coffered ceiling and arched windows. More arches lead from here to the main bar with its polished granite counter and to what was once the partner's room where dukes awaited an invitation to sit. It is all opened up now and there are lots of comfortable chairs for us all, I'm happy to say.

Open
All Week
Hours
11.00–23.00 Mon–Sat
(12.00–22.30 Sun)
Credit Cards
Access, Visa, Delta, Switch, AmEx
Bar Food Available
11.00–22.00 Mon–Sat
(12.00–21.30 Sun)
Special Features
Wheelchair access including lavatory
Beers Available
Youngers Scotch Bitter, Theakston Best Bitter, Theakston XB, Marston's Pedigree, Directors, Weekly Guest Beer
Nearest Tube Station
Charing Cross

So through the double doors in the far wall and the Mall is directly ahead, leading to the big house where the bank's most valued customers lived. Indeed, I suppose this could be the Queen's local. A stroll down the Mall and into the Lord Moon by the back door, who, apart from a few thousand tourists and the world's press, would notice?

The Lord Moon was Wetherspoon's 106th pub. It shares with the others the well-known Wetherspoon's characteristics – no music, a big no-smoking area, and a 99p pint of Younger's Scotch Bitter. It is open all the hours permitted and does food all day. Look carefully at the neo-Gainsborough facing you as you go in. The 18th-century blade leaning on the garden urn is the chairman and founder of Wetherspoons, Tim Martin. Through the glass doors, at the head of what used to be the stairs down to the vaults, stands an elegant man in a dinner jacket. That is Tim Martin too, a statue this time.

· THE LYCEUM TAVERN ·

354 Strand, WC2 **836 7155**

'The new Lyceum will find its old friend in good shape'

Open
All Week

Hours
11.00–23.00
(12.00–15.00 and 19.00–22.30 Sun)
Closed Christmas Day, Boxing Day

Credit Cards
Visa, Mastercard, Eurocard

Food Available
Bar 12.00–14.30
Restaurant 17.00–21.00

Special Features
Wheelchair Access (but not lavatory)

Beers Available
Samuel Smith variants

Nearest Tube Station
Covent Garden

In the days when Henry Irving's great Lyceum Theatre was alive and well, the little Lyceum Tavern was part of theatrical London. The pub backed onto the theatre, and actors and singers and backstage staff were in and out all the time.

They will surely be again and quite soon. A huge £14-million restoration is bringing the Lyceum to life again. Meanwhile the Lyceum Tavern couldn't sit around and wait. It has long since made another life for itself.

Samuel Smith got it with five others when it bought Hennekey's in 1980 and has done it over very nicely with cosy drinking booths in the main bar and a pleasant panelled bar overlooking the Strand upstairs. When the new Lyceum reopens at last it will find its old friend in very good shape.

· THE MAGDALA TAVERN ·

2a South Hill Park, NW3 **435 2503**

'Three bullet holes in the cream tile frontage'

Open
All Week

Hours
11.00–23.00
(12.00–22.30 Sun)

Credit Cards
None

There are three bullet holes in the cream tile frontage of the Magdala Tavern in South Hill Park and a notice explaining how they come to be there. It was here, it says, that Ruth Ellis shot and killed her lover David Blakeley on 10 April 1955.

This she did, standing over him and putting three more bullets into his body as he lay on the pavement, then quietly waiting for the police to come. She was the last woman to be hanged, and she gave this otherwise unmemorable local a sort of macabre glamour that still lingers.

The pub has a public bar and a saloon bar, each with its own entrance. It was from the saloon bar that David Blakeley emerged unsuspectingly that night to find the woman he had fatally offended waiting.

There is a theatrical gloss to it now with photographs of Alan Bates, Richard Attenborough, John Geilgud and others and a painting of Oscar Wilde. The star, quite rightly, is Ruth Ellis. She stares bleakly from the frame, blonde, ashen, heavily made-up in an open-neck shirt blouse with a silk scarf and a broad belt tightly fastened. Grouped with the photograph is a letter she wrote from Holloway.

It starts 'Dear Frank', sends thanks for lovely flowers, is sorry to hear of some accident he had had but she gets to herself in the end. 'No doubt you have heard I do not want to live,' she writes. 'You may find this very hard to believe but that is what I want. I am quite well and happy under the circumstances, I am very well looked after, I have plenty to amuse me. Well Frank this must be all for now. Thanks once again. Yours Ruth Ellis.'

Beneath it are two miniature certificates, one the official declaration that the judgement of death had been executed, the other the death certificate, signed by the prison surgeon on 13 July 1955.

Magdala was the Ethiopian hill fortress taken and destroyed by Sir Robert Napier in 1868. He became Lord Napier of Magdala. There is a painting of the battle on the side of the building.

Bar Food Available
12.30–14.30
(12.00–17.00 Sun)

Special Features
Tables outside seat 30

Beers Available
Young's Special, regularly changing guest ales, Carlsberg, Tennent's Extra, Tennent's Pilsner

Nearest Tube Station
Hampstead Heath

·THE MAGPIE AND STUMP·

18 Old Bailey, EC4 **248 5085**

'Only the name survives'

Few London pubs had a more macabre past than this one. It stood facing the gallows of Newgate Jail and would rent out its upper floors for all-night parties before an execution. Vast crowds whooped it up below while the nobs drank, played cards and at dawn watched the wretched prisoner slowly strangling on the gibbet while his relations hung on his legs to hasten his end. The sight gave them a good appetite for the Magpie and Stump's large execution breakfast.

In time the old pub had a pretty swift coup de grace itself. After being remodelled in 1931 it settled down to a

Open
Mon–Fri

Hours
11.00–23.00
Closed Bank Holidays

Credit Cards
All major cards except Switch

Food Available
Bar 11.00–23.00
Restaurant
12.00–15.00

Special Features
Wheelchair Access
Private Room seats 120

Beers Available
Hancock's Best, Well Hung, Bass

Nearest Tube Station
St Paul's

respectable old age as a tourist attraction and all was well until 1988 when it was sold to a developer and demolished. The deal was that a new Magpie and Stump should be part of the new building. This is it.

It would be easy to miss it. The Magpie and Stump keeps its old address but the only hint that there might be a pub in Old Bailey is an inn sign oddly attached to what looks like an office wall. The new pub's facia and entrance are hidden away round the corner in an alley called Bishop's Court.

The Magpie and Stump is now a large modern pub on three levels, the main bar on what estate agents call the raised ground floor, a wine bar under that, a restaurant under that. Under that are two more floors of kitchens and cellars.

The new pub is spacious, fully air-conditioned and handsomely equipped. There's a lift if you can't manage all the stairs. But nothing, not even the inn sign, was saved from the historic old tavern. Only the name survives.

Barmen have to explain that the name given to their new specially brewed ale refers to the gallows. It is Well Hung.

· THE MAN IN THE MOON ·

392 King's Road, SW3   352 2543

'An even more important fixture'

Open
All Week

Hours
11.00–23.00
(12.00–22.30 Sun)
Closed Bank Holidays

Credit Cards
None

Bar Food Available
12.00–19.00

Special Features
No-smoking Area
Wheelchair Access

Beers Available
John Smith's,
Theakston Best,
Theakston XB,
Theakston Old Peculier,
Wadworth 6X,
Carlsberg,
Kronenbourg, Foster's,
Holsten Pils, Guinness

Nearest Tube Station
Sloane Square

This big old Georgian pub in the far reaches of the King's Road lives in adventurous times. As I write, the popular little theatre at the back is being doubled in size, the basement is being turned into a theatre bar and new managers, Barry and Sarah Scarborough, are planning big changes to the food. They are themselves both ex-chefs.

The lively main bar on the ground floor isn't changing much. Well there are new carpets, curtains and bar stools, but it keeps its massive old oak counter, its solid tables, the satellite television, juke box and gaming machines, not to mention the cornice of beautiful hand-painted tiles by William de Morgan and the huge decorated and devilled mirrors covering the walls. They have been there for 200 years.

Fred is an even more important fixture. He has been going to the Man in the Moon for 55 years now and continues to sit in the same place at the bar every single day consuming his daily 10 pints. He is 79.

·THE MAPLE LEAF·

41 Maiden Lane, WC2 **240 2843**

'One bucket of chicken wings, one of ice-cold beer'

Canadian flags catching the breeze in Maiden Lane proclaim that here is the Canadian pub. It used to be a rather rackety English one called the Bedford Head but it's been the Maple Leaf for years now and known to Canadians everywhere, the London pub where you found Canadian beer, Canadian food and, most important, other Canadians.

It got a major refit recently and reopened on Canada Day with all sorts of Canadian hoopla. Everyone agreed it was hugely improved. For one thing it seemed about twice the size and there were reminders of Canada everywhere, also carefully placed television screens so no one need lose a moment of the ice hockey.

There was a strong Canadian accent at the bar too, with six Molsons, two of them on tap. It was, boasted the Maple Leaf, the only pub in the world outside North America to have draught Molson. It also does a lot of shooters. Shooters are lethal cocktails served in test tubes and you are meant to down them in one. They cost £1.95 a time and are guaranteed to get the party going. They are Canadian too.

Then there is the excellent Canadian food, the burgers and the steaks and the home-made meatloaf and brunch served all day with fresh juice, ham, griddled eggs, hash browns with pancakes and maple syrup. And ice hockey, did I mention ice hockey? Molson sends the Maple Leaf videos of every big match, flying them in, not wasting a minute, so throughout the season you can sit round a television screen in Covent Garden with your mates and watch the drama with one bucket of chicken wings and one of ice-cold beer. It's almost like being at home.

Open
All Week
Hours
11.00–23.00
(12.00–22.30 Sun)
Credit Cards
All major cards accepted
Food Available
12.00–22.00
Special Features
Tables outside seat 16
Beers Available
Molson Dry, Molson Canadian, Theakston, John Smith's, Brakspear, Directors, Gillespie's, Guinness, Molson Golden, Molson Ice, Foster's, Canada Light, Laurentide, Becks, Newcastle Brown Ale, Holsten Pils, Budweiser Cider: Scrumpy Jack
Nearest Tube Stations
Covent Garden, Charing Cross

·THE MARLBOROUGH·

46 Friar Stile Road, Richmond **0181-940 0572**

'The splendidest garden'

Thackeray described this pub in 1844 as one of the comfortablest, quietest, cheapest, neatest little inns in England. It was known as the Rose Cottage Hotel in those days and only became a pub when it at last got a licence in 1870. It hadn't had a licence? Perhaps the Rose Cottage had been a temperance hotel. It sounds like a temperance hotel.

Anyway it was now the Marlborough and there it is, 125 years on, the traffic-choked Richmond of today pressing round it, no longer the quietest little pub but still agreeable

Open
All Week
Hours
11.00–23.00
(12.00–22.30 Sun)
Credit Cards
Visa, AmEx
Bar Food Available
12.00–22.00
(12.00–14.30 and 19.00–21.30 Sun)

Special Features
No-smoking Area
Wheelchair Access
(but not lavatory)
Terrace and Beer
Garden seat 330

Beers Available
Thomas Hardy Country
Bitter, Tetley, Marston's
Pedigree, Eldridge
Pope, Carlsberg Export,
Guinness

Nearest Tube Station
Richmond

and quite unexpectedly bosky. It begins long and narrow, dividing evenly into three – first the public bar with wooden floors and high-backed settles, then the saloon, carpeted, curtained and set about with green leather chesterfields. Beyond that is a servery with an open grill selling steaks, chops and burgers. It is currently trying kangaroo steaks. Do they sell any? 'Some,' says Oisin Rogers, the new manager.

Until recently Oisin was running the Man in the Moon in the King's Road, which has a 120-seat theatre, but the Marlborough has something very special too. Beyond the terrace at the back with its corrugated polypropylene roof – yes I know, but it keeps the rain off – you find a huge garden with roses, trellis walkways, oak trees, a children's corner and tables to seat 300. It is leafy and peaceful by day, warmed by garden heaters in the winter, floodlit in the evening. It is really the splendidest garden. I'm surprised Thackeray didn't mention it.

·THE MARQUESS OF GRANBY·

51 Chandos Place, WC2   **836 7657**

'The thin end of the wedge'

Open
All Week

Hours
11.00–23.00
(12.00–22.30 Sun)

Credit Cards
Access, Visa,
Mastercard

Bar Food Available
11.00–21.00
(12.00–21.00 Sun)

Special Features
Private Room seats 50

Beers Available
Marquess Bitter, Tetley,
Adnams, Castlemaine,
Lowenbrau, Carlsberg

Nearest Tube Station
Charing Cross

The Marquess of Granby at the back of the Coliseum has a long imposing frontage that makes you expect a large imposing pub, but it is a sliver of a pub really, a wedge, all length and no width. Still, nothing wrong with wedges. At the thin end of the wedge is a very small snug. At the thick end of the wedge is a rather larger bar parlour. The main bar, getting gradually wider, is in between and the whole thing has been elaborately refitted. Back bar, bar counter, furniture, everything was replaced. It has been carefully done with a Gothic screen rescued from a demolished church put to good use.

The pub's rush hour is the Coliseum interval when opera-goers, cast and orchestra will suddenly erupt in the bar for a very quick one indeed. This is the answer given if anyone asks why there is no music. The orchestra, explains the landlord, won't have it.

There was a pub on this site in Charles II's day, the Hole in the Wall. Was it this shape? It was where Claude Duval the highwayman was caught sleeping it off. After his execution he was buried in St Paul's Church under a stone that reads:

Here lies Duval. Reader, if male thou art
Look to thy purse; if female to thy heart.

· THE MARQUESS TAVERN ·

32 Canonbury Street, N1   **354 2975**

'Restored to its former glory'

See this high-Victorian pub standing proudly by the New River Walk, Corinthian pillars reaching from first floor to balustraded roof, every inch a listed building and a credit to the Marquesses of Northampton whose pub it used to be.

The present Marquess has hung on to a lot of Canonbury, his substantial birthright, but for some reason his father sold the Marquess, which must have hurt its feelings at the time. Young's has it now. It bought it in 1979 and, as it says, restored it to its former glory.

It is truly a fine pub and well placed. The New River, originally designed to bring drinking water to the 17th-century City of London, now brings ducks and river walkers to its door. Picnic tables await them. Inside is a big, high-ceilinged saloon bar and the adjoining room is impressive too, a bar-cum-dining room with a high arched ceiling, eating and drinking booths and big mirrors. It was a pool room in its misspent youth.

The Marquess rightly prides itself on its beer and serves hearty traditional food. In keeping with the times it provides unhearty food as well. There's a good salad bar.

Open
All Week

Hours
11.00–23.00
(12.00–22.30 Sun)

Credit Cards
None

Bar Food Available
11.00–21.30

Special Features
Wheelchair Access
Tables outside seat 50
Private Room seats 80

Beers Available
Young's Bitter, Young's Special, Tennent's Extra, Castlemaine

Nearest Tube Station
Highbury and Islington

· THE MAYFLOWER ·

117 Rotherhithe Street, SE16   **237 4088**

'The dark little bar casts a powerful spell'

In the spring of 1620 the *Mayflower* up-anchored at Rotherhithe and sailed down the Thames on the first lap of her historic journey to the New World. She had been moored next to a riverside tavern called the Shippe. It would be nice to think that its customers cheered and waved as she started her great adventure.

The *Mayflower* was back at Rotherhithe eight months later, anchoring near the Shippe again. Surely the crew bowled into the bar that night but her glory days were over. Within a year her captain was dead. They buried him in the graveyard of St Mary's Church, hard by the Shippe, and the *Mayflower* lay rotting at her old moorings.

The Shippe stood another 100 years or so and was then rebuilt. They called the new pub the Spread Eagle and Crown, a serviceable name but the Shippe had been better and its new name is better still.

It changed to the Mayflower in the 1960s when, all patched up after the war – its top floor had been blown off

Open
All Week

Hours
11.00–23.00
(12.00–22.30 Sun)

Credit Cards
Visa, AmEx

Restaurant Food Available
12.00–14.30 and
18.30–21.30 (No food Sun or Mon evenings)

Special Features
Wheelchair Access
Tables outside seat 30
Private Room seats 35

Beers Available
Greene King, Bass, Stella Artois, Kronenbourg, Carling Black Label, Guinness

Nearest Tube Station
Rotherhithe

in the Blitz – it set its cap at American visitors who were understandably thrilled to find it still tucked away by the church among the wharfs and warehouses.

I must say the dark little bar with its old black settles and tables casts a powerful spell. You can buy British and American stamps there under a curious long-standing licensing arrangement and you get a good view of the river from the restaurant upstairs, newly refurbished after a change of owner.

The best view is from the deck at the back of the old pub. It juts out over the river and just over there, where the old Thames barges wallow, is more or less where the *Mayflower* was anchored. This is the place to drink to a gallant ship, a great voyage and the captain in the graveyard behind you.

·THE MELTON MOWBRAY·

18 Holborn, EC1 **405 7077**

'An arresting piece of kitchen theatre'

Open
Mon–Fri

Hours
11.00–23.00
Closed Bank Holidays

Credit Cards
All major cards accepted

Bar Food Available
11.00–21.00

Special Features
No-smoking Area
Wheelchair Access
Tables outside seat 20

Beers Available
Fuller's Ales, ESB, London Pride, Chiswick Bitter, Hock, Mr Harry, Summer Only, Golden Pride

Nearest Tube Station
Chancery Lane

For the third of its new Ale and Pie houses, Fuller's took over a big sports shop and, after the 12-week refit costing £407,000, Holborn had a spanking-new pub.

Its success took everyone aback. It went from nothing to highest trader in the company on Day One. Middle management from every office in sight converged on it each lunchtime, a highly desirable clientele, good-mannered, good-humoured, free-spending and, as a rule, quick-eating. They all have desks to get back to.

Melton Mowbray's instant popularity had some drawbacks. It could seat 80 people at lunchtime but many more came and within months Fuller's was spending another £120,000 providing seats for another 80 downstairs.

The space is well used, with different floor and ceiling levels and a gallery at the far end, and many a pub would envy the size of the cellars. It is all state of the art down there with electronic hoists for the beer and amazing computerized ovens in the kitchens. The pies rotate behind glass doors and cook in 2 minutes 45 seconds. It is an arresting piece of kitchen theatre entitled *The Rising and Browning of the Puff Pastry Lid*. They should sell tickets.

SMOKING CAUSES CANCER

Chief Medical Officers' Warning
1 mg Tar 0.1 mg Nicotine

SMOKING CAUSES FATAL DISEASES

Chief Medical Officers' Warning
5 mg Tar 0.5 mg Nicotine

·The Mitre·

24 Craven Terrace, W2   **262 5240**

'Brand new Victorian'

Whitbreads is a great refurbisher of pubs. Each Whitbread pub gets a turn every five years and if it waits long enough it may get a REAL going-over. The Mitre, a much-admired pub in Bayswater, a Grade II listed building, emerged from one such recently. It always was Victorian and it is sort of Victorian still, brand-new, pastiche Victorian.

There are five bars – the main saloon bar and four smaller ones – all decorated and handsomely furnished in the Victorian manner. Two have marble fireplaces, one has a stag's head, one a charming skylight formerly boarded up. The smallest at the back has a portrait of Disraeli, the coming man, they say, and one is a no-smoking bar with its own entrance to the hall and so to the street.

Down worn stone stairs, an original feature, is the piano bar, a maze of little drinking areas tucked under low ceilings with flagged floors, big barrels, an old kitchen range. It is full of atmosphere and is thought to have a friendly ghost. 'It is still there,' says Helen Watts who runs the Mitre with her husband. 'When we are in bed we can hear it banging doors in the basement.'

Open
All Week
Hours
11.00–23.00
(12.00–22.30 Sun)
Credit Cards
All major cards accepted
Bar Food Available
12.00–21.30
Special Features
No-smoking Area
Wheelchair Access
(but not lavatory)
Tables outside seat 50
Private Room seats 60
Beers Available
Boddingtons, Pedigree, Flowers IPA, London Pride, Heineken, Stella Artois, Murphy's, Guinness
Nearest Tube Station
Lancaster Gate

·The Monarch·

49 Chalk Farm Road, NW1   **916 1049**

'You just may catch the new Rolling Stones here'

In some music pubs you pay to get into the music room. In others, like the Monarch, you pay to get into the pub.

From Chalk Farm, this report: 'This small, intimate and unobtrusive music pub opposite the Roundhouse gets a clued-in crowd that is onto the up-and-coming bands that are the speciality of the maison. Indie-rock acts are on every night of the week, well-known bands such as Shed 7, Echobelly and SMASH, as well as exciting new pretenders. You may find yourself rubbing shoulders with the likes of Blur.

'Every other Saturday the Monarch transforms itself into Quintessence, which says it is a Sixties psychedelic super elastic bubble plastic party. It gets bands like Uncle Pablo's Giggling Leaf and My Drug Hell and groovy DJs accompanied by a light show. It is hugely popular.

'You can usually expect a crush at the Monarch. You just may catch the new Rolling Stones here between 8.30 and 11.00 pm. A DJ plays from 11.00 pm to 2.00 am on Fridays and Saturdays. Recommended.'

Open
All Week
Hours
20.00–24.00
(20.30–02.00 Fri & Sat)
Closed Christmas Day, Boxing Day
Credit Cards
None
Bar Food Available
All opening hours
Special Features
Tables outside seat 12
Beers Available
Lowenbrau, Kronenbourg, Chimay, Stella, Heineken, Duval
Nearest Tube Stations
Chalk Farm, Camden Town

· THE MONKEY PUZZLE ·

30 Southwick Street, W2   **723 0143**

'A young monkey puzzle tree in a sheltered corner'

Open
All Week

Hours
11.00–23.00
(12.00–22.30 Sun)
Closed Christmas Day

Credit Cards
All major cards accepted

Food Available
Bar 12.00–14.30
Restaurant 12.00–14.30 and 18.00–21.30
(12.00–21.00 Sun)

Special Features
Wheelchair Access
Beer Garden seats 60

Beers Available
Badger, Tanglefoot, Hard Tackle, Hofbrau, Guinness

Nearest Tube Stations
Edgware Road, Paddington

A very annoying thing happened to the Monkey Puzzle on the night of 16 October 1987. The great gale blew its monkey puzzle tree down. It was a large, handsome and impossible-to-climb monkey puzzle tree, pride of the garden, and the pub had been named after it. Now look.

Well, life in the Monkey Puzzle goes on. It is a modern pub built into the ground floor of an apartment block and lots of cheery red signs guide you in saying 'Welcome' in a dozen different languages. Private hotels abound in these parts and there are lots of tourists on the streets.

New owners have changed the beers but have kept the bar billiards and satellite TV, and the garden still has picnic tables, strings of coloured lights and regular barbecues in the summer.

There is also a young monkey puzzle tree in a sheltered corner with its fingers crossed.

· THE MOON AND SIXPENCE ·

185 Wardour Street, W1   **734 0037**

'Tony Hancock in a ferned grot'

Open
All Week

Hours
11.00–23.00
(12.00–22.30 Sun)

Credit Cards
Access, Visa, Delta, Switch

Bar Food Available
11.00–23.00
(12.00–21.30 Sun)

Special Features
No-smoking Area
Wheelchair Access

Beers Available
Theakston Best, Theakston XB, Youngers Scotch Bitter, Courage Directors, Marston's Pedigree, Becks, Foster's, McEwans

Nearest Tube Stations
Tottenham Court Road, Leicester Square

JD Wetherspoon has turned a cinema into a pub in Brent, a Woolworth's into a pub at Ruislip Manor, a post office into a pub in Southend. In Wardour Street it has done the business with a Barclays bank.

This Barclays had beautiful tall arched windows. They are still there but nothing else of the bank remains. Even the massive safe in the vaults has gone, though it was a titanic struggle. You don't mention vaults in the Moon and Sixpence. They are cellars now.

It is a roomy pub with busy lunchtimes, three kinds of hologram on the walls and a realistic portrait bust of Tony Hancock in a ferned grot. The manager is called Tadgh, pronounced Tie, Irish for Tim.

Friday lunch is Silly Tie Day. It is as well to know these things.

· THE MOON UNDER THE WATER ·

28 Leicester Square, WC2 **839 2837**

'Alas, there are no longer tables outside. Westminster Council...'

There's only one pub now in Leicester Square. This one. It used to be an Angus Steak House until 1992 when Wetherspoons took it over and from being a long thin restaurant with steaks it became a long thin pub with food all day.

It specializes in good cask ales, cheaper than most, but Wetherspoons' famous cut-price pint of Youngers Scotch bitter is not quite so cheap here. This being Leicester Square it is £1.40 a pint – '*still* the cheapest pint in the West End, ' says the new manager, Richard Hamilton. Overheads in such glossy positions mount steadily. Apparently the cost of just opening the doors in the morning has now reached £7,500 a week.

Still, it has a strong character, won't have music, has a big no-smoking bit and is full every night, and when the doors do open in the morning there are always people waiting. Alas, there are no longer tables outside. In spite of the heatwave this summer Westminster Council, at its most disagreeable, insisted they go.

Open
All Week

Hours
11.00–23.00
(12.00–22.30 Sun)

Credit Cards
Access, Visa, Delta, Switch

Bar Food Available
All opening hours

Special Features
No-smoking Area
Wheelchair Access

Beers Available
Theakston Best,
Theakston XB,
Youngers Scotch Bitter,
Courage Directors,
Marston's Pedigree,
Becks, Foster's,
McEwans

Nearest Tube Station
Leicester Square

· THE MORPETH ARMS ·

58 Millbank, SW1 **834 6442**

'Don't venture into the cellars'

The Tate Gallery delights some, sends others reeling down Millbank. They should reel to the right. In minutes they will find comfort and reassurance in this trusty and dependable Victorian pub.

All is traditional and familiar in the Morpeth Arms and will stay so. The summer is particularly busy with stout tables and wooden benches right across the front and down the side. The traffic roars by and you can hardly hear yourself speak but they do a decent lunch at the Morpeth Arms and it's a Young's pub so the beer is good too.

Don't venture into the cellars, though. They say that soon after the pub was built in 1845 a convict on the run hid in the labyrinth of vaults beneath the pub, lost himself and was never seen again. Visitors to the vaults though have felt a hand on their shoulder and have been chilled by an unseen presence dripping water. It has sent them dashing back to the Tate.

Stand with your back to the pub and look across the river. The extraordinary building facing you is the new headquarters of MI5.

Open
All Week

Hours
11.00–23.00
(12.00–22.30 Sun)

Credit Cards
All major cards accepted

Food Available
Bar 11.00–21.00
Restaurant
11.00–20.00

Special Features
Wheelchair Access
Tables outside seat 72
Private Room seats 50

Beers Available
Young's, Castlemaine, Stella Artois

Nearest Tube Station
Pimlico

·THE MUCKY DUCK·

108 Fetter Lane, EC4　　　　　　　　　　**242 9518**

'Red-nosed drunks, vicars and fat ladies in stripes'

Scene: Two ladies chatting outside a factory bearing the sign Sid Brown's Tool Works. One is saying to the other 'You're a very lucky woman, Mrs Brown.'

Partners Gareth Stones and Tony Crowe are proud of the framed seaside postcards at the Mucky Duck. All those bathing belles, landladies, red-nosed drunks, vicars and fat ladies in stripes with their *doubles entendres* are worth the detour from Holborn or Fleet Street.

The Mucky Duck has been so named only since July 1993, before which it was the Swan, a Fleet Street haunt with a strong presence from the neighbouring and now deserted Daily Mirror building. Gone are the hacks and also the stuffed swan that used to look down on the assembly at the bar.

Upstairs is Annie's Bar. Annie was a previous incumbent. It is a bright room with banquettes and tables, pink curtains at its several windows, and a busy lunch crowd. Parties are held here. The speciality upstairs as well as down is the Mucky Duck Doorstep, a sandwich measuring two inches thick.

With the Mucky Duck going strong, Stones and Crowe formed the Mucky Pub Co and looked around for a second pub. They found the Devonshire Arms in Duke Street and are usually there these days, leaving the Mucky Duck in the safe hands of Maurice Daley, the one-time Stoke City goalkeeper.

Open Mon–Fri
Hours 11.00–23.00 Closed Bank Holidays
Credit Cards None
Bar Food Available All opening hours
Special Features Private Room (evenings only) seats 35
Beers Available Bass, Worthington, London Pride, Adnams, Carling Black Label, Tennent's, Guinness, Caffrey's
Nearest Tube Station Chancery Lane

·THE MULBERRY BUSH·

Upper Ground, SE1　　　　　　　　　　**928 7940**

'Alarums and excursions'

After 50 years of furious dispute the new Coin Street is emerging. One redevelopment scheme after another has grappled with these 16 prime acres on the South Bank between Blackfriars and Waterloo Bridges. There were two public inquiries, countless court actions, constant protests and demonstrations but now the first groups of new houses and flats are finished and occupied. They have cafes, restaurants and shops, a riverside walkway, a park and a market. They also have a fine modern pub.

The Mulberry Bush sits on the outer rim of the Mulberry Co-op, which was the first of the housing co-operatives to be completed. The National Theatre and LWT are to the left,

Open All Week
Hours 11.00–23.00 (12.00–22.30 Sun)
Credit Cards All major cards accepted
Food Available Bar 11.00–23.00 Restaurant 12.00–15.00 and 18.00–21.30
Special Features No-smoking Area Wheelchair Access Tables outside seat 12

IPC Magazines and the Daily Express to the right and very stylish developments lie straight ahead. Something tells me that the Mulberry Tree won't be short of customers.

It is a Young's pub and very pleasant. Its big bar has a whole wall of glass doors that completely fold back, the conservatory at the back is a no-smoking area with air-conditioning and its own entrance and a broad spiral staircase takes you to the restaurant on the first floor. You can stand on the balcony there and wave to the Oxo tower. How great that after all the alarums and excursions it has survived.

Beers Available
Young's IPA, Young's Special, Dirty Dick's, Castlemaine XXXX, Stella Artois, London Lager, Premium Lager, Becks, Budweiser, Carlsberg
Cider: Scrumpy Jack

Nearest Tube Station
Waterloo

· THE MUSEUM TAVERN ·

49 Great Russell Street, WC1 **242 8987**
'Karl Marx is still suspected of having broken one of the mirrors'

The pub that first occupied this commanding corner in Bloomsbury was called the Dog and Duck. Well, that wouldn't do once the British Museum opened on the other side of the road and in 1761 it chose a daring new name. It became the British Museum Tavern.

It seems to have been a homely place. You could take your own pork or lamb and have it cooked for a penny. Clearly something grander was required and it was rebuilt in 1798 and again, grander yet, in 1855.

This time William Finch Hill, the theatre architect, was the designer. His building, renamed the Museum Tavern, had four entrances to five bars, with pool and billiards and rooms for lodgers upstairs. He suspended huge globes from ornate iron fittings above the main doors and gas lamps burned in every window. It is this building, the outside hardly changed, that you see today.

Generations of scholars have crossed the road from the British Museum to drink here. Among them was the museum's most famous student, Karl Marx, who is still suspected by the pub of having broken one of the mirrors in the bar's back fitting. Marx would presumably have approved of what has since happened to the pub interior, all divisions between public bar, private bar, jug bar and bar parlour abolished. No juke boxes or taped music lurk to alarm shy denizens of the British Museum who still come in. It remains a gentlemanly, scholarly pub surrounded by academic bookshops, and in nearby Coptic Street is what some people, i.e. me, consider the best pizza house in London.

Open
All Week

Hours
11.00–23.00
(12.00–22.30 Sun)

Credit Cards
All major cards except Diner's Club

Bar Food Available
11.00–22.00

Special Features
Wheelchair Access (but not lavatory)

Beers Available
Real ales, John Smith's, Courage Best, Courage Directors, Theakston, Wadworth 6X, Old Speckled Hen

Nearest Tube Stations
Tottenham Court Road, Russell Square

Open
All Week
Hours
11.00–23.00
(12.00–22.30 Sun)
Closed Christmas Day
Credit Cards
None
Bar Food Available
12.00–22.00
Special Features
Wheelchair Access
Beers Available
Adnams, Young's, Tetley, Benskins, Guinness
Nearest Tube Station
Hyde Park Corner

·THE NAG'S HEAD·

53 Kinnerton Street, SW1   **235 1135**

'Drinking and talking, eating and talking'

The Nag's Head, tucked away in this little mews in the most expensive part of town, is a very chatty pub. It isn't very big and the bar counter is a chatty sort of height, as high as your average kitchen table, the stools round it the height of kitchen chairs. Then there's the landlord, Kevin Moran, and his son Peter. They chat away to everyone.

Kevin was a successful stunt man before he hurt his back, and Peter describes himself as a jobbing actor, though he is mostly at the Nag's Head. Still, he says, a pub IS acting, and this is an extrovert and entertaining place. Conversation is general with much laughter and newcomers are soon part of it.

Kinnerton Street is smart now but it was mostly stables when it started in the 1820s. The Nag's Head was the ostlers' pub. It was tiny, a single bar not much bigger than a horse's stall, and this is how it stayed well into the 1960s. Len Cole, the formidable landlord of the day, would say that the Nag's Head was the smallest pub in London and that was how he liked it. His successors saw no point in unused space at the back and it is a bit bigger now and the Morans have made it a lot more comfortable. Pictures and photographs and mementoes of times past now cover the panelled walls, fires are lit in winter, and in the summer people take their drinks into the mews. The front bar is for drinking and talking and the back bar is for eating and talking with food from noon to 10.00 pm, unless they sell out first.

·THE NARROW BOAT·

Open
All week
Hours
12.00–23.00
(12.00–22.30 Sun)
Credit Cards
Access, Visa, Delta, Switch
Bar Food Available
12.00–21.30
Special Features
Wheelchair Access
Tables outside seat 35
Private Room seats 30

119 St Peter's Street, N1   **226 3906**

'Long, low and, you will be surprised to hear, narrow'

This is not, as you may think, a narrow boat made into a pub. It is a pub built to look like a narrow boat, a pretend narrow boat. You find it in Islington on the bank of the Regent's Canal, long, low and, you will be surprised to hear, narrow with a hardwood floor and long windows looking down at the towpath. There is water on one side and St Peter's Street on the other.

On the stern wall a mural shows the canal in its industrial heyday. Nautical objets abound. Sitting at one of the heavy wooden tables you might almost think you were in a narrow boat.

The Narrow Boat attracts a youngish crowd. There's

piped music and Sky TV and lots of gaming machines, and the food is youthful and reasonably priced. Live music fills the bar on Saturday nights, soul, rock 'n' roll, country, on fine Sundays there are barbecues outside and on Monday nights the Carling Premiership on Sky TV pulls in a football crowd.

The little terrace on the deck is pleasant in the summer and, in the basin beyond, narrow boats gather.

Beers Available
Grolsch, Caffrey's, Bass, Carling Black Label, Tennent's Pilsner

Nearest Tube Station
Angel

· THE NEW MOON ·

88 Gracechurch Street, EC3   **626 3625**
'The high Victorian hall fills with brokers'

This handsome, dignified City pub occupies a commanding position in Leadenhall Market, the lofty arcade in the heart of the money market where you can still find butchers, bakers and candlestick makers.

The high-Victorian hall with its long counter fills with brokers when the markets close and the big downstairs bar has busy lunchtimes. This is where the food is served.

During the pub's most recent refurbishment John Hall, the licensee, found an old menu dated 18 August 1900. In those days the pub was called the Half Moon and boasted the sort of restaurant that has printed, dated menus. You did well in this one: rump steak 1s, potatoes (boiled) 2d... Lunch in the New Moon costs rather more nowadays but Mr Hall considers his food to be more interesting than that.

Open
Mon–Sat

Hours
11.00–23.00
11.30–15.00 Sat
Closed Bank Holidays

Credit Cards
All major cards except Amex and Diner's Club

Bar Food Available
11.30–14.30

Special Features
Wheelchair Access (but not lavatory)

Beers Available
Boddingtons, London Pride, Wadworth 6X, Flowers IPA, Castle Eden, Brakspear, Wethered, Stella Artois, Heineken

Nearest Tube Stations
Monument, Liverpool Street

· THE NIGHTINGALE ·

97 Nightingale Lane, SW12   **0181-673 1637**
'Prizes for its flowers, its beer and its customers'

You aren't likely to hear a nightingale at the Nightingale. Not much woodland left in Balham, not many copses, that is what nightingales like. Still the Nightingale makes a pleasant rural impression and has a delightful and secluded paved garden, the perfect place for a quiet drink on a summer's evening. Its borders, window boxes and hanging baskets are luxuriant. It wins prizes for its flowers.

It has had a prize from Camra for the quality of its beer too, and last year it won one for the quality of its customers. The Association of London Brewers and Licensed Retailers had a contest to find which pub inside the M25 had raised most money for charity. It turned out to be the Nightingale.

In 16 years the money raised by its regulars had gone up

Open
All Week

Hours
11.00–15.00 Mon–Tue;
11.00–23.00 Wed–Sat;
(12.00–22.30 Sun)

Credit Cards
None

Bar Food Available
12.00–14.30 and
18.00–21.00

Special Features
Wheelchair Access
Beer Garden seats over 60

Beers Available
All Young's variants

Nearest Tube Station
Clapham South

to £220,000, a terrific achievement. This year's feats included face-painting, a 35-mile walk along the river bank and a sponsored haircut. One long-haired customer made the supreme sacrifice, had his head shaved and raised £1,000.

The pub itself is comfortable and welcoming with homemade soups, cottage pie and real sausages at lunchtime and an impressive wine list, ten reds, nine whites, two sparkling and a good house claret. It gets packed in the evening.

·THE O-BAR·

Open
All Week
Hours
13.00–1.00 Mon–Wed;
13.00–2.00 Thur;
13.00–3.00 Fri–Sat;
(14.00–22.30 Sun)
Closed Christmas Day,
New Year's Day
Credit Cards
None
Bar Food Available
18.00 to closing time
Beers Available
Bottled lagers
Nearest Tube Stations
Leicester Square,
Piccadilly Circus

83 Wardour Street, W1   **437 3490**
'It never happened to the Round House'

The Round House, built in 1892 on a fine corner site in Soho, was an alderman among pubs, large, dignified and five-storeyed, the personification of Victorian virtues. Ah, the sigh of the pumps as the careful pints were drawn, the top hats in the private bar, the corsets in the snug. If they could see it now!

The Round House has undergone an astonishing transformation. It is now the O-Bar, a glittering glam arena fuelled by holiday food and Costa cocktails, strutting its stuff through the Nineties with music thudding, disco, acid jazz, funk, and every table taken and outside the queues so long they need doormen with headsets and intercoms to control them. Couples only, please.

Queues? Doormen? It never happened to the Round House in all its days.

·O'HANLONS·

Open
Mon–Fri
Hours
11.00–23.00
Closed Bank Holidays
Credit Cards
None
Restaurant Food Available
12.00–14.30 and
18.00–21.00
Special Features
Wheelchair Access
Patio seats 30

18 Tysoe Street, EC1   **837 4112**
'It could be the most Irish pub in London'

John O'Hanlon from County Kerry bought a little pub called the Three Crowns three years ago and changed its name. He called it O'Hanlons. What else would he call it?

It could be the most Irish pub in London. It's just a little pub, you understand, a private house until 1939, but now the ground floor is painted cream and shamrock, the big front window says O'Hanlons in Celtic letters and inside it's all Ireland and rugby. There's a rugby ball signed by the 1982 Irish team, dozens of programmes of Irish Internationals, a bodhrán behind the bar and himself getting the crack going and taking infinite care with the Dublin Guinness.

There is only a handful of places in London importing

the real stuff and this is one of them. O'Hanlon charges £2.05 a pint and it takes a while to pour, but what's your hurry? Sit at a table and he'll let you know when it's ready. He has his own brew now, O'Hanlons Irish Ale, as fine an Irish bitter as was ever brewed in Borough. It is very popular in Islington.

There's the one big room in O'Hanlons with a bare wood floor and a mixture of tables and chairs and a covered beer garden out at the back with whitewashed walls and plants. You can eat out there or in the bar and lots do.

It is real Irish home cooking. John O'Hanlon's mother came over from Ireland to take over the kitchen when he got the pub and she does great food, baked Irish gammon with lots of potatoes, beef and Dublin Guinness pie, and, some say best of all, real Irish soda bread. She gets up at the crack of dawn to make it and it's still warm when the pub opens. Irish purists also appreciate the Cork Dry Gin, the Bushmills Whiskey and the Ballygown mineral water.

Beers Available
O'Hanlons Irish Ale, Crouch Vale, Bass, Tennent's, Guinness, Caffrey's, Carling Black Label

Nearest Tube Station
Farringdon

· OLD BANK OF ENGLAND ·

194 Fleet Street, EC4   430 2255

'The safest wine and spirit store in history'

Fuller's, which likes to turn banks into pubs, has excelled itself with this one. It is a magnificent Grade 1 listed building that for 87 years was the Law Courts' branch of the Bank of England. Now it is one of the most imposing pubs in London.

It was put here next to the Law Courts in 1888 at the suggestion of the Treasury. 'Sombre and opulent High Victorian,' was Sir Nikolous Pevsner's judgement. It replaced the Cock, one of London's most historic inns, which was obliged to move across the road. How ironic that, 100 years later, the grand usurper should have become a pub itself.

Outside nothing has changed; inside there has been an adjustment or two but High Victorian it remains, and great heavens the banking hall! Noble columns, high Italianate windows, a magnificent ceiling with chandeliers that have to be winched down from the floor above when a bulb goes, a room so high that it comfortably accommodates a new gallery. Confidently centre stage middle reigns its splendid new bar.

The floor above is now occupied by solicitors but it was once part of the 27-room apartment provided for the bank manager, such a personage was he. His one-time office in the bank is now a club room and the busy office next to it a restaurant with white tablecloths and waitress service. There

Open
Mon–Fri

Hours
11.00–23.00
Closed Bank Holidays

Credit Cards
Visa, Switch, Delta, Mastercard, AmEx

Bar and Restaurant Food Available
11.00–21.00

Special Features
Wheelchair Access (but not lavatory)
Private Rooms seat 16 and 25

Beers Available
London Pride, India Pale Ale, Summer Ale, Old Winter Ale, Golden Pride, plus guest beers from regional brewers

Nearest Tube Station
Temple

is less formal food too. You place an order at the bar and it is brought to you or, anyway, to the lawyers and bankers who crowd in at lunchtime. They are back in force on their way home in the early evening. Others look in for tea in the afternoon.

Fuller's says that what it wanted from its new bank was a sumptuous up-market eating and drinking emporium. This it has certainly got, though there were problems. Bank vaults always give builders headaches, but the vaults in this one eclipsed anything. Impenetrable strongrooms. Vast walk-in safes. A bullion room with steel-reinforced walls four-feet thick, armour-plated ceilings and mammoth steel doors. To get pipes from the new cellar to the bar took thermal lances and diamond drills.

The bullion room is the wine and spirit store now. It must be the safest wine and spirit store in history.

·THE OLD BELL TAVERN·

95 Fleet Street, EC4　　　　　　　　　　**583 0070**

'After the diaspora'

Open
Mon–Fri

Hours
11.00–23.00
Closed Bank holidays

Credit Cards
All major cards accepted

Bar Food Available
12.00–21.00

Special Features
Wheelchair Access
Private Room seats 30

Beers Available
Marston's Pedigree, Tetley, Wadworth 6X, Brakspear, Nicholson's Best, 6 real ales, Carlsberg, Castlemaine, Guinness

Nearest Tube Station
Blackfriars

What happened to Fleet Street's busy pubs when the newspapers left? We are nettled to report that this trauma had less effect on them than was expected. The newish Popinjay closed and the King and Keys, scene of much dramatic confrontation, was transformed into a Scruffy Murphy's, but the rest seem much as they were. Rather more so, if anything.

Here is the Old Bell Tavern, a senior Fleet Street pub, built in 1678 by Sir Christopher Wren as a hostel for his masons. He was rebuilding St Bride's Church, which had been burned out in the Great Fire, and he needed somewhere to lodge them, so up went the Old Bell.

You know St Bride's? It is a beautiful church and for all these years the Old Bell has been its nearest neighbour, just a lathe and plaster job, nothing very special but getting steadily more interesting with age. It has been a licensed tavern for 300 years and it, too, is now a listed building.

In the great days of Fleet Street, the Old Bell was a printers' pub, small but cosy, its bar tucked away behind its off-licence. After the newspaper diaspora in the late 1980s it had to find an entirely new clientele, as did all the pubs in Fleet Street. It is now a lawyers' and bankers' pub and is doing well again.

There have been changes. The off-licence has gone altogether, making the pub a little bigger. In its place is a comfortable snug and a handsome stained-glass window faces the street. Printers taking a trip down memory lane will notice such things and will be pleased to see that the triangular oak stools, a feature of the pub since its early days, are still there. These, according to the Old Bell, are unique to the Old Bell.

· THE OLD BULL AND BUSH ·

North End Road, NW3   **0181-455 3685**

'Come, come, come and make eyes at me...'

The Old Bull and Bush, declares the Old Bull and Bush, is probably the most famous pub in the world. It's right. It probably is.

After years of being altered, extended and refurbished it is a big, sprawly modern pub now, but never a month goes by without the saloon bar rocking again to the refrain that made Florrie Forde a fortune and the Old Bull and Bush a household name:

> *Come, come, come and make eyes at me*
> *Down at the Old Bull and Bush (ta ra ra ra ra)*
> *Come, come, drink some port wine with me*
> *Down at the Old Bull and Bush...*

The Bull and Bush had a long history before ever Florrie Forde, 15 stone and swathed in mauve brocade, began belting out her big hit round the halls. Booklets on the bar tell the story. Old farmhouse. Charles I. Medicinal springs. Hogarth. William Pitt. Gainsborough making his helpful remark – 'What a delightful little snuggery is this said Bull and Bush.' Then the pleasure garden and the music licence and concerts and sing-songs and half the East End heading for a day in the country and a good old knees-up down at the Old Bull and Bush. With Florrie Forde's smash hit they had the perfect song for it.

The Old Bull and Bush is still going great guns. There were huge changes to it in the 1920s and again in the 1980s when it closed for three and a half months for a major rebuilding job. The pub was changed from top to toe with new bars, new kitchens, new places to eat, jolly bits and quiet bits. One of the new bars might be a country house library. Another has a classic upright piano around which, every Tuesday evening and Sunday lunch, it's Cockney time. There are no prizes for guessing at least one of the songs...

> *Hear the little German band*
> *Just let me hold your hand*
> *Do do have a little drink or two*
> *Down at the Old Bull and Bush. Bush Bush.*

Open
All Week
Hours
11.00–23.00
(12.00–22.30 Sun)
Closed Christmas Day
Credit Cards
All major cards accepted
Restaurant Food Available
12.00–15.00 and 18.00–21.00
Special Features
No-smoking Area
Wheelchair Access
Tables outside seat 50
Private Room seats 30
Beers Available
Young's, Burton, Tetley, Castlemaine, Carlsberg, Guinness
Nearest Tube Station
Golders Green

·THE OLD COFFEE HOUSE·

Open
All Week
Hours
11.00–23.00
(12.00–15.00 and
19.00–22.30 Sun)
Closed Christmas Day,
Boxing Day
Credit Cards
None
Bar Food Available
12.00–15.00
Special Features
Wheelchair Access
Private Room seats 30
Beers Available
Courage Best, Courage
Directors, Marston's
Pedigree, Kronenbourg,
Foster's, Holsten,
Guinness, Beamish
Nearest Tube Stations
Piccadilly Circus,
Oxford Circus

49 Beak Street, W1 **437 2197**

'You can still get coffee'

The Old Coffee House, people are sometimes bemused to discover, is a pub. It started life as a coffee house, true, but that was in the 18th century. Many a future pub was a coffee house then. The others changed their names when they started selling best bitter, but the Old Coffee House saw no reason to. The Old Coffee House it stayed.

Some think it could be called the Old Antique Shop. The bar is filled with stuffed animals, brass things hanging from the ceiling and such rare and curious items as the boxing gloves used by Dave Charnley to knock out David 'Darkie' Hughes when defending his lightweight title in 1961. It was the shortest ever British title fight. It lasted 40 seconds.

It is proud of its range of lunches, 20 main courses on offer every day, trad pub grub, and you can still get coffee in the Old Coffee Shop. Filter only.

·THE OLD DR BUTLERS HEAD·

Open
Mon–Fri
Hours
11.00–23.00
Closed Bank Holidays
Credit Cards
All major cards
accepted
Bar and Restaurant Food Available
11.00–14.30
Special Features
Wheelchair Access
(but not lavatory)
Private Room
seats 120
Beers Available
Boddingtons, Flowers,
Marston's Pedigree,
Brakspear, Heineken,
Stella Artois
Nearest Tube Station
Moorgate

Masons Avenue, EC2 **606 3504**

'Add piles of dung and you could almost be in the London of James I'

Masons Avenue gives you a good idea of how things would have looked in 17th-century London after a miracle clean-up. Add piles of horse dung and emptied chamber pots, don't look too closely and you could almost be in the London of James I.

It is a narrow flagstoned alley, a black and white five-storey half-timbered mansion on one side and the Old Dr Butlers Head a few feet away on the other. The half-timbered mansion is actually an office block built in 1928 and the pub, burned down in the Great Fire and then rebuilt, has been restored and restored again. It has survived, that is the great thing.

There is now one big bar with old timbers, bare floorboards, ancient-looking panelling to the ceiling, old barrels, stout wooden furniture and every lunchtime the bar is full of smartly dressed City men and City women, drinking and talking ten to the dozen. Up two steps at the back there are tables and chairs and girls making good-looking sandwiches and upstairs are two floors of restaurant with roasts and Dr Butler's Daily Specialities. The good doctor's steak and kidney pudding in the Tudor Room or much bigger Balcony Room on the top floor costs £9.85, veg or salad extra.

The doctor himself, neat grey beard, embroidered cap, twinkles down from the inn sign in the alley. He was a dreadful old fraud, suddenly firing off pistols inches away from the ears of patients to cure epilepsy and dropping poor souls with ague into the river.

The great cure that got him in with King James was his medicinal ale, good for your tum, he said. He bought several ale houses to sell it in. He got this one in 1616. It is the last remaining and it hasn't sold the doctor's ale for 300 years.

At weekends the City of London belongs to security guards and caretakers and Old Dr Butler does not open.

· THE OLD KING LUD ·

78 Ludgate Hill, EC4   **329 8517**

'Macho competition is the thing'

Some tremendous rebuilding has been going on around Ludgate Hill. Five major new office blocks and a new station have appeared, the old railway bridge has gone, the whole place has changed. So what, you will be asking, has happened to the King Lud? It was, after all, bang in the middle of all this.

Well, it disappeared for a year or two but when all the scaffolding and hoardings came down at last there it was. More or less. Its uninhibited five-storey façade had been saved, so hurray for that. The rest of the building had been totally demolished. In its place was a concrete shell for Whitbread to turn into whatever it had in mind.

What it had in mind was another pub for its Hogshead chain, so it was ancient timbers, old flagstones and a great gantry loaded with barrels for the new Old King Lud. Country benches and old wooden tables were brought in.

Its character changed too. The King Lud I remember had a disco and did pizzas but it was never as lively or as thirsty as this. A minimum of 20 different cask ales are on tap every day, and vast quantities are downed, customers using two-pint tankards and four-pint jugs to save time.

A young and largely antipodean staff throws itself into the spirit of the thing, particularly on Friday nights when the place is jumping. Macho competition is the thing. The current bet is that you can't get 30 halves of ale down in three hours. If you do you get your money back. Many try. Some succeed. Can they still stand up, though? Shome can.

On Sundays a deep peace descends on the King Lud. Sunday papers are on offer. The four-pint jugs doze behind the bar counter. You might almost think this was one of those quiet sleepy old pubs you hear about.

Open
All Week

Hours
11.00–23.00
(12.00–22.30 Sun)
Closed Christmas Day

Credit Cards
Visa, Mastercard

Bar Food Available
All day till closing time

Special Features
No-smoking Area
Wheelchair Access
(disabled lavatory)
Tables outside seat 6

Beers Available
London Pride, Fuddles, Gale's, Boddingtons, Old Speckled Hen, Flowers Original, Flowers IPA, Abbot Ale, Brakspear, Castle Eden Ale, Marston's Pedigree, Wadworth 6X, Heineken, Stella Artois, Guinness, Murphy's

Nearest Tube Station
Blackfriars

· THE OLD RED LION ·

Open
Mon–Fri
Hours
11.00–23.00
Closed Bank Holidays
Credit Cards
Visa, Mastercard, AmEx
Bar Food Available
12.00–14.00
Special Features
Wheelchair Access (but not lavatory)
Tables outside seat 8
Private Room seats 25
Beers Available
Greene King, Flowers IPA, Rayments, Abbot Ale, Stella Artois, Kronenbourg, Harp, Carling Black Label, Guinness
Nearest Tube Stations
Holborn, Chancery Lane

72 High Holborn, WC1   **405 1748**

'The ghosts of the Lord Protector and his cronies won't know where they are'

This Red Lion has a rather grisly claim to fame. After the restoration of Charles II it was felt necessary to punish the three men considered most responsible for his father's execution – Oliver Cromwell, his son-in-law Henry Ireton and the judge who sentenced Charles I to death, John Bradshaw.

They were dead already as it happened, buried in Westminster Abbey, but they were punished all the same. They were disinterred, taken to Tyburn and strung up. On the way there the cart stopped off at the Red Lion where the three bodies lay overnight. They can hardly have been very welcome guests. Ireton, the youngest of the three, had been dead ten years.

The old pub has been rebuilt, restored and refurbished any number of times since then. The latest renovation closed the pub for six weeks. In the saloon bar they kept the good-looking Victorian back bar but everything else was replaced. It is still remains Victorian after a fashion and very comfortable, but brand new. The first-floor bar was turned into a small restaurant.

· THE OLD RED LION ·

Open
All Week
Hours
11.30–15.00 and 17.30–23.00
11.00–15.00 and 19.00–23.00 Sat
(12.00–22.30 Sun)
Closed Christmas Day
Credit Cards
None
Bar Food Available
11.30–15.00 and 17.00–19.00
Special Features
Wheelchair Access
Patio seats 18
Beers Available
Bass, IPA, Caffrey's, Grolsch, Tennent's, Carling Black Label
Nearest Tube Station
Angel

418 St John Street, EC1   **837 7816**

'Miracles on a stage the size of an in-tray'

Lively Islington pub with a theatre upstairs that can sit 50 comfortably, 60 if everyone breathes in. Actors, directors and designers perform miracles on a stage the size of an in-tray.

Downstairs one set of the original Victorian partitions has survived to give two big bars. Both get packed. Not so long ago there was a small and sunless beer garden in the alley at the back. Derelict buildings on either side have been demolished and now daylight pours in and sometimes the sun. The new managers, Joanne and Paul Pavitt, plan a beer garden there with grass and flowers and lots more tables. Permissions, as I write, are anxiously awaited.

Joanne's parents used to manage the Old Red Lion and she has lived there since she was seven. Paul worked in a bank down the road and would come into the Red Lion at lunchtime. So they met and fell in love and married and they are running the place now. You never know where romance will bloom.

·The Old Shades·

37 Whitehall, SW1   **930 4019**

'Almost any parade does wonders for trade'

Walk up Whitehall from Trafalgar Square and you pass three interesting pubs almost next door to each other, the Silver Cross, the Old Shades and the Clarence. The Old Shades is the one in the middle.

It is a Grade II listed building, which means that you get told off if you pull it down. You wouldn't want to do that. It is Flemish-Gothic with carved spandrels, cross-mullioned leaded casements and an elongated gable, a long thin pub put up in 1898.

Yes it seems older, and there was, in fact, a tavern on the spot long before that. I dare say that the crowd that watched the execution of Charles I just up the road came in for a drink afterwards, but the Old Shades believes in letting bygones be bygones and there is a nice portrait of the Queen on a horse over the mantelpiece at the far end.

Old Shades gets a lot of tourists and welcomes Big Occasions. Almost any parade down Whitehall does wonders for trade. Riots of the poll tax sort don't.

It has had success with real-ale festivals lately. Tourists like them. Very olde they think. It had a very successful Welsh festival recently. Reverend James bitter sold well. So did Son of a Bitch ale.

Open
All Week
Hours
11.00–23.00
(12.00–22.30 Sun)
Closed Christmas Day
Credit Cards
Visa, Mastercard, Delta
Bar Food Available
12.00–14.30 and
17.00–21.30
(12.00–18.00 Sun)
Special Features
Wheelchair Access
(but not lavatory)
Private Room seats 40
Beers Available
London Pride,
Worthington's,
Caffrey's, Bass,
Grolsch, Carling Black
Label, Staropramen
Nearest Tube Station
Embankment

·The Old Ship·

25 Upper Mall, W6   **403 4243**

'It used to be on the sleepy side but no longer'

The Old Ship is probably the oldest pub in Hammersmith, a 17th-century riverside hostelry at one time steeped in history and tradition. It was on the sleepy side really, but no longer. A new lessee, Paul Bann-Murray, has changed just about everything – character, appearance, customers.

The new Old Ship, now called The Old Ship, Ranger on the River, has been painted arcade green with pop art signs in yellow and red. The saloon bar has been opened up, its counter moved, a new bar opened in what was the landlord's sitting room upstairs. The wide first-floor balcony, also once the landlord's private domain, is now crowded with lunchers whenever the sun shines, every seat taken.

There is a big new kitchen, new lavatories, a nappy-change room, a barbecue by the front door doing a roaring trade in bargeburgers, and there is music from opening to closing time, getting louder as the day progresses.

Open
All Week
Hours
10.00 (breakfast)–
23.00
(12.00–22.30 Sun)
Credit Cards
All major cards
accepted
Bar Food Available
10.00–23.00
Special Features
Wheelchair access
Tables outside
seat 100
Private Room
seats 200

Beers Available
London Pride, Old Speckled Hen, Wadworth 6X, Foster's, Kronenbourg, Sol, Budweiser, Molsen, Foster's Ice, Guinness

Nearest Tube Station
Hammersmith

Open
Mon–Fri

Hours
11.30–20.00

Bar Food Available
Lunchtimes only

Beers Available
No draught beers. Bottled lagers. Over 150 wines

Nearest Tube Station
Cannon Street

Open
All Week

Hours
11.00–23.00
(12.00–15.00 Sun)
Closed Bank Holidays

Credit Cards
All major cards accepted

Not all the locals like the changes, but Mr Bann-Murray has pressed ahead, and though the new Old Ship has lost old customers it has clearly won many new ones. The new customers are by and large young and like their music loud and they and Bann-Murray are of one mind. His customers like the new Old Ship, he says, and so does he.

· THE OLD WINE SHADES ·
6 Martin Lane, EC4   **626 6876**
'It asks for jackets and ties as it has always done'

A public inquiry at Guildhall pivoted on the value of this small City pub. A major development depended on the outcome. It would mean the end of the Old Wine Shades if it went ahead. Architects and lawyers locked in argument. But this was the only City tavern to survive the Great Fire said one side; it had been in continual use since 1663; it was a listed building and was unique. All right, said the other side. The developers would preserve it. They would put it behind a glass screen as a draught lobby in their new building.

Happily the pub that was mistaken for a draught lobby is still there, so let's drink to that. It is owned by El Vino, which also has the famous bar in Fleet Street, and it is more of a wine bar itself these days. It asks for jackets and ties as it has always done and keeps its gentlemanly shabbiness, the old carpet runner, the assorted tables and chairs. The substantial City people who eat and drink there find this very agreeable.

Things don't change much at the Old Wine Shades. The wine list is as sound as ever, the food as good and Victor Little who runs it, silver-haired, courteous but an unmistakable figure of authority, has been there since 1961.

Note the address. People and deliveries often go to the wrong place. It is Martin Lane near Cannon Street, not St Martin's Lane near Trafalgar Square.

· YE OLDE CHESHIRE CHEESE ·
Wine Office Court, 145 Fleet Street, EC4   **353 6170**
'By the time it reopened it had doubled in size'

The Cheshire Cheese is one of London's most celebrated taverns. It is the archetypal 17th-century chop-house, small cosy rooms, black settles, sawdust-covered floors, creaking stairs, open fires and good old boys in the chimney corner. In the Cheshire Cheese's case the old boys happened to be Dr Johnson in the chop room and Charles Dickens in the bar, so its position as a long-running tourist attraction is secure.

The original tavern burned down in the Great Fire of London but was rebuilt the following year, 1667, and there were no major changes for the next 300 years. The Yorkshire brewer Samuel Smith bought it in 1986 and found it, it must be said, distinctly unsteady on its pins. Also, perhaps, a little small for its commercial possibilities...

So in 1990 it did something about both problems. In the next 18 months the pub was underpinned and tightened up, totally refurbished and effectively extended. By the time it reopened it had just about doubled in size.

The old tavern now has six separate bars, three restaurants and a private dining room. A modern kitchen on the top floor supplies food to them all, sending it down by dumb waiters. There are three sets of toilets where there was only one before and six staff rooms.

By and large it has been a mannerly restoration. Dr Johnson might have a thing or two to say about the rock music in the cellar bar. Still, you can't hear it anywhere else. He might also want to know why his chair was standing on a table in the chop-room with a notice saying Dr Johnson's Chair, but I think Dickens would be happy in the ground-floor bar. It seems hardly changed at all, even keeping the faded gilt notice above the door saying Gentlemen Only. The management hope women customers will ignore this.

The building itself has stopped leaning and groaning. The floorboards, still swept and freshly scattered with sawdust twice a day, have lost their creak. It is now ready for the next 200 years.

Food Available
Bar
12.00–15.00 Mon–Sun;
18.00–21.00 Mon–Thur
Restaurant
12.00–21.30 Mon–Sat

Special Features
Private Room seats 60

Beers Available
Samuel Smith variants,
Ayingerbrau variants

Nearest Tube Station
Blackfriars

·YE OLDE COCK TAVERN·

22 Fleet Street, EC4   353 8570

'Oh plump headwaiter at the Cock to which I most resort'

Ask not why the chicken crossed the road. The Olde Cock crossed the road in 1887 to make way for a bank, uncommonly civil. It was, then as now, a famous old tavern. Pepys, Goldsmith, Sheridan and Dickens all knew it well and Tennyson had written a poem about it, not perhaps his best but its first verse is hard to beat:

*Oh plump headwaiter at the Cock
To which I most resort
'How goes the time?'
'Tis five o'clock'
'Go fetch a pint of port.'*

Open
Mon–Fri

Hours
11.00–23.00
Closed Bank Holidays

Credit Cards
All major cards accepted

Bar and Restaurant Food Available
12.00–15.00

Special Features
Wheelchair Access
(but not lavatory)
Private Room seats 120

Beers Available
Theakston Best,
Theakston XB,
Theakston Old Peculier,
Courage Directors,
Wadworth 6X, Foster's,
Holsten

Nearest Tube Station
Aldwych

The Olde Cock rescued as much as it could from the old building – pictures, furniture, the fireplace and its overmantel (Grinling Gibbons, they say) and resumed its role in life which was filling poets with port and others with strong ale.

It was comfortably past the 100th anniversary of its great move when, in April 1990, a disastrous fire broke out in the bar and most of the things that had been rescued from the old tavern were destroyed. Still the building itself, a copy of the old one and a landmark in Fleet Street, was saved. So, happily, was the old fireplace and, after eight months in the hands of the builders and restorers, Ye Olde Cock reopened looking every bit itself again. Some in Fleet Street even reported improvements. The upstairs restaurant was lighter, they said, and in some ways nicer and still had its excellent carvery at lunchtime.

As for the Dickens Room on the second floor with its old panelling and Dickens mementoes, this was untouched by the fire. It is a pleasant period room used for special occasions. Take with a pinch of salt tales of Dickens dining there. He died before the olde cock crossed the road.

·Ye Olde Mitre Tavern·

Ely Court, Hatton Garden, EC1　　　　　　**405 4751**

'The Black Prince...Henry VIII...Elizabeth I...'

Open
Mon–Fri

Hours
11.00–23.00
Closed Bank Holidays

Credit Cards
None

Bar Food Available
11.00–22.30

Special Features
Private Room seats 20

Beers Available
Burton, Friary Meux,
Tetley, Carlsberg
Export, Carlsberg
Pilsner, Guinness,
Castlemaine

Nearest Tube Station
Chancery Lane

Few pubs have had closer brushes with great events than Ye Olde Mitre Tavern. The medieval bishops of Ely were vastly rich and powerful. Their palace was hereabouts and in 1547 one of them, the well-named Bishop Goddrich, built this little tavern for his servants.

It was all go in the bishops' palace. The Black Prince stayed there, John of Gaunt died there, Henry VIII feasted there and Elizabeth I danced round its cherry tree and gave most of the estate to her favourite, Sir Christopher Hatton.

Things went from great to disastrous for the bishops and in 1772 their palace was pulled down. The little tavern came down too, but it was speedily rebuilt and to the original plan, and here it is, one of London's most picturesque pubs with a stone mitre from the bishops' gatehouse in the wall and the trunk of the cherry tree in a corner of the bar.

The two small panelled rooms with their high settles and are as they have always been. They share a counter, and sometimes a shoe horn could get in one more City gent.

Up the narrow winding stairs is the Bishop's Room, rather larger. You have a good chance of getting a seat there. Or poke about outside. There's a narrow yard with barrels for tables if you don't mind standing.

It is well tucked away, this old pub. Ely Court, a narrow covered alley off Hatton Gardens, is the best way to it. Leave by the even narrower alley, which will take you to Ely Place, and there, turning left, you will find the Mitre's most distinguished neighbour, St Etheldreda's, the 13th-century bishops' church. You used to have sanctuary in both church and pub. Until quite recently the police could not enter either. Note for villains: they can now.

·Ye Olde Surgeon·

183 Tottenham Court Road, W1   **631 3618**

'Cutting bits off and sewing bits on'

A theme pub and what do you suppose the theme is? An operating theatre. Honestly.

It's all *Spitting Image*-type surgeons and patients at Ye Olde Surgeon, jokes involving cutting bits off and sewing bits on, humorous skulls, funny bandaged bits, real-life ads for Ex-Lax, a cocktail called Lop It Off, a bar snack called Double Hernia.

The staff of the hospital round the corner like it but the prognosis is not good. Another Ye Olde will be wheeled in as soon as it is felt that this particular joke has worn thin. Ye Olde Cadaver? Ye Olde Dangling Bitte? Anything seems possible.

Open
Mon–Sat
Hours
11.00–23.00
Closed Christmas Day
Credit Cards
All major cards accepted
Bar Food Available
All opening hours
Special Features
Wheelchair Access (but not lavatory)
Tables outside seat 16
Beers Available
Theakston XB, Theakston Old Peculier, Theakston Best, Old Speckled Hen, Guinness, Gillespie's, Becks, Coors, McEwan Lager, McEwan Export
Nearest Tube Stations
Warren Street, Goodge Street

·The Orange Brewery·

37 Pimlico Road, SW1   **730 5984**

'A spectacle that lacks drama'

A head of Bacchus looks down from the arch over the corner doorway to the bar of the Orange Brewery, a fine four-storey Victorian pub in the bit of London where Chelsea meets Pimlico.

The Orange Brewery makes all its own ale in a brewhouse directly underneath the bar. It is a most satisfactory arrangement, leading, as you can see, to a big saving in brewer's drays. Three main house ales are brewed there: SW1, the pub's best-selling bitter; SW2, which is rather stronger; and Pimlico Porter, a revival of the rich dark ale that was the principal beer drunk in London in the 18th and

Open
All Week
Hours
11.00–23.00
(12.00–22.30 Sun)
Closed Christmas Day
Credit Cards
Access, Visa, Diner's Club, AmEx
Bar Food Available
12.00–22.00;
11.00–23.00 Sat
(12.00–15.00 and
19.00–22.30 Sun)
Special Features
Wheelchair Access
Tables outside seat 30

Beers Available
SW1, SW2, Pimlico
Porter, Theakston, Leff
Blond, large selection
of bottled beers

Nearest Tube Station
Sloane Square

19th centuries. John Horne, the young brewer, also does new ales for special occasions. He has one involving oranges and coriander that he thinks has a great future. He regularly takes parties round.

As for the pub itself, this has just emerged from a root-and-branch improvement that has actually improved the place, not always the case. The bar itself seems hardly to have changed since Victorian times. It even has gas light. The dark old dining room, though, is now a comfortable second bar with a glass-topped platform looking down on big vats in which SW1 and SW2 slowly ferment. It is a spectacle that lacks drama but always has a happy ending.

Mozart composed his first symphony round the corner in Ebury Street. No 180. He was eight years old.

· THE ORANGE TREE ·

45 Kew Road, Richmond　　　　　　　　**0181-940 0944**

'Got its name from a superstar'

Open
All Week

Hours
11.00–23.00
(12.00–22.30 Sun)
Closed Christmas Day

Credit Cards
All major cards accepted

Food Available
Bar 12.00–15.00 and 18.00–23.00
Restaurant 12.00–15.00 and 18.00–23.00
(12.00–15.00 Sun)

Special Features
No-smoking Area
Tables outside seat 40
Private Room seats 65

Beers Available
Young's Bitter, Young's Special, Dirty Dick's, Young's London, Young's Premium, Stella, Castlemaine, Oatmeal Stout, Guinness, Beamish

Nearest Tube Station
Richmond

The Orange Tree that stood here in the 18th century got its name from the first orange tree to be brought to Britain, a superstar in Kew Gardens. It is a friendly name for the large dignified Victorian public house that replaced it in the 1890s. A man might raise his hat if he had one to this imposing pub with its fine brick and terracotta façade obligingly standing so near Richmond Station.

It is very Victorian inside with red walls covered in pictures, a very large L-shaped bar and big bulbous mahogany pillars, but everything is big about this pub. Indeed in 1971 they found there was any amount of room on the first floor for a theatre seating 80 people, the first ever licensed pub theatre of its kind.

For the next 20 years the Orange Tree Theatre staged plays and sometimes musicals there. Some got transferred to the West End and it became quite famous. It dreamed of more space, though, and in 1989 converted a little school nearby into a theatre-in-the-round. It still uses the theatre in the pub a lot too – new writers, experimental productions, that sort of thing.

There's jazz in the big wine bar in the cellars of the pub every Sunday evening and a new terrace opened at the back in the heatwave this summer. The eight tables there and the ten at the front were a smash hit as the days got increasingly tropical. It is very enterprising, the Orange Tree, as befits a former *Evening Standard* Pub of the Year.

·The Outback Inn·

11 Henrietta Street, WC2   **379 5555**
'Oz and Kiwi travellers far from home'

In the heart of the great outback called Covent Garden, a small beleaguered outpost awaits Oz and Kiwi travellers far from home. It is a long thin pub called the Outback Inn and it runs from Henrietta Street right through to Maiden Lane with an entrance and indeed an exit at each end.

It is possibly the most Australian of all the Australian pubs in London, with plain wooden floors, stout wooden tables, squat wooden stools and a bar counter that looks as if it was knocked together last night. There's a drinking bit, an eating bit and a huge games bar in the basement. Videos of all major sporting events back home are flown over straight after the match and enthralled crowds watch them on big screens upstairs and down.

This used to be the Rickshaw, a long thin Indian restaurant, but it has not left the lightest footprint in the sand. It has been the Outback since December 1994, since when it has been steaks, burgers and Roy's home-made sausages served with fries and mushy peas. Roy is the Kiwi chef. There is live music five nights a week and cold lager all day and every day.

You don't have to be an Oz or indeed a Kiwi to drink in the Outback, but it helps. You know what a dunny is? You will be pleased to hear the Outback has one of each sort.

Open
All Week
Hours
11.00–23.00
(12.00–22.30 Sun)
Credit Cards
Access, Visa
Bar Food Available
12.00–21.00
Mon–Thur;
12.00–20.00 Fri–Sun
Special Features
Wheelchair Access
ground floor only
(but not lavatory)
Beers Available
Brakspear, John Smith's, Foster's, Foster's Ice, 4X, Victoria Beer, Tooheys, Boags, Steinlager, Lion Ice, Lion Red, Caffrey's, Budweiser, Molson Dry, Cooper's Sparkling Ale, Castle Lager, Newcastle Brown Ale, Murphy's
Nearest Tube Station
Covent Garden

·The Outpost·

Burdett Road, E3   **0181-981 7717**
'Tattooed from shoulder to wrist'

This is the bikers' pub, a pub for bikers run by bikers, as they will tell you. The bikes occupy the forecourt, kings of the road from Italy, America, Japan. The bikers line the bar inside.

The Outpost sticks out conspicuously on the park side of Burdett Road. It is black with pale blue motorbike murals, and if the bikes are a formidable sight so too are the bikers, filling the bar and the pool room, Jack Danielses or bottled lagers in their hands.

Drinks tend to last at the Outpost. Bikers are not, as it happens, big drinkers. Well, the bikes outside can cost a bomb and they are loved with a passion. To ride them needs a strong nerve and a clear head, so it's lucky for the Outpost that non-bikers go too sometimes. They get a guarded welcome.

Open
All Week
Hours
11.00–23.00
(12.00–22.30 Sun)
Credit Cards
None
Bar Food Available
11.00–23.00
Special Features
Wheelchair Access
(disabled lavatory)
Beer Garden seats 15
Private Room seats 60

Beers Available
Pedigree, Tetley,
Grolsch, Newcastle
Brown Ale, Holsten,
Foster's, Guinness,
Carling Black label,
Stella Artois

Nearest Tube Station
Mile End

A big spread of snaps on the wall features bikers, bikers' women and bikers at one with nature, bikers getting tattooed, bikers having their nipples pierced. The notice board is largely occupied by ads for tattooists and body piercers. Behind the bar stands the manager, Des Clarke. He is tattooed from shoulder to wrist on both arms, and wears an earring and a nose stud.

·THE PAXTON'S HEAD·

153 Knightsbridge, SW1　　　　　　　　　**589 6627**

'Any pub that bore his name had to glitter'

Open
Mon–Sat

Hours
11.00–23.00
Closed Christmas Day,
Boxing Day, New Year's
Day

Credit Cards
AmEx, Visa,

Food Available
Bar 12.00–14.30
Restaurant
12.00–16.00

Special Features
No-smoking Area in
dining room
Wheelchair Access
(but not lavatory)
Private Room seats 45

Beers Available
Nicholson's, Wadworth
6X, Tetley, Brakspear,
Bass, Castlemaine,
Lowenbrau, Carlsberg,
Tennent's Pilsner

Nearest Tube Station
Knightsbridge

Sir Joseph Paxton was the Victorian landscape gardener who designed and built the Crystal Palace. Any pub that bore his name had to glitter as this one splendidly does.

Of course it would have been bigger if he had built it. His conservatory for the Duke of Devonshire was 300-ft long, his Chatsworth fountain 237-ft high. A pub he built would have been more like the Albert Hall. He would surely have approved of the brilliant decorated mirrors, though. They cover the walls of the bar. Some have had to be replaced with plain glass but most of the originals have survived and sparkle as they always did. The polished mahogany bar counter and the listed ceiling are terrific too, and as for the huge Victorian mantle clock on the fireplace, that certainly approaches his scale.

The Paxton's Head was a hotel to begin with but the upper floors are offices now. The good news is that the fine room on the first floor is a restaurant again. It stood empty for ages. The original restaurant was quite famous in its day but a murder cast rather a shadow on the silver service. It was out of hours. But all the same…

·PHARAOH AND FIRKIN·

90 Fulham High Street, SW6　　　　　　　**731 0732**

'Flagship of the booming temperance movement'

Open
All Week

Hours
12.00–23.00
(12.00–22.30 Sun)
Closed Christmas Day

Credit Cards
None

Bar Food Available
Full meals during all
opening hours

In 1910 the new Temperance Billiard Hall opened in Fulham High Street. There were speeches and applause and I rather think a band. There was surely ginger beer. This was a flagship of the booming temperance movement, exuberant and stylish with parallel ranks of billiard tables stretching from end to end. Hopes ran high that this fine new dry pub would coax the working man from the far-from-dry pubs on every side.

Other Temperance Billiard Halls carried the battle to

Clapham, Wandsworth, Balham and Lewisham and fought the good fight for half a century and more, but they have all gone now. The one in Fulham was the last to give up, and what has happened to it must be keenly felt by the shades of its founders. It has become one of London's biggest and most successful pubs, a pub with its own brewhouse producing vast quantities of ale in what used to be the temperance kitchen. It is the Pharaoh and Firkin now.

The size of the place astonishes newcomers, the height of it and the spread of it, also the size of the crowd. Even on a quiet night there will probably be a couple of hundred, and at the weekends it is home to 800 and more, everyone apparently having a party, a sing-along pianist going strong and everyone joining in. It's not so much the rafters they shake as the handsome Edwardian girders still, after 100 years, keeping the high-pitched roof on.

Firkin food is sold all day. There's a window to the brewhouse to let you see the Pharaoh Ale, the Cam Ale (camel, geddit?) and the Dogbolters being brewed, and the telephone is housed in one of the classic red telephone kiosks that once stood on every other street corner. It weighs a ton. It took ten men to manhandle it in.

Special Features
No-smoking Area
Wheelchair Access
Live Music Fri and Sat, solo and sing-a-long

Beers Available
Dogbolter, Pharaoh, Cam Ale, Firkin Mild, Golden Glory, Castlemaine XXXX, Carlsberg Export, Lowenbrau, large variety of bottled beers

Nearest Tube Station
Putney Bridge

· THE PHENE ARMS ·

9 Phene Street, SW3   352 3294

'Thank you, Dr Phene'

Dr John Samuel Phene – it rhymes with meany – was an eccentric old boy in many ways but he had a lasting claim to fame. He was the first man to plant trees in the streets of large towns. No one seems to have thought of it before. Queen Victoria warmly commended him for it and so do we. Thank you, Dr Phene and thank you for this nice little pub at the corner of these two leafy Chelsea streets.

Dr Phene built the streets and the pub in 1851 and planted lots of trees of heaven saplings around them, also groves of acacia, and I'm pleased to say he lived another 60 years so he saw them grow into mature trees. He also saw his pub pass to Watney's just before he died at a great age in 1912.

The pub is very much as he left it with its tall Victorian bar and its tiny dining room. They serve lunch here all week but on Sundays you go upstairs for the roast beef with all the trimmings. There is a much bigger room up there. There is also a charming little roof terrace for supper on summer evenings.

Three of Dr Phene's trees of heaven still grow in the

Open
All Week

Hours
11.00–23.00
(12.00–22.30 Sun)

Credit Cards
All major cards accepted

Bar and Restaurant Food Available
12.00–14.30
(12.00–15.00 Sat;
12.30–16.00 Sun) and
19.30–22.30
(19.30–22.00 Sun)

Special Features
Beer Garden seats 100
Private Room seats 40

Beers Available
Webster's, Adnams, Ruddles County, Ruddles Best, Guinness, Carlsberg, Foster's, Holsten Budweiser

Nearest Tube Station
Sloane Square

pub's front garden, a lovely place to sit and drink on a sunny day. Elizabeth Hurley was filmed there doing just this in *Mad Dogs and Englishmen*. The garden has been a great asset to the pub and, indeed, to the streets around for 140 years, and absurd attempts to stop customers from drinking in it were swiftly thrown out by the High Court.

Wesley Davis who has had the lease for some years now reports that the pub's renowned cricket team, the Phene Philanderers, is in a Saturday league now and has actually won a game or two.

·PHOENIX AND FIRKIN·

Windsor Walk, SE15 **701 8282**
'He'd rather Mrs Train than Mrs Bovril'

Open
All Week

Hours
11.00–23.00
(12.00–22.30 Sun)

Credit Cards
All major cards accepted

Bar Food Available
12.00–23.00

Special Features
No-smoking Area
Wheelchair Access
Beer Garden seats 10
Private Room seats 30

Beers Available
Rail Ale, Firkin Mild, Dogbolter, Castlemaine, Carlsberg, Lowenbrau

Nearest BR Station
Denmark Hill

The Phoenix and Firkin is, as I think you will agree, a remarkable pub. It used to be a railway station. Not many pubs can say that.

You don't get away from trains at the Phoenix and Firkin. Trains run under it, a model train runs inside it, trains take you almost to the door. You get on at Victoria or London Bridge, get out at Denmark Hill and there it is straddling all four platforms.

It was always a good-looking station. *The Times* called it a glorious 1866-vintage Tuscan palazzo, but one night early in 1980 some rotter set fire to it. The palatial ticket hall, the ladies' waiting room, the Station Master's house, all went up in smoke and flame. British Rail was going to pull the whole thing down, but there was a tremendous local outcry. Instead the builders moved in and, Phoenix-like, the Tuscan palazzo rose from the ashes to start a new chapter, this time as a lively and popular public house.

So have a look at the building before you enter it. Inside it is all classic London, Chatham and Dover, classic Firkin too, plain wooden furniture, a big practical 58-ft bar, nice old railway posters – 'He'd rather Mrs Train than Mrs Bovril' – and a station clock rescued from Llandudno Junction.

There's live blues and jazz on Mondays and Thursdays in winter, and on summer evenings draught scrumpy is the thing and just about everyone sits outside on the steps.

What is really special is the beer, brewed in a brewhouse in the cellar. So while you drink your ale, think of the big vats of English beer coming to fruition beneath your feet – the famous Dogbolter, the Firkin Mild and the pub's best seller, Phoenix Rail Ale. I find it a cheering thought myself.

The Phoenix and Firkin was the *Evening Standard*'s Pub of the Year in 1994.

· THE PINEAPPLE ·

53 Hercules Road, SE1   **928 6579**

'A cheerful, workaday Lambeth local'

Look to the right next time your train approaches Waterloo and you may spot a golden pineapple among the rooftops of Lambeth. This is the crowning glory of the Pineapple, a once ambitious Victorian gin palace, now a cheerful, workaday Lambeth local.

It has imposing marble pillars in pairs, four front doors and a foundation stone laid by Henry Finch in 1870. Maddigan's, the Dublin pub-owner, bought it in 1985 and brought Sean O'Neill over from Ireland to run it. He is still there cheerily dispensing pints of Murphy's. Lunchtimes are his busy time. 'Basic food,' says Mr O'Neill, 'but cheap.'

William Blake was born along the road.

Open
All Week

Hours
11.00–23.00
(12.00–22.30 Sun)

Credit Cards
None

Bar Food Available
12.00–21.30

Special Features
Wheelchair Access
Beer Garden seats 30

Beers Available
Greene King, Abbot, Ruddles County, Courage Best, Marston's Pedigree, Whitbread IPA, Foster's, Heineken, Stella Artois, Budweiser, Holsten, Guinness, Murphy's

Nearest Tube Station
Lambeth North

· THE PLUMBERS ARMS ·

14 Lower Belgrave Street, SW1   **730 4067**

'Belgravia has had its share of horror and mystery'

The Plumbers Arms, despite its robust tradesman's name, is distinctly above stairs. Not too many plumbers live in Lower Belgrave Street, though those that do may well commend the house champagne, a very reasonable £14.95.

The Plumbers Arms is said to be so called because of the army of plumbers who helped transform five fields and a stretch of river into Belgravia. The pub itself was one of the first of the new buildings. It was put up in the 1820s to cater for the builders and, of course, the plumbers, and when their work was done it served the servants of the grand new houses they had built. Strict class distinctions applied.

Today it is a pleasant single-bar pub with a Lincrusta ceiling, a splendid mahogany bar counter, old plates, old prints and smart young barmen in white shirts and grey waistcoats polishing up the gleaming beer pulls. It has well-kept cask ales and denizens of Lower Belgrave Street find it a very good place for lunch.

But it is not its cellar or its kitchen that has given the Plumbers Arms its celebrity. This stems from the events of the rainswept November night in 1974 when, bleeding and soaked to the skin, Lady Lucan stumbled into the pub. She had a shocking story to tell. An intruder had murdered her nanny and had then attacked her. He was still in the house.

Open
All Week

Hours
11.00–23.00 Mon–Fri;
12.00–18.00 Sat;
(12.00–15.00 Sun)
Closed Christmas Day

Credit Cards
Visa, Mastercard

Bar Food Available
12.00–22.00 Mon–Fri;
12.00–18.00 Sat;
(12.00–15.00 Sun)

Special Features
Beer Garden seats 24
Private Room seats 25

Beers Available
John Smith's, Wadworth, Courage Directors, Theakston, Foster's, Carlsberg, Holsten, Miller, Budweiser, Molsen, Guinness

Nearest Tube Station
Victoria

The police were called and found the nanny dead in the Lucan family home. Later that night Lord Lucan turned up briefly in a friend's house in Sussex, then drove away. He has never been seen since.

The episode has left a lasting mark on the Plumbers Arms, which obliquely refers to it in a brief history of Belgravia in its menu. 'In more recent years,' it writes, 'Belgravia has had its share of horror and mystery, not only Belgravia but also the Plumbers Arms.'

·THE PRINCE ALFRED·

Formosa Street, W9   286 3027

'A perfect period piece. Well almost'

Open
All Week

Hours
12.00–23.00
(12.00–22.30 Sun)
Closed Christmas Day, Boxing Day

Credit Cards
None

Bar Food Available
12.00–14.30 and
19.00–22.30

Special Features
Wheelchair Access

Beers Available
Burton Ale, Tetley, Young's Special, Young's PA, Flowers IPA, Lowenbrau, Castlemaine, Carlsberg

Nearest Tube Station
Warwick Avenue

The Prince Alfred is a true rarity, a working Victorian pub in full fig. It has hardly changed from the day in 1862 when it first opened its various doors.

It was always a good-looking pub, a cut above and still is. It was called after Queen Victoria's second son. He was only 18 but had already had four years in the navy and as soon as he could he grew one of those Players cigarettes naval beards. That was the pub sign solved. He was elected King of Greece that year too. He turned it down.

The pub is a remarkable sight. They have kept everything – the beautiful curved and etched glass, the original 15-ft-high centrepiece with its shelves and clocks and ornamental flourishes, the massive mahogany counter, best of all the splendid carved and glazed partitions. These divide the space into five separate bars: the Public, the Gentlemen's, the Ladies', the Private and the Snug.

All but one has its own street entrance. The exception was the Snug. Ladies using that had to duck into it through little doors in the partitions, only three feet high, but once in they had perfect privacy. Rotating snob screens hid them from even the bar staff.

It is a perfect period piece. Well, almost. There has been one change over the years. The stables at the back have been made into a sixth bar, open plan in the modern way and kitted out with a pool table. This is the bar that persons Prince Alfred's age like. It is the one that gets crowded.

·THE PRINCE BONAPARTE·

80 Chepstow Road, W2 **229 5912**

'Not a bistro, not a brasserie, a pub with food'

There used to be a local in Notting Hill Gate called the Artesian. It was a very bad neighbour. Rough. In the 80's, though, it changed hands, was smartened up and got a new name. As the Prince Bonaparte it quietened down and now, continuing its journey up-market, it has changed a lot more. It has become one of the new born-again foodie pubs of London in the 90's.

It seemed to happen all at once. It closed for just a fortnight last summer and when it opened again it had been remodelled, redecorated, rejuvenated. The two bars had been knocked together, light flooded through the restored conservatory roof, the rented pool tables, gaming machines and juke box had been sent back and a splendid open kitchen had replaced a stretch of the counter and was producing delicious Mediterranean food.

The new partners, the chefs Beth Coventry and Phillip Wright, and the manager Mark Harris, insist that this remains a pub, not a bistro, not a brasserie, but a pub with food, and it holds on to pub-like ways. There is draught ale and draught lager on the handpumps, you can't book a table, they don't take credit cards and if you are eating you order your food at the bar.

The food, though, cooked before your eyes, is quite unpub-like. It is a wonderful thing that has happened to the Prince Bonaparte.

Open
All Week

Hours
11.00–23.00
(12.00–22.30 Sun)
Closed Christmas Day

Credit Cards
None

Restaurant Food Available
12.00–15.30 and
18.00–22.30

Special Features
Wheelchair Access
(but not lavatory)
Private Room seats 30

Beers Available
Bass, London Pride, Old Speckled Hen, Worthington, Caffrey's, Carling Black Label, Grolsch, Staropramen, Guinness

Nearest Tube Station
Westbourne Park

·THE PRINCE OF TECK·

161 Earls Court Road, SW5 **373 3107**

'Djavagidweegend?'

Pity homesick Oz expats stranded among the poms in the Earls Court Road. Happily there is an abiding certainty to cheer them. They know that if they stand at the bar in the Prince of Teck long enough they will meet everybody they know.

There are other Oz pubs in London but the Prince of Teck has claimed his kingdom. His is a handsome pub with griffins and gargoyles on the outside not to mention a portrait of the prince, harum scarum brother of Queen Mary. She would forgive him almost anything but when he gave the Cambridge emeralds to his Irish mistress… But back to his pub.

Ah Australia! Posters bring it all back. There's a map

Open
All Week

Hours
11.00–23.00
(12.00–22.30 Sun)
Closed Christmas Day

Credit Cards
None

Bar Food Available
11.00–15.00 and
17.00–21.00
(12.00–20.00 Sun)

Special Features
Wheelchair Access

Beers Available
Australian beers, Young's Bitter, Young's Special, Courage Best, Webster's Yorkshire Bitter, Foster's, Kronenbourg

Nearest Tube Station
Earls Court

and boomerangs and Oz road signs featuring kangaroos and crocodiles, and sitting on the bar is a stuffed and very male kangaroo wearing a short Wallabies Australian Rugby shirt and carrying an empty can of Victoria VB beer, and in case you've been away from home too long there's a handy glossary of the language. Gidday. Cow's hoof. Djavagidweegend?

There are no carpets and very little furniture in the Prince of Teck apart from bar stools along the bar and round the walls. The lager is cold. There are three juke boxes, the new flat digital sort that hang on the wall, two of them featuring the hilarious Kevin Bloody Wilson. Loos are labelled Sheilas and Bruces and the notice board reflects other urgent needs. Some Ozzies want places to live, some want flat mates, quite a few want to sell campervans, a travel firm has cut-price fares to the US. 'If you can beat these prices start your own damn airline,' it snaps.

There is a very different room upstairs, the Princess Lounge, where they serve traditional pom pub food. It has a fitted carpet, comfy seats, swagged curtains. Swagged curtains? You're sure this bit isn't for cow's hoofs, Bruce?

· THE PRINCE OF WALES ·

Open
All Week

Hours
11.00–23.00
(12.00–22.30 Sun)

Bar Food
12.00–17.00

Special Features
Outside area seats 35

Beers Available
Boddingtons, London Pride, Pedigree, Flowers, Stella, Heineken, Murphy's, Guinness
Cider: Scrumpy Jack

Nearest Tube Station
Clapham Common

Clapham Old Town, SW4   **622 4789**

'A sailor on the roof'

You can't miss the Prince of Wales. POW POW POW is painted in large letters on the parapet, the Union Jack flies from the flagpole and there's the jaunty figure of a sailor sitting on the roof.

It is just as extrovert inside with a vast collection of curios and objects collected around the world by the landlord's father in his seafaring days. They hang from the ceilings and cover every inch of the walls. Happily there remains some room for the customers, though not a lot.

The Prince of Wales is a small, cosy sort of place with a loyal following. Musicians, actors, artists and students crowd in and lots goes on – regular pub outings, the Derby, Wimbledon and such, Saturday cabaret once a month, pancake races on Shrove Tuesday and at closing time they play 'Land of Hope and Glory'. Not many pubs do that.

· THE PRINCE OF WALES ·

48 Cleaver Square, SE11   **735 9916**

'Where the hard men drank'

Cleaver Square is an agreeable place to live, a backwater of nice houses, Georgian mainly, near enough to the City and Houses of Commons to be popular with both. The middle was once a garden but is now used by the residents to park their cars. A game of boules and you might be in any small French town except, of course, for the pub in the corner.

The Prince of Wales could not be more English. There was a pub here before the square but the original one was rebuilt in 1909 and here it is, a comely Edwardian local named for the prince who became George IV. It is a small, intimate pub, the public bar at the front and saloon bar behind it knocked into one and still not much room. It seems a peaceful and friendly place but you would hardly believe the troubles it has seen.

For years it had a dire reputation. It was where the hard men drank, where the Richardson gang met the Krays for summit meetings, and when Kate Emmett, an actress from Australia, arrived as the new tenant ten years ago she found it distinctly unjolly. It had no furniture at all. People sat on the floor and the caretaker manager had a stick with a hook on it behind the bar to protect himself.

Either she had to go or the roughs did, so she took them on. She banned them, refused to serve them, stood her ground and she was threatened, bullied and physically attacked. These battles were followed by legal battles over the freehold, and at the time of writing they have been going on for six long years and are still unresolved.

Still, at least peace has broken out in the pub itself. This must be a relief for Cleaver Square, not to mention the actors, musicians and politicians in the streets roundabout and the ginger tom who rules the bar...

Open
All Week

Hours
11.00–23.00
(12.00–22.30 Sun)
Closed Bank Holidays

Credit Cards
None

Beers Available
Young's Bitter, Young's Special, Dirty Dick's, Stella, Castlemaine, Guinness
Cider: Dry Blackthorn

Nearest Tube Station
Kennington

· THE PRINCE OF WALES ·

150 Drury Lane, WC1   **240 9935**

'Moving with the times'

The Prince of Wales rather boasts of its proletarian background. It was, says the potted history on the outside wall, formerly a potato warehouse. In 1852, though, it went up in the world, became a pub, a well-appointed pub, good position, heart of theatreland and all that, and assumed the rank of the Queen's eldest son.

Open
All Week

Hours
11.00–23.00
(12.00–22.30 Sun)
Closed Christmas Day, Boxing Day

Credit Cards
All major cards accepted

Bar Food Available
11.00–22.00
(12.00–15.00 and
19.00–22.00 Sun)

Special Features
Wheelchair Access
(but not lavatory)
Tables outside seat 20
Private Room
seats 100
Function Room
seats 100

Beers Available
Theakston, Courage
Directors, Carlsberg,
Holsten, Foster's,
Guinness, Gillespie's

Nearest Tube Station
Covent Garden

Time passes: cut to tramcars, rolling presses, newsboys shouting, and it is 1982. The Prince of Wales is now full of stuffed animals and cobwebs and is looking tired and down at heel. What's this? A gang of revolutionary persons is taking it apart. Farewell Victoriana, farewell Prince of Wales. It reopens as a trendy bar-café with lowered ceilings, red walls, chrome fittings, artificial plants, a juke box and a new name. It is now Charley's. The kids pour in. It is a big hit.

It does not last. Another decade and Charley's has dated badly too, so it gets another new personality. It closes for six weeks, reopens and good lord it is the Prince of Wales again.

This time, though, it is one of Scottish and Newcastle's modish T and J Barnard pubs, in the style of the moment: 1990s early ale house. So it is wooden floors and plain wooden furniture at the Prince of Wales, pies with meat, potatoes and veg all under the same puff pastry lids, seven English ales on tap and 20 different bottled beers, some quite exotic, in a rack behind the counter. Barbara Fitzgerald, the extremely experienced landlady, thought they would never sell, not at that price, but they go extremely well.

Fruity bottled ale brewed by Trappist monks in a remote monastery is part of 1990s early ale house and, after its conventional beginnings, the Prince of Wales is moving with the times.

· THE PRINCESS LOUISE ·

208 High Holborn, WC2   **405 8816**

'They are tough old birds, these Princesses Louise'

Open
All Week

Hours
11.00–23.00
12.00–15.00 and
18.00–23.00 Sat
(12.00–14.00 and
18.00–22.30 Sun)
Closed Christmas Day,
Boxing Day

Credit Cards
None

Restaurant Food Available
12.00–14.30 Mon–Fri only

Special Features
Wheelchair Access
(but not lavatory)
Private Room seats 50

Princess Louise was the fourth daughter of Queen Victoria. She was the Queen's great-great-aunt. She was unhappily married to the Duke of Argyll. She talked a lot, and in 1891 they named this pub after her.

It was a splendid pub and still is, though it has changed a bit of course. Instead of parading round lots of little rooms, the massive mahogany bar makes its deep U-turn in the middle of one big open space. But the polished granite pillars, the richly engraved windows, the walls of gilt mirrors, elaborate tiling, fine plaster ceilings and plush banquettes, the polished mahogany and brass have all survived.

It is a miracle really that the Princess Louise is still with us. There was the Blitz, of course, but much more dangerous were the redevelopers of the 60s and 70s. The Princess Louise was on the point of coming down to make way for an office block when an outcry from the good guys, cheered on by the *Evening Standard*, saved the day. A preservation order arrived in the nick of time, making it a Listed Building Grade II*.

Mark the star, it is important. The regal Victorian gents is separately listed. You don't often meet a listed gents.

The Louise, we'll not stand on ceremony here, has seen various owners come and go. It is now owned by Regent Inns, a lively independent, and it does nine cask ales at last count, a lot of which gets drunk outside on the pavement on sunny days.

It seems very odd that they were actually thinking of pulling it down not long ago, but then the Princess whose name it bears lived to 91. They are tough old birds these Princesses Louise.

It was the *Evening Standard* Pub of the Year in 1986.

·THE PROSPECT OF WHITBY·

57 Wapping Wall, E1   **481 1095**

'A haunt of smugglers, thieves and other low-lifers'

The Prospect of Whitby is the oldest riverside pub in London and probably the most famous. Its flagstoned bar with its pewter-topped counter sitting on old barrels must have been used by half London in its long day. There's a separate section for bar snacks now, a good restaurant up creaking stairs and a jolly riverside terrace with picnic tables under an old weeping willow. It has been the high point of many a day out.

The old inn was built around 1520 and was no better than it ought of have been, a haunt of smugglers, thieves and other low-lifers. Indeed, it boldly called itself the Devil's Tavern. Misbehaving sailors were hanged along the low watermark, a popular entertainment drawing big crowds. Samuel Pepys came to the pub on official business. Judge Jeffreys came to dine and enjoy the hangings.

The pub was burned, rebuilt, changed its name – the Prospect (from Whitby) was a merchant ship that moored nearby – and, slowly, slowly, it started to get respectable.

It is very respectable now as you can see from the two chairs by the dining-room door. A notice on one of them reads: 'This chair was occupied by HRH Princess Margaret when dining here on June 26, 1949.' Prince Rainier has had dinner here too, and Kirk Douglas. Where are their chairs?

It was as well the Princess was not dining here on 14 January 1953 when Robert Harrington 'Scarface' Sanders and his red scarf gang raided the Prospect of Whitby. Capt John Cunningham was giving a small dinner party. He and his guests were relieved of their watches, jewellery and money at pistol point. Scarface was caught soon afterwards when, doing another job, he shot at a policeman. He got life.

Beers Available
Brakspear Bitter, Brakspear Special, Bass, Theakston Best Bitter, Theakston Old Peculier, Gale's HSB, Adnams Broadside, Bateman XB, plus an unusual changing guest beer

Nearest Tube Station
Holborn

Open
All Week

Hours
11.30–15.00 and 17.30–23.00
(12.00–22.30 Sun)
Closed Christmas Day, Boxing Day

Credit Cards
All major cards accepted

Bar and Restaurant Food Available
11.30–15.00 and 17.30–23.00

Special Features
No-smoking Area
Wheelchair Access (but not lavatory)
Beer Garden seats 80
Private Room seats 60

Beers Available
Courage Directors, Courage Best, Theakston Best, Theakston XB, Kronenbourg, Foster's, Holsten, Molsen, Guinness

Nearest Tube Station
Wapping

Open
All Week
Hours
11.30–23.00
(12.00–22.30 Sun)
Closed Christmas Day,
Boxing Day
Credit Cards
Visa, Access
Restaurant Food Available
12.00–17.00
Special Features
No-smoking Area
Tables outside seat 30
Private Room seats 200
Beers Available
Courage Best, Courage Directors, Theakston Best, Theakston XB, Foster's, Kronenbourg, Beamish
Nearest Tube Station
Covent Garden

·THE PUNCH AND JUDY·

40 The Market, Covent Garden, WC2   **379 0923**

'A balcony of royal proportions'

When the famous old flower and vegetable market moved out of Covent Garden in 1974 a miracle happened. Instead of being knocked down, the old market was put to wonderful use and when we saw it next the Punch and Judy was occupying a prime site in Charles Fowler's elegant market hall.

It was a brilliant place for a pub and the Punch and Judy was a smash hit from the word go. It had a section of the cellars that had once provided overnight storage for vegetables, and with its flagged floor and vaulted arches this made a perfect cellar bar. It led into a courtyard in the glass-roofed arcade, another coup. Customers could sit and drink there whatever the weather and still think they were in the open air.

Someone else got the ground floor but the Punch and Judy re-emerges on the floor above with a light modern bar opening onto a balcony of royal proportions. It stretches the whole width of the building with a shelf for drinks-in-progress all the way along.

Below is the West Piazza, London's first square, originally designed by Inigo Jones. Now street entertainers perform there to big crowds all summer long and customers of the Punch and Judy, cheerfully crowding the balcony, have the front row in the circle.

The Punch and Judy was one of many prizes in Scottish and Newcastle's purchase of the big Chef and Brewer chain. It was showing signs of wear, but the new owners have spent £200,000 on it lately, a lot of it, as the pub says, to improve customer flow. Not all customers warm to the emphasis on business efficiency. Be this as it may, trade has increased by 20 per cent.

The food remains hearty and traditional and the Punch and Judy is still a major lager house.

·THE PUNCH TAVERN·

Open
All Week
Hours
11.30–23.00 Mon–Fri;
11.30–18.00 Sat;
(12.00–15.00 and
19.00–22.30 Sun)
Closed Christmas Day,
Boxing Day, New Year's Day

99 Fleet Street, EC4   **353 6658**

'The gilded Mr Punch smiles on'

Some of us remember the days when the entire nation read *Punch* at the dentist. For more that 100 years it was the national sense of humour but then, quite suddenly it seemed, it wasn't. Sad really.

When it started in 1841 the staff of the new mag took to

a pub in Fleet Street called the Crown and Sugarloaf. It, in turn, took to them, so much that it changed its name. It became Punch's Tavern.

Unlike the magazine and the newspapers that enlivened Fleet Street, Punch Tavern is still there, though it seems to have lost its apostrophe along the way. In the mid-1980s new owners spent £250,000 doing it over so thoroughly that it now looks more splendidly Victorian than ever. The ornately tiled Fleet Street façade might have been put up yesterday, and regular customers were pleased as Punch, particularly when they went to the gents. Before the restoration this was something to be postponed as long as possible.

After the pub's great refurb, Alan Coren, penultimate editor of *Punch*, came to reopen it. He found a brand-new pub sign with a gilded Mr Punch smiling wickedly down at him. Mr Coren left *Punch* soon afterwards and *Punch* closed for ever soon after that. The gilded Mr Punch smiles on.

Credit Cards
All major cards accepted

Bar Food Available
12.00–14.30

Special Features
Wheelchair Access (but not lavatory)

Beers Available
Tetley, Brakspear, Worthington, Bass, Carling Black Label, Guinness, Caffrey's, Staropramen, Tennent's Pilsner

Nearest Tube Station
Blackfriars

·THE QUEEN MARY·

Victoria Embankment, WC2   **240 9404**
'A famous sight criss-crossing the Clyde'

The Queen Mary, or the TS *Queen Mary* as she is known on formal occasions, is an extremely pleasant pub some yards offshore between Waterloo and Hungerford bridges. TS stands for Turbine Steamer.

Other working ships retiring to the Thames have sometimes done well as restaurants, and the Queen Mary and its immediate upstream neighbour, the Tattershall Castle, have restaurants too. They are true pubs all the same. They have pub licences. They keep pub hours. They call themselves pubs and operate as pubs. Their saloon bars are populated by persons of distinction sitting at small tables, pints of beer before them. If that's not a pub what is?

The Queen Mary is a truly shipshape ship with two jaunty red, white and blue funnels and two tiers of square portholes. When she was launched on the Clyde in 1933 she was the most luxurious pleasure steamer the river had ever seen. She was a famous sight criss-crossing the Clyde, but in 1977 she was reluctantly retired. The breakers yard loomed but happily Bass stepped in. The old girl was given a £2-million refit in Chatham Docks and started a new life on the Thames.

So there she is with three public bars all with marvellous river views, particularly the one on the top deck. The wardroom bar is the smart one with big banquettes and widely spaced tables. You can get bar food in here. The Thames bar

Open
All Week

Hours
11.00–23.00
(12.00–22.30 Sun)
Closed Bank Holidays, Christmas

Credit Cards
All major cards except Diner's Club

Food Available
Bar 12.00–18.00
Restaurant 18.00–21.00
(18.00–22.00 Fri)

Special Features
Tables outside seat 50
Private Room seats 150

Beers Available
Worthington, Charrington variants, Caffrey's, Grolsch, Guinness

Nearest Tube Station
Embankment

has discos twice a week there and attracts a younger crowd. All three are supplied with beer from the tender moored alongside.

There is a good carvery and everything moves gently the while, rising and falling with the tides and rocking just a bit whenever the river police speed by. 'They do it on purpose,' says the Queen Mary, not really minding. The Thames is a millpond compared with the Clyde.

· THE QUEENS ·

49 Regent's Park Road, NW1 **586 0408**

'Thus Sir Kingsley is well suited'

Open
All Week
Hours
11.00–15.00 and 17.00–23.00 Mon–Fri; 11.00–23.00 Sat; (12.00–22.30 Sun)
Credit Cards
All major cards accepted
Bar Food Available
11.30–14.30
Special Features
Wheelchair Access (but not lavatory)
Tables outside seat 18
Private Room seats 45
Beers Available
Young's Bitter, Young's Special, Young's Oatmeal Stout, Young's Premium Lager, Young's London Lager, Tennent's Extra, Red Stripe, Castlemaine, Guinness
Nearest Tube Station
Chalk Farm

My man on Primrose Hill sends this report: 'The Queens stands on a corner at the very heart of Primrose Hill village, home over the years to writers, actors, musicians, artists, and, in more recent times, environmentally friendly shop people. Robert Stephens gets in. Denis Quilley has a drink here. So does Gayle Hunnicutt, Simon Jenkins, Robert Plant of Led Zeppelin. Kingsley Amis once wrote an article about it for the *New York Times*. It is his local too.

'Nine out of ten of the 170 or so Young's pubs in and around London play no music. So it is with the Queens. This does not dissuade young hearties from piling in after cricket, softball or whatever on the hill. It can get very busy.

'Manager Dave Williams looks on his domain as a place to which sensible older people resort. Thus Sir Kingsley is well suited.'

· THE QUEEN'S ARMS TAVERN ·

94 Draycott Avenue, SW3 **589 4981**

'Where's the pool table gone?'

Open
All Week
Hours
11.00–23.00
(12.00–22.30 Sun)
Closed Christmas Day
Credit Cards
All major cards except AmEx
Bar Food Available
12.00–22.00
Special Features
Wheelchair Access (but not lavatory)
Tables outside seat 20

People used to say that the Queen's Arms was just a pool table with a pub round it. But Chelsea is Chelsea and Charles Wells Ltd, the Bedford brewer, recently paid half a million pounds to get it and then spent another £150,000 doing it over. There certainly have been changes made. Where's the pool table gone?

Charles Wells is a family firm still run by the great-great-grandsons of the founder, three first cousins. They are clearly chips off the old block. They have a fine new brewery on the outskirts of Bedford, which produces 550,000 barrels of beer a year, and they have more than 300 pubs now, 22 of them in London. The Queen's Arms Tavern, its original name now restored, is the 22nd.

The place is much improved, with a big island bar counter, new carpets, wallpapers and copious bric-a-brac and Carole McCabe, the new manager, has introduced a tapas bar that runs all day. There is traditional pub food too, and, of course, Bombardier Best Bitter and Eagle IPA, the company's well-known cask beers, not to mention its lager, Fargo, and Red Stripe, the famous Jamaican lager it makes in Bedford under licence.

Beers Available
Eagle IPA, Bombardier Best Bitter, Fargo, Red Stripe, Bitberger, McEwan's, Guinness

Nearest Tube Station
South Kensington

·THE RAILWAY·

18 Clapham High Street, SW4   **622 4077**

'The first pub on the Internet?'

There was once a pub on this corner of Clapham High Street called the Railway Tavern. It had a railway station outside, and a thick pre-war fug inside. I described it in this guide as a Railway Tavern's Railway Tavern.

You see what happens? No sooner was the guide on the streets than Ann and Tom Halpin took over the old pub, closed it, completely changed it and opened it again. It isn't anything like a Railway Tavern now.

The Halpins describe their new decor as hippy-de-luxe. This means multi-coloured walls and oriental fixtures and fittings. The food, no longer British Railways stodge, is Italian. The newly decorated bar is young and hip and there are remarkable plans for the old upstairs bar. It will become a Cyberia room with ten computer terminals where customers will be able to roam the Internet. This could be the first such pub in London.

A pub on the Internet? Clearly a new name was needed. So it is the Railway now.

Open
All Week
Hours
12.00–23.00
(12.00–22.30 Sun)
Bar Food Available
12.30–15.00 Mon–Sat
Beers Available
Bass, Charrington IPA, and a guest
Nearest Tube Station
Clapham Common

·THE RAILWAY TAVERN·

15 Liverpool Street, EC2   **283 3598**

'The grand Railway Tavern of the main-line terminus'

Is there a self-respecting town in all the land that does not have a Railway Tavern? London has 18. Let this and the one that follows stand for them all.

First the grand Railway Tavern of the main-line terminus. This one is opposite Liverpool Street, a big, impressive high-ceilinged bar with recent Victorian fittings, an island of booths in the middle and partitions around the outside walls. There is a roomy games room upstairs – pool table, pinball

Open
Mon–Sat
Hours
11.00–23.00
(12.00–15.00 Sat)
Credit Cards
All major cards accepted
Food Available
Bar lunchtimes
Mon–Sat
Restaurant
11.00–21.00

Beers Available
Boddington, Flowers Original, London Pride, Castle Eden, Heineken Export, Stella Artois, Murphy's, Guinness

Nearest Tube Station
Clapham Common

machines, fruit machines and a loud juke box – and pizzas to eat here or take away, a Pizza Hut franchise. There is also a small wine bar, recently redecorated with Moulin Rouge murals. Service in all parts is swift and efficient. The staff knows well that customers have either a job to go to or a train to catch.

This Railway Tavern has been so much a part of Liverpool Street station for so many years that it has become known as Platform 19. 'Meet you on Platform 19,' say older commuters, showing they know a thing or two. Liverpool Street, you will gather, has 18 platforms.

·THE RAILWAY TAVERN·

Open
All Week
Hours
11.00–23.00
(12.00–22.30 Sun)
Credit Cards
None
Bar Food Available
11.00–21.00 Mon–Sat;
(12.00–15.00 Sun)
Special Features
Wheelchair Access
(but not lavatory)
Beers Available
Fargo, Bombardier, McEwans, Red Stripe, Carling, Guinness
Cider: Scrumpy Jack
Nearest BR Station
Hackney Central

339 Mare Street, E8   **0181-985 4184**
'A sky-blue locomotive belching smoke'

For a classic Railway Tavern go to somewhere with a railway station. This is Hackney's. It is on the corner opposite Hackney Central on British Rail's North London line, is painted a rather smart navy blue and has a sky-blue locomotive belching smoke on its inn sign.

There has been a go at making the bar look like a railway station with the counter cast as the buffet and the loos marked Men's Waiting Room, Women's Waiting Room, but what it is mainly like is a Railway Tavern with its dartboard, gaming machines and red velour banquettes. It is popular with British Rail staff from the station and the bus staff from the nearby Clapton Pond depot, it is proud of its doorstep sandwiches, has Irish music on Fridays and jazz on Saturdays and raises money for the fund that brings exchange students to Hackney from Barbados. Hackney is twinned with Barbados.

·THE RAJ·

Open
All Week
Hours
12.00–23.00
(12.00–22.30 Sun)
Closed
Christmas Day
Credit Cards
None
Special Features
Wheelchair Access
Tables outside seat 36

40 Holland Park Ave, W11   **727 6332**
'The day belongs to pool'

For most of its life this big Victorian public house was the Mitre, a good-looking red brick Victorian pub devoting itself, I have no doubt, to good works and the prosperous stucco villas around it.

A decade or so ago it got a radical going-over. It briefly closed and reopened as the Raj, one of the early theme pubs. Nostalgia for British India, that was the theme, and the big lounge at the back became an Indian restaurant. Alas it was not the hit that had been expected, so out went British India, out went the restaurant with its gazebo and Indian waiters, in came pool tables, arcade games, a juke box permanently on, Sky TV never off.

Traces of each passing civilization can be found. Portland stone mitres from its days as the Mitre decorate the roof. Framed 70-year-old gossip about Sir Hari Singh hangs in the bar. The day belongs to pool, though. While the juke box competes with Sky TV, the five tables are in constant use and the two bars, a short flight of steps between them, get packed with wall-to-wall people as the week wears on.

The Raj seems due for a new name again, the Cue Ball, perhaps, or Inn Off the Black? In the meantime its customers may find reassurance in the large handwritten poster pinned behind the bar counter. It bears an existential message: I Drink Therefore I Am.

Beers Available
John Smith's, Courage Directors, Carlsberg, Holsten, Budweiser, Foster's, Becks

Nearest Tube Station
Holland Park

· THE RAT AND PARROT ·

24 Tavistock Street, Covent Garden, WC2   **497 2796**
'Loud music and lager'

There are a number of Rat and Parrots. There's a rather rakish one in Kensington Church Street, a lively one in Putney High Street, a smart one in Earls Court Road and others in West End Lane, Parkway, Queensway and Park Street, Croydon. This one is the noisy, boozy one in Covent Garden.

To look at it now you'd think it had always been a pub, but actually it found its true vocation late in life. For its first 100 or so years this Rat and Parrot was part of the old fruit and veg market, a long, narrow warehouse crammed with cut flowers, open at Tavistock Street at one end and Exeter Street at the other. Latterly Joe Allens has been underneath.

Chef and Brewer made it into a pub in the late 1980s and there's still quite a lot of the warehouse left. The stout wooden floor, the heavy double doors, the black metal windows and the obligatory warehouse ramp could hardly be improved upon Rat and Parrotwise...

The week starts quietly in Tavistock Street as a rule but it rapidly gains momentum and is soon rocketing towards Friday, THE day of the Rat and Parrot week. On Friday nights the place heaves with people, all the seating removed, impatient queues outside, strong men at the door and music at full blast.

Young members of the scrum have two things in mind, to reach the bar and to meet the immediate just-glimpsed object of their desire. Most manage these feats repeatedly. The drink is bottled lager and the new landlord Tony

Open
All Week
Hours
11.00–23.00 Mon–Sat
(12.00–22.30 Sun)
Credit Cards
All major cards accepted
Bar Food Available
11.00 onwards
Mon–Sat
(12.00 onwards Sun)
Special Features
Wheelchair Access
(but not lavatory)
Beers Available
Theakston, Courage Best, Courage Directors, John Smith's, Holsten Export, Foster's, Kronenbourg, Gillespie's

Nearest Tube Station
Covent Garden

Jackson likes to see his customers enjoying themselves. 'It is the best party atmosphere in Covent Garden,' he says.

There's food at lunchtime, mainly Tex-Mex these days, but people don't go there to eat. Concept is the buzz-word in brewery circles at the moment, pubs have to have a concept. The Rat and Parrot concept in Covent Garden seems to be right on target. Loud music and lager.

·THE RED LION·

Crown Passage, SW1   **930 4141**

'The Red Lion remembers Charles I but knew Charles II better'

Open
Mon–Sat

Hours
11.00–23.00
(11.00–16.00 Sat)
Closed Bank Holidays

Credit Cards
Visa, Access

Bar and Restaurant Food Available
12.00–14.30

Special Features
Wheelchair Access (but not lavatory)
Tables outside seat 8
Private Room seats 25

Beers Available
London Pride, Ruddles County, John Smith's, Webster's, Kronenbourg, Carlsberg, Foster's, Guinness

Nearest Tube Station
Green Park

Crown Passage is a narrow alley just opposite St James's Palace. It is lined with useful little shops. Some go up it for the ironmonger or the cobbler, others use it as a short cut from Pall Mall to King Street. Quite a few never get past the Red Lion.

This tiny black timber-fronted pub with its leaded-glass windows, hanging baskets and antique lanterns looks too picturesque to be true but it is every bit as old as it seems. It has been there for more than 400 years, has the second oldest beer licence in London and is still very much in business.

The small, panelled bar is open all day and fills up quickly at lunchtime and again when people finish work. There is a small pleasant room upstairs that serves good plain pub food and on the last Saturday of every January the pub is packed with splendidly attired Cavaliers. They come together to mark the execution of their hero, King Charles I, on 30 January 1649.

The Red Lion remembers this well but it knew King Charles II better. He lived in St James's Palace over the road and his lively mistress Nell Gwyn lived round the corner at 79 Pall Mall. Some discretion seemed appropriate so Nell would slip into the Red Lion, go down the cellar steps and through a tunnel. At the other end the King would be waiting. Is it true? Unromantic surveyors doubt it. They have had a good poke around the cellar and there's no tunnel, they say.

THE RATS WERE FIRST NOTICED DURING THE GREAT PLAGUE

·THE RED LION·

Duke of York Street, SW1   **930 2130**
'A small Victorian gin palace of a most superior kind'

This is the most glittering of Red Lions. On all sides brilliant-cut and bevelled glass flashes and sparkles. It is a real star, a small Victorian gin palace of a most superior kind, almost totally unspoiled. 'Uncommonly well preserved,' wrote Sir Nikolaus Pevsner. That was high praise from him.

Did I mention it was small? It is small. There is just 300 square feet of it, not a lot. In summer it spills onto the pavement but the rest of the year sees Londoners reverting to one of their most profoundly held beliefs: there's always room for one more inside.

Mr Michael Browne who has run the pub for ten years likes to see it really full. He will tell you that he sells more beer per square foot than any other pub in Piccadilly.

In its bohemian past Jermyn Street flower girls would offer their services for 2d a time in the private bar. The Red Lion, robbed of its private bar, is the height of respectability these days and you see unexpected people pushing through the crush. Clint Eastwood seems to feel at home here, Andrew Lloyd Webber too. Mr Lloyd Webber is said to like it because there is never any music of any sort.

You can eat here too. Well, you can get a sandwich – oh, and home-made fish and chips on Fridays and Saturdays.

Open
Mon–Sat
Hours
12.00–23.00
Closed Bank Holidays
Credit Cards
None
Bar Food Available
12.00–14.30
Special Features
Wheelchair Access
Beers Available
Tetley, Burton, Nicholson's, Alsop Stout
Nearest Tube Station
Green Park

·THE RED LION·

318 High Street, Brentford   **0181-560 6181**
'The pub doesn't open at all during the day'

In 1967 the Red Lion, Brentford, was just two years old, not just a new pub, a new kind of pub. The *Evening Standard* at the time described it as a socko, roll-em-in-the-aisles, top-of-the-pops fun palace and most controversially announced that this was its first-ever Pub of the Year.

It divided the judges like nothing has since. We had seen some lovely old pubs and here was this young, noisy, uppity pub where you could hardly move and couldn't hear yourself speak. There were two live bands every night, country and western in one bar, rock 'n' roll in another, and the cocktail bar upstairs linked to the saloon bar by closed-circuit television. And that wasn't all. 'When groups weren't playing,' I wrote in surprised tones, 'gramophone records were.'

Then 26 years passed and I went back.

Graffiti on the cement rendering. Heavy curtains drawn

Open
All Week
Hours
18.00–late Mon–Sat
(12.00–22.30 Sun)
Beers Available
London Pride, Chiswick, draught and bottled lagers, Heineken, Tennent's, Carling, Guinness Cider: Strongbow
Nearest BR Station
Brentford

all day. Posters stuck in every pane of glass advertising the bands that would be playing that week. The pub, I was told, didn't open at all during the day. It didn't bother with food either. The only remaining bar opened at 6.30 pm. The music room opened at 9.00 pm and the bands were on till late.

That was last year. Another year passed and I went back again. Someone's been tidying it up a bit, the outside has been repainted and I rather think the windows may have been cleaned. The curtains are still drawn all day but a different set of names is trailed behind the bar counter: Luther Alison, Steve Simpson, Barrance Whitfield, Limehouse Lizzie.

'This is the best,' breathes a girl drinking lager at the bar. It opens at 6.00 pm now and the music room opens at 8.00. She'll be there till late.

·THE RED LION·

48 Parliament Street, SW1 **930 5826**

'A glass of the Genuine Stunning if you please'

Open
All Week

Hours
11.00–23.00
(12.00–22.30 Sun)
Closed Christmas Day

Credit Cards
All major cards except AmEx and Diner's Club

Food Available
Bar 11.00–15.00
Restaurant 12.00–14.45

Special Features
Wheelchair Access (but not lavatory)
Tables outside seat 70
Private Room seats 35

Beers Available
Tapsters Choice, Tetley, Burton, Eldridge Pope Best Bitter, Carlsberg, Lowenbrau, Castlemaine, Oranjeboom

Nearest Tube Station
Westminster

Of all the Red Lions this one lies nearest to the corridors of power. Around it are great ministries of state. Across the road is the Prime Minister. Round the corner are the Houses of Parliament themselves. This is the MPs' pub, the one they nip into before some brisk legislating.

It is a very handsome pub indeed, Eclectic Flemish Baroque as you can see, a Grade II listed building, a very classy pub and historical, my goodness. The original Red Lion was built on this site in 1733, a similar pub actually, nervously visited by Charles Dickens when he was only 11. The adventure appears in David Copperfield: 'What is your best – your VERY best – ale a glass?' 'Twopence-halfpenny,' says the landlord, 'is the price of the Genuine stunning ale.' 'Then,' says I, producing the money, 'just draw me a glass of the Genuine Stunning if you please…'

They pulled this Red Lion down in 1899 during the great pub boom and built a new one, this one, in its place, the very latest in pubs, no cost spared. It has changed hardly at all since then. Most of the original fittings are still in place and it's pretty well full all day, the bar walls covered in drawings, cartoons and photographs of famous politicians.

There's a nice old-fashioned dining room upstairs with old-fashioned English food and a comfortable cellar bar. It was liked by demonstrating miners and the licensee liked them right back. 'Top-quality customers,' he says. The pit banners they have presented to the pub are now part of its history.

· THE RED LION ·

1 Waverton Street, W1 **499 1307**

'Quite unspoiled,' people say. That's not it

There's a proud pride of Red Lions in London, at least 24 of them, but socially this is surely the one that has done best. It is the Mayfair Red Lion and it is very smart these days. To see it now with its quiet restaurant, its old prints, its panelled walls and its well-heeled regulars, it is hard to imagine its ragged-trousered beginnings.

In those days – it is the 17th century we are talking about now – it stood on a muddy unmade road just by the boundary of Chesterfield House, lordly seat of the Earls of Chesterfield. Its customers were toughs from the notorious May Fair, street traders from Shepherds Market, grooms from the big house. Then the workmen building Berkeley Square, Hill Street and Chorley Street made it their own. That was a step up all right and, as the exclusive Mayfair of the 19th century took shape, it was the great army of domestic servants that kept the place going.

Now, of course, the basements they worked in and the attics they slept in are exclusive Mayfair apartments and it is the occupants of these who fill today's totally gentrified Red Lion with a hum of quiet conversation.

It is a charming pub the year round. In winter the seats to get are the winged settles near the fire, in summer people crowd the forecourt, and the food is a cut above at any time. How lucky to have such a local. 'Quite unspoiled,' people say. That's not it. Vastly improved is what it is. Chesterfield House, though, is nowhere to be seen. They pulled it down in 1937.

Open
All Week

Hours
11.00–23.00 Mon–Fri;
12.00–15.00 and
18.00–23.00 Sat;
(12.00–15.00 and
19.00–22.30 Sun)
Closed Christmas Day,
Boxing Day

Credit Cards
All major cards accepted

Bar and Restaurant Food Available
12.00–22.00
(restaurant closed Sat lunch)

Special Features
Wheelchair Access

Beers Available
Theakston XB,
Gillespies, Greene King
IPA, Courage Directors,
Wadworth, Foster's,
Kronenbourg, Guinness,
Coors

Nearest Tube Station
Green Park

· THE RING ·

72 Blackfriars Road, SE1 **928 2589**

'The talk is all of boxing, then and now'

Photographs of boxers, chins in, fists up, cover the walls of this small, serious boxers' pub – Bombadier Billy Wells, Seaman Tommy Watson, the great Tommy Farr. Ben Ford waves from the train at Waterloo. Jack Doyle, boxer, singer, movie star, shakes hands with Len Harvey, and in the bar old fighters gather and the talk is all of boxing then and boxing now.

The Ring is run by Neville Axford, one-time army champion, 25 professional fights and still in the game. He's a coach now with young boxers in training. They work in the gym over the bar, no frills up there, a ring, some well-used

Open
All Week

Hours
11.00–23.00 Mon–Fri;
11.00–15.00 and
19.00–23.00 Sat;
(12.00–22.00 Sun)

Credit Cards
None

Bar Food Available
11.00–15.00

Special Features
Wheelchair Access
(but not lavatory)

Beers Available
Tetley, Burtons, Castlemaine, Skol, Lowenbrau, Guinness

Nearest BR Station
Waterloo

punchbags and young hopefuls toiling and pummelling.

From the gym windows you can see the corner of the crossroads where the Blackfriars Ring once stood. 'London's Premier Arena' said the posters, 'Turbulent Centre of Boxing' said the papers of the day.

It was run for 25 years by Bella Burge, the world's only woman boxing promoter, but it was reduced to rubble in an air raid in 1940 and after the war an office block, Orbit House, replaced it.

It has been useful. The British Library keeps its Oriental and India Office collections there. But it's not the same, somehow.

·The Rising Sun·

Open
All Week

Hours
11.30–23.00
(12.00–22.30 Sun)
Closed Christmas Day, Boxing Day

Credit Cards
Visa, Access

Bar Food Available
12.00–14.30

Special Features
No-smoking Area
Wheelchair Access (but not lavatory)
Private Room seats 50

Beers Available
All Sam Smith variants, Taddy Porter Stout, Oatmeal Stout, Natural Lager, Old Brewery Bitter, Museum Ale

Nearest Tube Station
St Paul's

38 Cloth Fair, EC1   **726 6671**
'A rapscallionly youth'

This old Smithfield pub used to be picturesque to the point of almost falling over. Now it is very chipper, having been giving a thorough going-over by Samuel Smith, the Yorkshire brewer.

The general feeling in the bar is now modishly Victorian, beefed up with non-stop music and flashing fruit machines. There is a quieter room above where you can have lunch. You feel you could almost touch St-Bartholomew-the-Great, the oldest church in the City outside the Tower, from the upstairs windows.

The Rising Sun had a rapscallionly youth with body-snatchers slipping laudanum into drinks at the bar. This would not be allowed today. Nothing is allowed to spoil Sam Smith's good beer.

·The Rising Sun·

Open
All Week

Hours
11.00–23.00
(12.00–22.30 Sun)
Closed Christmas Day, Boxing Day, New Year's Day

Credit Cards
Mastercard, Visa, AmEx, Eurocard

Bar Food Available
12.00–22.00

Special Features

46 Tottenham Court Road, W1   **636 6530**
'A masterpiece rescued'

Next time you are in Tottenham Court Road, you are bound to be there sometime, have a look at the Rising Sun. It is just getting over a rather unhappy experience but it is, as you will see, a most remarkable pub.

It was designed by Treadwell and Martin, Victorian architects who are increasingly admired, and the Rising Sun is said to be their masterpiece. The style is elaborate art-nouveau Gothic and architectural critics speak with admiration of its delicate mouldings, its heraldic beasts and cupids' heads, its rising suns, its decorative gables and elegant bartizans.

A bartizan is an overhanging turret. The Rising Sun had two, still has one.

In the early Eighties the owners of the day made what seems to be a bizarre decision. They changed its name to the Presley, as in Elvis, lowered the ceiling by about two yards, anointed the walls with pictures of Elvis and turned it into a rock 'n' roll bozo. The next owner, Scottish and Newcastle, speedily put this eccentric interlude behind it and closed the Presley for two months. When it reopened it was the Rising Sun again.

Or almost. Treadwell and Martin would be pleased with the outside, carefully restored and painted cream, but very little was left of the once luxuriant Victorian fittings inside, and the designers started more or less from scratch. It is what is described as Ale House now, which means bare boards and a generous roster of real ales and speedy pies.

So there is good news from this generally ill-favoured thoroughfare. Outside, a minor masterpiece rescued. Inside, well, at least the ceiling is back where it belongs.

· THE RIVER RAT ·

2 Lombard Road, SW11   **978 4161**
'Peaceable times'

London has a new hobby. Helispotting. Helispotters spot helicopters and cross their numbers off in a little book. To spot helispotters helispotting you could not do better than this pleasant new riverside pub. With Battersea Heliport so near, the terrace of the River Rat is a helispotter heaven.

It is nice to be able to report such peaceable times at the River Rat. Not long ago it was the Chandler and far from peaceable, which surprised people at the time. It was such a pleasant-looking pub and it had a great site. It was on Battersea's new river walk and you looked across the river to Chelsea Harbour and the marina. It opened in December 1988 with the highest hopes.

Well they say that new pubs take time to settle down, but things went wrong at the Chandler almost from the start and got worse. In 1993 the brewers closed it for almost a whole year.

Then Dennis and Denise Timms who have the Water Rats in Chelsea took it over. It got a new name and a new personality. Out went the pool table and the pinball machines, in came peaceable wooden tables, upholstered chairs, friendly barrels to sit round in the bar and a kitchen that stayed open all day. In, too, came a new manager, their son Gavin. Gavin Timms is 6' 4" and 18 stone.

Wheelchair Access
(but not lavatory)
Tables outside seat 30

Beers Available
Theakston Best,
Theakston XB,
Theakston Old Peculier,
Courage Best, Courage
Directors, Gillespie's,
Holsten, Carlsberg

Nearest Tube Stations
Tottenham Court Road,
Goodge Street

Open
All Week

Hours
11.00–23.00
(12.00–22.30 Sun)
Closed Christmas Day,
Boxing Day

Credit Cards
Visa, Mastercard

Bar Food Available
12.00–22.30

Special Features
Wheelchair Access
Tables outside
seat 120

Beers Available
Bass, London Pride,
Wadworth 6X,
Staropramen, Grolsch,
Carling Black Label,
Caffrey's, Guinness;
Cider: Dry Blackthorn

Nearest Tube Station
Clapham Junction

·THE ROBERT BROWNING·

15 Clifton Road, W9 **286 2732**

'Would this wine had washed all over that body of yours'

Open
All Week

Hours
11.00–23.00
(12.00–22.30 Sun)
Closed Boxing Day,
New Year's Day

Credit Cards
None

Bar Food Available
12.00–14.30 and
17.30–21.00

Special Features
Wheelchair Access
(but not lavatory)
Tables outside seat 60
Private Room seats 90

Beers Available
Old Brewery Bitter,
Ayingerbrau

Nearest Tube Station
Warwick Avenue

On one of his sorties from his Yorkshire stronghold seven years ago Sam Smith bagged a down-at-heel Victorian pub called the Eagle. He refurbished it from top to toe as he does and here it is now, a glossy Sam Smith pub called the Robert Browning. Locals still call it the Eagle.

As a young man Browning lived briefly nearby, overlooking the canal, and he would have been astonished to hear that pictures of him and his beloved would one day cover the upstairs bar of the boisterous new pub down the way, not to mention his passionate love letters and some of the passionate poems he wrote for her. His marriage certificate too. 'Age: of full age. Rank or Profession: Gentleman.'

It is a nice pub, this reborn Robert Browning. The main bar downstairs is where the serious drinking is, but the first-floor bar is where I see Robert and Elizabeth, a comfortable Victorian sitting room with long windows, button-backed leather sofas, mahogany tables, lamps, mirrors, portraits. He wrote:

There you stand
Warm too and white too;
Would this wine
Had washed all over that body of yours
Ere I drank it.

Is this what goes on at the Robert Browning?

·THE ROSE AND CROWN·

55 High Street, Wimbledon Village, SW19 **0181-947 4713**

'A notoriously dissipated poet'

Open
All Week

Hours
11.00–23.00
(12.00–22.30 Sun)

Credit Cards
None

Bar Food Available
12.00–14.30 and
17.30–22.00 Mon–Sat;
(phone pub for Sunday
opening hours)

Special Features
No-smoking Area
Wheelchair Access
Beer Garden seats 100

The Rose and Crown in Wimbledon Village is one of south London's great pubs. The *Evening Standard* Pub of the Year judges thought so and gave it the crown in 1970.

It is an old pub; 1640 is old. Charles I still had his throne and his head in 1640. It is as pretty a pub as you could hope to find, a beautiful house of old brick, lovely in its proportions inside and out. It keeps its powerful appeal for generations. In its days as a coaching inn – the London coach began and finished here – it was as popular as it is now.

Inside are old maps of Wimbledon, prints of 18th-century London and a complete set of Hogarth's 'Idle Prentice'. They add to the pub's historical feel, but nothing does this more than the benign, ghostly presence of its two most famous regulars.

Leigh Hunt and Swinburne were both leading figures in Bohemian London. Swinburne was actually famous. He was not only a poet but a notoriously dissipated poet. Such was the life he led, it was whispered, that his health had broken down. That is why he lodged at 2 The Pines, Putney, and walked across heath and common to the Rose and Crown.

Sightseers started gathering at the Rose and Crown to see the dying poet, a predicament as familiar then as now. He found a satisfactory solution. He simply moved his chair upstairs. The chair is still upstairs, though his table continues to do service in the bar. He lived to 72.

The bar goes on drawing crowds. It is not the stage coaches for London or celebs walking from Putney. It is, I can only suppose, the atmosphere, the congeniality and the beer.

There is a small no-smoking area in the Rose and Crown now, a light, plain lounge and a buttery serving hot and cold food. At the back a conservatory leads to a little garden, paved, ivy-walled and thoroughly charming. Families recuperate here after constitutionals on the common, young lovers hopefully seek a quiet table, people read papers and chat. Poets, their health ruined by dissipation, may also take their chances.

Beers Available
Young's, Castlemaine, Tennent's Extra

Nearest Tube Station
Wimbledon

· THE ROSE OF YORK ·

Petersham Road, Richmond   0181-948 5867

'A view so beautiful it has been painted by Turner and Reynolds and thousands of times by the rest of us'

When Samuel Smith, the Yorkshire Brewers, set its cap on London its first pub was this one. It was an old cavalry barracks that had been made into a pub called Tudor Close, and Sam Smith really went to town on it. The Tudor fakery was stripped away, new cellars were excavated, and a team of craftsmen from Yorkshire worked on it for 16 months. The Rose of York emerged as from a chrysalis and almost at once became the *Evening Standard* Pub of the Year.

Fifteen years later it is still a most appealing country pub with its big comfortable bar, its good traditional food, its lovely sheltered courtyard and a view of Petersham Meadows and the bend in the Thames so beautiful it has been painted by Turner and Reynolds and thousands of times by the rest of us.

The Rose of York has been letting a few rooms for bed and breakfast as old inns used to. It now has nine bedrooms with en suite bathrooms. En suite bathrooms? You would have done well to get a bowl and a jug of hot water in the old inns of England.

Open
All Week

Hours
11.00–23.00
(12.00–22.30 Sun)
Closed Christmas Day, Boxing Day

Credit Cards
All major cards except AmEx

Bar Food Available
12.00–15.00 and
18.30–21.30
(12.00–15.30 Sun)
Set-price lunch Sun

Special Features
No-smoking Area
Wheelchair Access
Beer Garden seats 150

Beers Available
All Samuel Smith variants, including Old Brewery, Museum Ale, Ayingerbrau

Nearest Tube Station
Richmond

·THE ROUND HOUSE·

1 Garrick Street, W1   **836 9838**

'Not round. Elbow-shaped'

Open
All Week

Hours
11.00–23.00
(12.00–22.30 Sun)

Credit Cards
None

Bar Food Available
12.00–16.00

Special Features
Wheelchair Access
(but not lavatory)

Beers Available
Theakston Best,
Theakston Old Peculier,
Marston's Pedigree,
Younger's IPA, Leffe
Blond, Becks,
McEwans, Guinness

Nearest Tube Stations
Leicester Square,
Covent Garden

The Round House, the substantial Victorian pub on the corner of Garrick Street, had got distinctly rowdy, not to say rough. It can happen. So what do you do?

This is what Scottish and Newcastle did. Having bought the pub it closed it down, gave it an entirely new interior and reopened it as the first of its new real-ale houses. This meant a nice wooden floor, plain wooden furniture, eight draught ales on the handpumps and pies with puff pastry tops floating up from the kitchen. It also meant short shrift for troublesome customers. Troublesome customers weren't keen on any of this, particularly the short shrift, and agreeable new customers replaced them. How has business been lately? 'Tremendous,' says the new manager David McKinstry.

A potted history on the front has a theory about the name. For its first 75 years, it says, the pub was called Petters Hotel. It was then renamed the Round House because of its shape. But it isn't round, it's elbow-shaped. It should be called the Elbow.

·THE ROUND TABLE·

St Martin's Court, WC2   **836 6436**

'A doorman to discourage horsy and fighting men'

Open
All Week

Hours
11.00–23.00
(12.00–22.30 Sun)
Closed Christmas Day

Credit Cards
None

Bar Food Available
12.00–15.00 and
18.00–21.00

Special Features
Wheelchair Access
(but not lavatory)
Tables outside seat 30

Beers Available
Theakston, Theakston
Old Peculier, Youngers
IPA, Marston's
Pedigree, Bulmer's,
Belgian Trappist beers,
Becks, McEwans

Nearest Tube Station
Leicester Square

St Martin's Court, the little pedestrians-only cut between St Martin's Lane and Charing Cross Road, has old book shops, Sheekey's restaurant and oyster bar, the stage doors of the Albery and Wyndham's and this extremely pleasant Victorian pub.

There is a history of it on the outside wall, rather rumbustious, apparently. These parts were the resort of 'horsy and fighting men' and prize fights were arranged in local taverns. The original Round Table put up the American champion John C Heenan to contest the belt with the valiant Tom Sayers. It doesn't say who won.

Those days finished with the Queensberry Rules, and anyway the Round Table was rebuilt in 1877 and with theatres on all sides it became more theatrical than sporting. So it is today – a civil, good-looking pub with downstairs and upstairs bars, both very busy at times.

It has become known for its cask ales. Big blackboards have lists of the guest beers coming soon, and serious beer drinkers can have two-pint or four-pint jugs. It is a reasonable place to eat too. Good pies.

·The Running Footman·

5 Charles Street, W1 **499 2988**

'Showing what fine fellows their masters were'

This interesting Mayfair pub, properly called I Am The Only Running Footman, commemorates a job no longer on offer in the Job Centres of the nation.

In the 18th century seriously grand persons employed footmen to run before their carriages, lighting the way, paying tolls, preventing collisions and generally showing what fine fellows their masters were. The running footmen, and indeed footmen of all kinds, met in this old Mayfair pub.

It was originally the Running Horse but it was renamed by the fourth Duke of Queensbury, the one they called Old Q. He was a great swell, infamous, wrote his biographer, for his shameless debaucheries. A footman always ran ahead of his carriage.

The new name has served the pub well for 200 years and it still brings people in. The pub itself is totally changed. It was almost entirely rebuilt in the 1930s but it looks as old as you could wish with its dark panelling and bottle-glass windows. Tourists love it.

The pub sign shows a running footman, of course. He seems most unsuitably dressed. He wears a powdered wig, a feathered hat, knee breeches and buckled shoes. The running footman in the painting inside is even more encumbered. He carries a tall cane topped with a silver ball containing a little something to keep him going as he lopes along.

Open
All Week
Hours
11.30–23.00 Mon–Fri;
18.00–23.00 Sat;
(12.00–22.30 Sun)
Closed Bank Holidays
Credit Cards
All major cards accepted
Restaurant Food Available
11.00–15.00 and 18.00–21.30 Mon–Fri;
18.00–21.30 Sat;
(19.00–21.30 Sun)
Special Features
Wheelchair Access (but not lavatory)
Tables outside seat 20
Private Room seats 20
Beers Available
Courage Best, Courage Directors, John Smith's, Theakston Best, Foster's, Kronenbourg, Holsten, Budweiser, Guinness
Nearest Tube Station
Green Park

·The Rutland·

Lower Mall, W6 **0181-748 5586**

'Oriel College, Oxford, bags the balcony'

The Rutland, a big lively pub on Hammersmith's riverside, was an early recruit to the olde English alehouse look. It has been bare boards and ancient timbers there for some years. The regulars like it, so do tourists.

It has a great position with a double rank of tables along the river wall. The sun has just to shine for ten minutes and every table is occupied. This is just half way along the course, and the crowds are prodigious. Oriel College, Oxford, bags the wide balcony on the first floor, a big marquee goes up at the side and half London seems to be there waving, cheering and trying to drink the Rutland dry.

The coat of arms on the side wall, motto *Pour Y Parvenir* (In Order to Accomplish), is the Duke of Rutland's. There are clearer messages.

Open
All Week
Hours
11.00–23.00
(12.00–22.30 Sun)
Closed Christmas Day
Credit Cards
Access, Visa
Bar Food Available
All Day
Special Features
No-smoking Area
Wheelchair Access
Beer Garden
Beers Available
Theakston Best,
Theakston XB, Courage Directors, John Smith's
Nearest Tube Station
Hammersmith

175

· THE SALISBURY ·

90 St Martin's Lane, WC2   **836 5863**

'Most people accept that in The Salisbury you stand'

Open
All Week
Hours
11.00–23.00
(12.00–22.30 Sun)
Credit Cards
All major cards accepted
Bar Food Available
12.00–19.30
Special Features
No-smoking Area
Wheelchair Access
(but not lavatory)
Tables outside seat 32
Private Room seats 26
Beers Available
Theakston, Tetley, Burton Ale, Dorchester, Carlsberg, Castlemaine, Lowenbrau
Nearest Tube Station
Leicester Square

The Salisbury is sometimes said to be the most beautifully preserved Victorian public house in London. It has lovely windows, brilliant-cut, acid-etched, delicately engraved, and Nikolaus Pevsner admired its Lincrusta ceiling, the art-nouveau bronze figures of alluring maidens, the flower stalks and flowers out of which electric bulbs grew.

You have to go early to get a proper look at this famous pub as it is packed to the doors a lot of the time. Every evening and often lunchtimes doormen check who comes in and on occasion who goes out, an anti-riff-raff move apparently. Well you can't get *everyone* in.

The surprising thing is that anyone can get a drink at all in a pub so popular and so populated. In the thick of the crush, however, with theatre-goers talking ten to the dozen all round you, a path to the bar mysteriously opens before you when the need is greatest.

Some very patient customers actually find seats. Curved banquettes form shallow niches with copper-topped tables, one of the bronze figures Pevsner liked between each, but most people accept that in the Salisbury you stand. There is a rather dull room at the far end, often partitioned off for private parties, and an excellent little theatre bar with a door onto St Martin's Court. It is easier to get a seat in these.

The Salisbury has had various owners since the third Marquess of Salisbury sold the lease in 1892. He was usually Prime Minister, but not then actually. It is his face on the pub's inn sign. It is currently owned by Scottish and Newcastle who got it and 1,653 other pubs when it did the famous deal with Chef and Brewer. This means you can get Newcastle Brown Ale in the Salisbury now, something no one ever thought they would live to see.

· THE SALUTATION INN ·

154 King Street, W6   **0181-748 2365**

'The Queen Mother pulled a few pints'

Open
All Week
Hours
11.00–23.00
(phone pub for Sunday opening hours)
Credit Cards
None
Bar Food Available
12.00–14.00

Walk far enough along King Street in Hammersmith and you will come to this agreeable pub. Old coaching inn, rebuilt 1909, listed building. Go in. I think it will surprise you.

First the bar, all polished and gleaming, an excellent bar, and the home-cooked meals are good, and I expect you'll like the conservatory. What is so unexpected, though, lies beyond.

It is a beautiful walled garden, colourful, tranquil, the perfect place for a quiet bosky drink on a warm afternoon away from the workaday reality of Hammersmith. It has earned the Salutation Inn umpteen accolades. It has been Fuller's Garden of the Year seven times and has won London in Bloom contests time and again. So much admired is this garden that the Queen Mother, patron of the Horticultural Society, came to see it in 1989, congratulated everyone in sight and pulled a few pints.

A nice pub with a lovely garden. If you work in King Street or live nearby what luck.

Special Features
Wheelchair Access
Beer Garden seats 40
Beers Available
All Fuller's variants
Nearest Tube Stations
Ravenscourt Park, Hammersmith

· THE SCARSDALE ·

23a Edwardes Square, W8   **937 1811**

'The pub that might have been Napoleon's local'

The Scarsdale is one of London's most admired pubs – if there is an award going it gets it. It has been the *Evening Standard* Pub of the Year, of course. It is a lovely pub.

You find it in Edwardes Square in Kensington, a French Arcadia, said the poet Leigh Hunt, who lived at No 32. The square was built in 1812 by a speculative French builder, and people whispered that it was for officers of Napoleon's army when they arrived. Happily they didn't and the pub that might have been Napoleon's local settled down to long peaceful years in this quiet and increasingly exclusive backwater.

People warm to the Scarsdale as soon as they see it. As season follows season its impeccable Georgian façade is covered in flowers and greenery, watered all night when necessary by an ingenious arrangement devised by the landlord, Fred Hill. It is just as attractive inside with high ceilings, a rich gleam of mahogany and brass, wooden fans and the original etched glass.

It is all traditional cask beers here, though, this being Edwardes Square, there is a brisk gin and tonic trade. They do well with wine too, and lunchtimes are busy with steaks, chops and burgers from a grill at the far end. There's no music of any sort but some years ago two fruit machines slipped in somehow. They are hidden away round a corner at the back.

The Scarsdale has no more devoted fan than the landlord. Fred Hill actually left it in 1990 to run other pubs but five years later he was back. He says with conviction that he intends to stay at home now.

Open
All Week
Hours
12.00–23.00
(12.00–22.30 Sun)
Credit Cards
Access, Visa
Bar Food Available
12.00–14.30 and
18.15–21.30
(12.00–14.00 and
19.00–22.00 Sun)
Special Features
Tables outside seat 30
Beers Available
John Smith's, Courage Directors, Ruddles Best, Theakston, Foster's, Holsten, Carlsberg, Guinness
Nearest Tube Stations
High Street Kensington, Earls Court

· SCRUFFY MURPHY'S ·

15 Denman Street, W1 **437 1540**

'Not scruffy in the least'

Open
All Week
Hours
11.30–23.00
(12.00–22.30 Sun)
Closed Christmas Day,
Boxing Day
Credit Cards
All major cards accepted
Bar Food Available
11.30–16.00 full Irish Food menu, also available for functions
Special Features
Private Room
Live Music on key Irish days – St Patrick's Day and
the rest
Beers Available
Kilkenny Ale, Guinness, Carlsberg Pilsner, Carlsberg Export, full range of Irish whiskeys and Irish products
Nearest Tube Station
Piccadilly

Pubs change. This one, next door to the Piccadilly Theatre and a full minute's walk from Piccadilly Circus, was the Queen's Head one day, Scruffy Murphy's the next, or so it seemed. It was a great surprise for Denman Street so it was.

There is a clutch of Scruffy Murphy's in London now, all opened by Taylor Walker in the past few months to gee up old pubs that were marking time. One occupies the premises of the King and Keys in Fleet Street, once the *Daily Telegraph* pub, famous in its day. Another has taken over the Gunter's Arms in Chelsea, a fourth the Griffin in Whetstone. If these succeed more will follow.

The idea is to give London some typical Dublin bars, a long-felt want, some think. Such, apparently, are these. They are as alike as peas in a pod. Each has an old delivery bike firmly chained to the front, an Irish greeting set in the tiles of the lobby – *slainte*, it says, Irish for cheers – and what appears to be an old Irish dresser behind the counter.

They are all as Irish as can be, a choice of draught Guinness (brewed in Park Royal) and Kilkenny bitter (brewed in Kilkenny) and any number of Irish whiskeys. The managers are Irish, as too are the bar staff, the music and the food – Bantry Bay mussels, Dublin Coddle, Irish stew and the like.

Lots of the customers are Irish too. They pack in and talk ten to the dozen with the cheerful bounce of Irish fiddles and drums in the background, sometimes recorded, sometimes live.

Tom Kieley, the one-time Irish civil servant who is now landlord in Denman Street, is pleased with all he surveys. 'No fruit machines,' he says, 'no cigarette machines, no condom machines in the loo. They wanted to put in a condom machine, but I explained that in Ireland they're not legal.'

This Scruffy Murphy's, I should mention, is not scruffy in the least. Nor, I believe, are the others.

·THE SEKFORDE ARMS·

34 Sekforde Street, EC1　　　　　　　　　**253 3251**

'A real village pub'

This is a pleasant street-corner local in Clerkenwell, a bit of London that has had more than its share of ups and downs. It is having a distinct up at the moment. The surrounding streets have never seemed more prosperous, and the Sekforde wears a confident air with window boxes and fresh paint and new tables on the pavement.

It is a real village pub and it plays a central part in local life. The local Rotarians meet in the first-floor restaurant and the staff and students from the City University seek daily inspiration in its comfortable bar.

There is a Sekforde Arms in the little Suffolk town of Woodbridge too. Thomas Sekforde, a 16th-century worthy, was a lawyer there, then retired to Clerkenwell. Many years later the two pubs, so many miles apart, quite independently took his name.

Open
All Week
Hours
11.00–23.00
(12.00–16.00 Sun)
Closed Bank Holidays
Credit Cards
All major cards accepted
Food Available
Bar 12.00–21.00
(12.00–16.00 Sun)
Restaurant
12.00–15.00
Special Features
Wheelchair Access (but not lavatory)
Private Room seats 38
Beers Available
Young's, Dirty Dick's, Labatts, Becks, Guinness, Beamish, Steinlager, Rolling Rock, Castlemaine, Tennent's Extra, Stella Artois, Lowenbrau
Nearest Tube Stations
Farringdon, Angel

·THE SEVEN STARS·

53 Carey Street, WC2　　　　　　　　　**242 8521**

'Heading for Carey Street?'

You're not doing too well? You're heading for Carey Street. This little back street is where the bankruptcy courts are, and many a man facing financial disaster has slipped into the Seven Stars to buck himself up a bit.

It is a charming little wooden-fronted old pub, one of the smallest in London, two small bars, a few tables and chairs, much used by lawyers. It has been there since 1602. John Crawley has had the lease for 12 years now. He allows no music or gaming machines and does all the cooking himself.

Open
Mon–Fri
Hours
11.00–21.30
Closed Bank Holidays
Credit Cards
None
Bar Food Available
11.00–19.00
Special Features
Wheelchair Access (but not lavatory)
Beers Available
Courage Best, Courage Directors, Foster's, Kronenbourg, Guinness, Beamish
Nearest Tube Stations
Chancery Lane, Holborn

· THE SHAKESPEARE'S HEAD ·

29 Great Marlborough Street, W1 734 2911

'As Tudor as you could wish'

Open
All Week
Hours
11.00–23.00
(12.00–22.30 Sun)
Credit Cards
Access, Visa, Mastercard
Food Available
All day
Special Features
Wheelchair Access (but not lavatory)
Tables outside seat 40
Beers Available
Directors, XB, John Smith's, Theakston Best, Foster's, Kronenbourg, Coors, Holsten Export, Guinness
Cider: Strongbow
Nearest Tube Station
Oxford Circus

There is something very appealing about this picturesque Tudor pub built in the 1920s with the figure of the Bard himself leaning thoughtfully from a little window and gazing down Carnaby Street. His poor hand is still missing. He lost it in the war.

The Shakespeare's Head had a thorough face-lift recently but is still as Tudor as you could wish and very keen on Shakespeare. There are quotes all round the bar. '*Et tu Brute?*' and, more to the point, 'We'll teach you to drink deep ere you depart.'

The Bard might well have approved of the dining room upstairs, a sombre, rather noble room where you can have a roast-beef dinner at a very moderate price. The good-humoured new manager can't understand why so few people do, and neither can I.

This is one of the pubs that English Heritage is currently thinking of listing.

· SHELLEY'S ·

10 Stafford Street, W1 493 0337

'Percy Bysshe? Or Fred?'

Open
Mon–Sat
Hours
11.00–23.00
Closed Bank Holidays
Credit Cards
Access, AmEx, Visa, Switch
Bar Food Available
12.00–15.00
Special Features
Wheelchair Access (but not lavatory)
Beers Available
Adnams Extra, Tetley, Brakspear, Kilkenny Ale, Lowenbrau, Castlemaine, Carlsberg
Nearest Tube Station
Green Park

This most tasteful and elegant public house is named, you might well suppose, after Percy Bysshe Shelley, poet and good egg. His likenesses are all over, also pictures of his wife, his holiday home, his tomb. Several of his poems are on the walls too; his portrait in oils hangs above the fireplace in the panelled doubles bar; and there he is, at his most romantic, on the inn sign outside.

He might have known the house. He did stay at Cooke's Hotel round the corner in Albermarle Street, indeed a letter he wrote from there hangs near the bar counter. It is an interesting letter about money and his great expectations. All the same I think Shelley's was named after Fred Shelley. You may laugh. You may think I'm making Fred Shelley up, but I promise you there was a Fred Shelley and he bought this pub in Stafford Street in 1862, 40 years after poor Percy Bysshe had drowned.

It was called the King John's Head in those days. It was still the King John's Head when someone called J Shelley assigned it to E H Barnes in 1888. By 1895, though, it had been upgraded to Shellcy's Hotel. So which Shelley was this? Percy Bysshe? Fred? J?

There has been many a change of owner since, the hotel bit has long since been dropped and Percy Bysshe has carried the day, the current owner, Nicholsons, is quite adamant about that. And anyway it is nice to have a pub named after a poet, and such a poet.

This one is very pleasant with its basement wine bar, its busy Victorian bar and its handsome function room upstairs. Sir Nikolaus Pevsner included it in his great book on London. He called it 'a pub in a thoroughly debased style'. Sir Nikolaus! Language!

·THE SHERLOCK HOLMES·

10–11 Northumberland Street, WC2   **930 2644**

'The most-photographed pub in London'

Sherlock Holmes has us in thrall. The stories sell round the world. They are tirelessly staged, filmed and televised, and members of far-flung Sherlock Holmes societies arrive all summer to pay tribute to the great man.

They all end up with notebooks and cameras at the Sherlock Holmes in Northumberland Street to find the bar filled with other Sherlock Holmes tours, locals on Sherlock Holmes walks and television crews interviewing everyone, filming everything. Robert Davie, the licensee, and his family are no longer surprised to be woken at 3.00 am by someone in the street taking pictures. 'This must be the most photographed pub in London,' he says.

The Sherlock Holmes is a smartly turned out pub in the modern Victorian style with a comfortable restaurant, a hidden roof garden and a unique tourist attraction: Holmes' study as it appeared one foggy night in *The Empty House*, every item supplied by the Conan Doyle family. There it is, the cosy room and Holmes by the window shot through the head by the vile Col Moran. See the hole the bullet made. But of course Holmes had foreseen it all. Moran had shot a mannequin. He was no match for Holmes.

This tableau was one of the big hits of the Festival of Britain in 1950 and subsequently toured America. Then, happily, Whitbread's bought it and installed it in its pub where it has been much enjoyed by students of Holmes' law ever since. The smallest change and they are on it like a shot.

In Sir Arthur Conan Doyle's day the pub was part of the Northumberland Hotel. He liked it and put it into *The Hound of the Baskervilles*. He also had Holmes' and Watson use the Turkish Bath next door. This is now a branch of Barclays Bank.

Open
All Week
Hours
11.00–23.00
(12.00–22.30 Sun)
Closed Christmas Day,
Boxing Day
Credit Cards
All major cards accepted
Food Available
Bar 12.00–22.30
Restaurant
12.00–15.00 and
17.30–10.45
Special Features
No-smoking Area
Wheelchair Access
(but not lavatory)
Tables outside seat 30
Beers Available
Sherlock Holmes Ale,
Boddingtons, Flowers
Original, Brakspear,
Murphy's, Stella Artois,
Heineken
Nearest Tube Station
Embankment

The Northumberland Hotel did not survive the 1920s. Part of it – this part – then became the Northumberland Arms and in 1957 changed its name again. Calling it the Sherlock Holmes was a brilliant stroke. It ensured customers in droves.

·THE SHIP·

10 Thames Bank, SW14 **0181-876 1439**

'The day of days in Mortlake'

From the saloon bar of the Ship at Mortlake you get a fine view of a yellow pole sticking out of the river. This is the finishing post for the Oxford and Cambridge Boat Race and for one moment on boat race day it becomes the most important post sticking out of any river anywhere.

Boat race day is when it all happens at the Ship. By the time it opens its doors there's a wall of people on both sides of the river and right across Chiswick bridge and the pub is under siege. Boat race watchers get through a lake of lager and an ocean of bitter and keep a team of cooks working flat out at the barbecue long after the two crews have collapsed over their oars.

The Ship closes early that night and a huge clear up begins. By the time everyone gets to bed the Ship is ship-shape again. The staff, though, is ready to bale out. 'We all need a holiday after boat race day,' says David Morgan the manager.

The Ship is a handsome pub on the Surrey side of the river with deep bay windows and balustrading right round the eaves. It is painted cream and has a substantial bar, a patio that can seat 300 and a garden with rabbits and a slide and a bouncy castle for children. 'We like to think this is a family pub,' says Morgan.

The Ship has plenty of big occasions through the year. The river overflows. Summer pig roasts draw the crowds. There's St Patrick's Day with Irish session musicians and Burns Night with the haggis, the ode to the haggis and David Morgan from Limerick in a kilt. There are ale festivals and quiz nights. 'Anything to celebrate we celebrate it,' says Morgan.

But it's the boat race that has made the Ship famous, the boat race that gets the adrenaline going. Two girls skinny-dipped right in front of the pub last time. It is the day of days in Mortlake.

Open
All Week

Hours
11.00–23.00
(12.00–22.30 Sun)

Credit Cards
Mastercard, Visa, AmEx

Bar Food Available
12.00–14.30 and
18.00–21.30
(12.00–21.30 Sun)

Special Features
Wheelchair Access
Beer Garden seats 100
Private Room seats 20

Beers Available
Courage Directors,
Old Speckled Hen,
Marston's Pedigree,
Theakston Old Peculier,
Young's Special,
Ruddles County,
Foster's, Carlsberg,
Budweiser, Holsten

Nearest BR Station
Mortlake

· THE SHIP INN ·

41 Jews Row, SW18 **0181-870 9667**

'Parachute in'

The one problem presented by this remarkable pub is finding it. This is not easy. It is set back from the river, hemmed in by a cement works, a bus depot and a car park, and no one lives in Jews Row or has any idea where it is. The faint-hearted have been known to give up.

All the same on a sunny summer's afternoon there might be fully 600 customers in and around the Ship Inn at Wandsworth so it can be reached. Try this. Drive across Wandsworth Bridge, go round the roundabout and just before you reach the bridge again take the little slip road on the left. That's the Ship on your right with the figurehead. On the other hand you could parachute in.

There have been major changes lately. The public bar at the front and the big conservatory overlooking the garden are still there, but a fine new restaurant has been added at the back with a long open kitchen. Chefs toil away in full view producing modish holiday food in the fashionable way – asparagus frittata, spaghetti puttanesca, mussel and squid stew. You have this either in the restaurant or in the riverside garden.

Sunday lunch on a summer's day is when it all comes together, everyone outside in the sun, the river slipping by, the barbecue in full spate producing prodigious quantities of steaks and chops, sausages and burgers. The garden has long had its own bar. Now it has a riverside marquee too, green and white stripes, lovely.

This garden is a great place for parties and you get an extraordinary number of people there. More than a thousand have been known to mill round the 12-ft television screen, which is put up for the Last Night of the Proms, extroverts conducting, everyone swaying, waving arms and belting out Land of Hope and Glory. Thousands come for the fireworks show on Guy Fawkes' Night and there was a tremendous bash for VE Day.

The beer is Young's, which shares the credit with Charles and Linda Gotto who rescued the place from what seemed like certain oblivion. The Gottos are now tenants of four Young's pubs. (See also the Alma and the Coopers' Arms.)

An *Evening Standard* Pub of the Year.

Open
All Week

Hours
11.00–23.00
(12.00–22.30 Sun)

Credit Cards
All major cards except Diner's Club

Restaurant Food Available
12.00–15.00 and 19.30–22.00

Special Features
Wheelchair Access
Tables outside seat 400
Private Dining Room seats 14

Beers Available
Young's Special, Young's Bitter, Stella Artois, London Lager, Castlemaine
Draught Cider: Scrumpy Jack

Nearest BR Station
Wandsworth Town

· THE SILVER CROSS ·

Open
All Week

Hours
11.00–23.00
(12.00–22.30 Sun)

Bar Food Available
All Day

Beers Available
Courage Best, Courage Directors, John Smith's, Theakston Best Bitter, Foster's, Holsten, Carlsberg

Nearest Tube Station
Charing Cross

33 Whitehall, SW1   930 8350

'Still being haunted'

This lively old pub, a brothel in the reign of Charles I, a tavern since the reign of Charles II, is the repository of much myth and legend including, quite possibly, the brothel bit.

Is it really haunted by the Tudor maid whose portrait hangs above the carved fireplace, murdered, they say, dumped in the Thames and not best pleased? 'We're still being haunted,' says the Tony Whitehead, the new Irish landlord, cheerfully.

There are three pubs in a row in this bit of Whitehall and this is the oldest, also the smallest. Now that the bar has been moved to the far end, though, there's room enough. Alterations of this sort can be made but preservation orders are in place to protect the important bits, the ceiling for instance. The ceiling is the great prize of the Silver Cross. It is a beautiful *barrel vaulted* ceiling. Barrel vaulting is special. The barrels over the bar are just barrels.

When these three pubs were built they were within what was called the Verge of the Court and all three licensees must present themselves at Buckingham Palace once every three years to face the Board of the Green Cloth.

They arrive at 11.00am, just after the changing of the guard when the crowds of sightseers outside are thickest, going in by the front entrance and being escorted along corridors to the room where, behind a table covered by green cloth, the Master of the Household and his colleagues wait.

The licensees get closely questioned. Their licences depend on this examination so it is a bit of an ordeal. Still it's better than going to the licensing justices as everyone else has to. 'I got lost and there was the Queen coming towards me,' says Mr Whitehead.

· THE SIR GEORGE ROBEY ·

Open
All Week

Hours
11.00–00.30
Mon–Thur;
11.00–06.00 Fri & Sat;
(12.00–22.30 Sun)
Closed Christmas Day

Credit Cards
None

240 Seven Sisters Road, N4   272 5356

*'They are too young to have heard of
George Robey at the Sir George Robey'*

George Robey, Prime Minister of Mirth, observes the comings and goings at the Sir George Robey from the inn sign with his once-famous quizzical smile. He wears his once-famous bowler, collarless frock coat and black eyebrows but he needn't have bothered. They are too young to have heard of George Robey at the Sir George Robey and just call it the Robey. I expect there are annoying people around who still call it the Clarence. which is what it used to be.

From the Robey comes this report: 'The Robey is near Finsbury Park station. Everyone knows it. Johnny Rotten gets there. It has a bar and a music room and two beer gardens, one at the front, one at the back. The music room is dark with black walls, a fair-sized stage and there's room to dance. You can get 300 ravers in. It closes at 11.00 pm during the week but on Friday and Saturday it turns into a club and stays open till 6.00 am. Soft drinks only after 2.00 am.

'On Friday nights it's the Freaky Club, which is indie-dance, and on Saturdays it's Another Night of Madness, which is trippy, trancey, techno, deep house. You don't have to be a member. They aren't clubs like that.'

Bar Food Available
All opening hours
Special Features
Wheelchair Access
Beer Garden seats 150
Beers Available
Grolsch, Newcastle Brown Ale, Labatts, Rolling Rock, Budweiser, Becks, Castlemaine, Lowenbrau, Tetley, Guinness
Nearest Tube Station
Finsbury Park

·THE SLUG AND LETTUCE·

16 Putney High Street, SW15   0181-785 3081

'Goodbye giant slugburger'

The Slug and Lettuce would seem the pub name least likely to succeed. It has, in fact, proved quite otherwise. There are 15 of them now, eight in London, and more in the offing.

Most of them are a bit like this one, big Victorian pubs restyled and renamed. This is a Slug and Lettuce class of '93. It was the White Lion until then and a full-sized white lion still stands high on the decorative Victorian facade looking like neither a slug nor a lettuce.

All the Slugs and Lettuces are being thoroughly spruced up at the moment, each in turn closing for five or six weeks and reopening with a lighter, brighter look. This one has a new colour scheme – cream, orange and blue – and has lost the wooden railings that divided it up. Its front windows have clear glass now, the air-conditioning has been improved, ceiling fans installed, the great expanse of wooden floor stripped and restored and the food has moved distinctly up-market.

So goodbye giant slugburger, an old favourite. Now it is smoked salmon tabbouleh, warm onion and Parmesan torte, tagliatelle with red pepper pesto. There's champagne on the wine list and an up-to-the-minute coffee-making machine on the bar.

The live bands that used to play two evenings a week are gone, also the fruit machines. For Slugs and Lettuces, as for many another London pub, the times they are a-changing as they inevitably do.

Open
All Week
Hours
11.00–23.00
(12.00–22.30 Sun)
Credit Cards
Visa, Access
Bar Food Available
11.00–23.00
Special Features
Wheelchair Access
(but not lavatory)
Beer Garden seats 40
Private Room
seats 150
Beers Available
Courage Best, Courage Directors, Wadworth 6X, Kronenbourg, Foster's, Miller Lite, Beamish Cider: Dry Blackthorn
Nearest Tube Station
Putney Station

·The Spaniard's Inn·

Spaniard's Road, NW3　　　　　　　　　　　　　　**0181-455 3276**

'Where Mrs Bardell plotted Mr Pickwick's downfall'

Open
All Week
Hours
11.00–23.00
(12.00–22.30 Sun)
Credit Cards
Visa, Access,
Mastercard
Bar Food Available
12.00–15.00 and
18.00–21.30;
12.00–21.30 Sat;
(12.00–21.30 Sun)
Special Features
Wheelchair Access
(but not lavatory)
Beer Garden seats 250
Private Room seats 30
Beers Available
Adnams Extra, Bass,
London Pride,
Hancock's,
Worthington, Carling
Black Label, Tennent's
Extra, Grolsch,
Caffrey's, Guinness
Nearest Tube Stations
Hampstead,
Golders Green

The Spanish Ambassador to the Court of James I is said to have lived here. Well, it would explain the name. It is a 16th-century weatherboarded house on the road that cuts through Hampstead Heath, and none of the many additions and alterations has spoiled it in any way.

It has been a tavern for 400 years, most of that time deep in the countryside. All the same life has not been without drama or glamour. Highwaymen, who, like modern New Yorkers, could be good company when not actually shooting you, were often there. Dick Turpin stabled Black Bess in the toll gate that still juts into the road causing daily traffic jams in both directions, and a musket ball he fired while holding up the Royal Mail is on show in the bar. They used to have his pistols too but they were pinched, as were the rifles left behind by the Gordon rioters. The rioters had been boozing in the bar when soldiers arrived and marched them off to Newgate Jail. They'd got into trouble for losing their rifles.

Things are usually more peaceful in the Spaniard's Inn. Shelley, Keats and Byron all went there and so, you will not be surprised to hear, did Charles Dickens. In The Pickwick Papers this was where Mrs Bardell and her friends plotted Mr Pickwick's downfall.

You can imagine Mr Pickwick in the saloon bar with its low ceilings, old panelling and cosy alcoves. Bar stools surround the old wooden bar and there is a charming panelled room upstairs with original beams and shutters and a splendidly sloping floor. There are real fires in winter and in the summer one of the best pub gardens you will ever see, with raised lawn and roses, a fine pergola and a big terrace of picnic tables. At the bottom of the garden more than 100 budgies lead busy lives in a big aviary. Children love them and are welcome here.

It is a pub worth making any sort of detour to visit. Mind the toll gate.

·The Sporting Page·

Camera Place, SW10　　　　　　　　　　　　　　**376 3694**

'Friendly, extrovert and sporty'

Open
All Week
Hours
11.00–23.00
(12.00–15.00 and
19.00–22.30 Sun)

Life in the Sporting Page is, as the name suggests, friendly, extrovert and sporty. The crowd is clearly there to enjoy itself and so is the staff.

It is a light cheerful modern pub between the King's Road and Fulham Road, formerly the Red Anchor. Outside it is whitewashed walls and new Bollinger canopies, this time bright red – a patriotic effect if the sky is blue. Inside a lot of varnished pine – floors, furniture and bar. There are lighthearted sporting prints, sporting paintings and sporting murals and rugby internationals on a big screen fill the bar to scrum-like capacity.

The tables and benches from the bar appear outside in the summer, and the kitchen is busy all year round. Espresso coffee is on offer, and with luck you may hit the night when the free hot snacks circulate.

Bollinger, as you might imagine, is the house champagne – £28 a bottle, £6 a glass. Jeriboams are also on offer at £135 per bottle, and Anthony Ratcliff, the new manager, is considering stocking a Nebuchadnezzar. This is Chelsea.

Closed Christmas Day, Boxing Day
Credit Cards Visa, Mastercard, Eurocard
Bar Food Available 12.00–14.30 and 19.00–22.00
Special Features Wheelchair Access (but not lavatory) Beer Garden seats 40
Beers Available Boddingtons, Wadworth, Webster's, Holsten, Foster's, Carlsberg, Guinness
Nearest Tube Stations Sloane Square, South Kensington

· THE SPREAD EAGLE ·

71 Wandsworth High Street, SW18   **0181-877 9809**

'A temple of Victoriana'

The Wandsworth one-way system is the heart of the Young's empire. At its centre is the old Ram Brewery itself and around it orbits a solar system of attendant planets making up a mighty pub crawl – the Brewery Tap; the Brewers Inn, which used to be the vast Two Brewers but is now a substantial pub and a 16-room hotel; the King's Arms, with its big garden running down to the river; smaller satellites like the Crane and the Grapes; the comfortable Queen Adelaide; the Old Sergeant, built and owned, would you believe it, by John Nash; the Alma; and the Ship.

The Spread Eagle stands four square in the heart of the High Street. There has been a Spread Eagle there for almost 300 years, but the first one was rebuilt at great cost in 1892 and there it is, a temple of Victoriana. The mahogany bar counter, backed by a fine display of etched mirrors and ornate woodwork, curves over the bare boards of the public bar, through the upholstered comforts of the saloon bar and into the old dining room, now the wine bar. Each area is separated from its neighbour by splendid etched-glass partitions and doors.

The Spread Eagle has played a central part in Wandsworth life. It was a coaching inn, provided stables and a ballroom, served as a magistrates court and hosted town meetings. Lord Spencer's agent met tenants and collected rents here, and the pub's usefulness continues with wedding receptions, private parties and the Half-Wits Comedy Club.

Open All Week
Hours 11.00–23.00 (12.00–22.30 Sun)
Credit Cards Switch
Bar Food Available 12.00–21.00 Mon–Fri; (13.00–15.30 Sun)
Special Features No-smoking Area Wheelchair Access (but not lavatory) Function Room Car Park
Beers Available Young's Bitter, Young's Special, Dirty Dick's, Winter Warmer, Young's London Lager, Young's Premium Lager, Castlemaine, Stella, Oatmeal Stout, Guinness
Nearest Tube Station Wandsworth Town

Look at the big square building at the back. In the 19th century this was the Assembly Rooms for dances, concerts and music hall. Then, sensationally, it became a bioscope. The recessed bookcase in the saloon bar was the door from the pub. Bioscopes everywhere were killed off by the cinema, and the Spread Eagle's has lain idle since. This year, though, Young's hopes to make it a venue for music and comedy all over again.

The manager, Tom Pheby, is all for it. He loves the Spread Eagle. 'There aren't many like this around,' he says.

· ST PAUL'S WINE VAULTS ·

29 Knightrider Street, EC4 **236 1013**

'Thankfully the ground floor at least is still a pub'

Open
Mon–Fri

Hours
11.00–20.00

Credit Cards
All major cards except Diner's Club

Bar and Restaurant Food Available
12.00–15.00

Special Features
Private Dining Room seats 16
Air Conditioning
Wine Bar

Beers Available
Hardy Country Bitter, Royal Oak Strong Ale, Eldridge Pope Light Ale, Miller, Grolsch, Budweiser, Becks, Swan Light, Guinness

Nearest Tube Station
Mansion House

St Paul's Wine Vaults? What's going on? This is the famous Horn Tavern, the historic old London pub that Mr Pickwick knew, burned down in the Great Fire of London, almost lost in the Blitz, nearly pulled down after the war. After all this to be changed to the St Paul's Wine Vaults? What can Eldridge Pope be thinking of ?

Well, a lot of changes have been made. The old cellar bar is certainly a wine vault now. Thankfully, though, the old bar parlour is still recognizably itself. Racks of wine fill the wall space behind the counter but people still go in for a pint in the evening. Eldridge Pope is a Dorchester brewer and sells its own cask ale there, so the ground floor at least is still a pub.

The Horn Tavern can take heart. It is still there, sound in wind and limb, more sound than before, I dare say. What would Mr Pickwick have made of the air conditioning? So there are plusses and it will be the Horn Tavern again some day.

· THE STAR AND GARTER ·

4 Lower Richmond Road, SW15 **0181-788 0345**

'Every window filled with faces'

Open
All Week

Hours
11.00–15.00 and
17.00–23.00 Mon–Fri;
11.00–23.00 Sat
(12.00–22.30 Sun)

Credit Cards
None

On the last Saturday of March getting on for a thousand people press into the Star and Garter on the river at Putney. It is a huge Victorian pile, a landmark, five storeys high with a tower making six, and windows on every floor have a brilliant view of the start of the Oxford and Cambridge boat race.

The Star and Garter is well prepared. It takes all the furniture out, puts away the real glasses and produces big boxes of plastic ones. A platoon of barmen lines the 40-ft counter in the saloon bar.

Then the doors are open and every window on the river frontage is wide open and filled with faces, their owners beside themselves with excitement as the race begins. The boats are around the bend and away in no time but they can be seen all the way to the finish on the big television screens over the bar counters.

The rest of the year, you might think, must be an anticlimax. Still it is a busy pub with a big young following, and ordinary weekends can be hopping at the Star and Garter. The ground-floor bar is quite a sight at any time of the day. So thickly covered in every kind of object is the high ceiling that it is years since anyone has ever had the opportunity to see it.

Its original architects had great social plans for the Star and Garter. The entire first floor was a ballroom, high, wide and elegant with classical mouldings and long windows overlooking the river. This is now the home of the Riverside Gymnasium: gold-card membership £245 a year.

Cross the road and there is Putney Pier: river trips daily to Hampton Court, Kew Gardens, Westminster and Richmond all summer long.

Bar Food Available
12.00–14.30 and
17.00–19.30
Special Features
Wheelchair Access
(but not lavatory)
Private Room seats 100
Beers Available
Tetley, Courage
Directors, Kronenbourg,
Foster's, Budweiser,
Miller, Guinness
Nearest Tube Station
Putney Bridge

·THE STAR TAVERN·

6 Belgrave Mews West, SW1   **235 3019**
'A rich mix in the saloon bar'

The Star Tavern was built for the household servants of the nobility. There were plenty of both in 19th-century Belgravia. Four dukes lived round the corner in the newly built Belgrave Square and the local servant population was enormous. The Star Tavern had to be big and it was every bit as hierarchical as the great town houses around it. Saloon bar, private bar, public bar or snug – the butlers, valets, footmen and coachmen understood exactly which was for them and which was not.

A couple of wars and the partitions came down and after that you didn't know whose shoulder your shoulder might be rubbing. Actors, gangsters, the Gaekwar of Baroda, it was a rich mix in the saloon bar of the Star Tavern and you were never sure if Paddy Kennedy would even let you inside his domain. He ruled the Star Tavern in the 1950s and 1960s and would not serve you if he decided he did not like the cut of your jib. He was particularly particular about who used the upstairs bar, where, they say, the Great Train Robbers planned their deed.

Open
All Week
Hours
11.30–15.00 and
17.00–23.00
Mon–Thur;
11.30–23.00 Fri;
11.00–23.00 Sat;
(12.00–15.00 and
19.00–22.30 Sun)
Closed Christmas Day,
Boxing Day
Credit Cards
None
Bar Food Available
12.00–14.30 and
18.30–20.45 Mon–Fri
Special Features
Wheelchair Access
(but not lavatory)
Private Room seats 30

Beers Available
ESB, London Pride,
Chiswick Bitter,
Carling, Heineken,
Grolsch, Guinness

Nearest Tube Station
Knightsbridge

Kennedy made a few bob in his day, lived well, spent freely but the horses were his undoing. Sadly he died broke in the licensed trade's home.

Bruce and Kathleen Taylor run the pub now and it is comfortable, familiar, agreeably old-fashioned. On winter evenings you still look for a table near one of the open fires and on a summer evening customers like to take their drinks into the mews where there are tubs of geraniums, hanging baskets of lobelia and very little traffic. Other London pubs have had to stop their customers from drinking outside in recent months, often after the complaint of a single neighbour, but hopefully, in spite of rumbles, this pleasant old custom will continue in Belgrave Mews West.

The Star Tavern's food is a draw and this is a Fuller's house so the beer is a big plus. Like the ESB it sells, the Star Tavern is a pub of Extra Strong Character. It was the *Evening Standard* Pub of the Year in 1992.

·THE STARGAZEY·

Open
All Week

Hours
11.30–23.00
12.00–23.00 Sat
(12.00–22.30 Sun)

Credit Cards
Access, Visa,
Mastercard

Bar Food Available
12.00–21.00
Mon–Thur;
12.00–20.00 Fri–Sat;
(12.00–14.30 Sun)

Special Features
No-smoking Area
Wheelchair Access
(disabled lavatory)

Beers Available
London Pride, ESB,
Chiswick Bitter,
Grolsch, Tennent's
Extra, Heineken,
Carling Black Label,
Guinness
Cider: Scrumpy Jack

Nearest Tube Station
Earls Court

236 Fulham Road, SW10   376 5827

'A new generation'

The Stargazey was the first of Fuller's new brainwave chain, the Ale and Pie Houses, a new generation of pubs, much discussed, carefully designed and marketed. There are eight of them in London now but some still like the Stargazey best…

First there's the building. It was a National Westminster bank until Fuller's took it, and what a prize – 2,000 sq ft, twice the size of your average pub and on a big main road corner site with vaults perfect for cellars, kitchens and store rooms. It was murder drilling through the thick reinforced walls, but apart from that it seemed clear that banks were made for pubs. Were there any more going?

There were indeed, but the Stargazey set the scene for things to come. It is a wide open, youthful pub, the outside walls a continuous run of sliding doors that fill it with light and slide open in a most satisfactory way on sunny days, and on every side the designers have given a modern gloss to traditional pub features. How nice to see granite counter tops, leather benches, Welsh chapel chairs, and modern partitions forming big bays for eating and drinking. One of them is a non-smoking bay. Non-smoking bits in pubs are still few and far between.

The ale is Fuller's, of course, so that's all right, and the pies, central to the success of the exercise, are pretty good too. A stargazey is apparently a sort of Cornish pie in which little fish poke their heads through the pastry. Thankfully they don't do this dreadful-sounding pie at the Stargazey, but the fish pie they do do – white fish, smoked fish and prawns – is very good.

Like all the pies it comes on an ash trencher, a wooden plate with grooves to keep the pies and the veg apart. But pies are by no means the only things on offer and you can eat here very reasonably until 9.00 pm. After that the pub side really takes over.

I would rather like one of these near me. There are lots of banks but none of them, alas, seems inclined to budge.

· THE SUN ·

47 Clapham Old Town, SW4   **622 4980**
'A sweate place'

Samuel Pepys moved to Clapham Old Town. That was how grand and rich he became. He lived there, wrote John Evelyn, 'in a very noble house and sweate place where he enjoyed the fruit of his labour in great prosperity'. This is still the way of it in Clapham Old Town.

Some fine old houses have survived and it has at least seven pubs of varying sweatness – the extrovert, bohemian Prince of Wales, the traditional Rose and Crown, the big, boozy Alexandra, Mistress P's that used to be the North Pole, the Frog and Forget-Me-Not that used to be the Cock, and the Fresian and Firkin that used to be the Bull's Head, hence, it is said, the cock and bull story. And this one, the Sun. Like the others it came too late for Sam Pepys. It would, I suspect, have surprised him the most.

The Sun is a fine Victorian building, a landmark in the old town. It is run by Ann and Tom Halpin and has been decorated in amazing style by the artists Caroline Ward and John Hammond. The large downstairs bar is a riot of colour with unusual wrought-iron tables and chairs and upstairs is an even more vividly decorated room with an extraordinarily painted ceiling, a sort of Sistine chapel in the jungle. Not to be missed is the lavatory, perhaps the most vivid room in the place. Amazonian is the word. Outside the flagged beer garden is cheered up by an arty wrought-iron fire escape. The garden has its own bar now.

The astonishing decor seems to have worked. The Sun is extremely popular and very lively in the evenings.

Open
All Week

Hours
11.00–23.00
(12.00–22.30 Sun)

Credit Cards
All major cards except AmEx

Bar Food Available
12.00–19.00

Special Features
Wheelchair Access
(but not lavatory)
Beer Garden with bar
6 outside tables
Function Room
seats 100

Beers Available
London Pride, Bass, Grolsch, Tennent's Extra, Tennent's Pilsner, Staropramen, Caffrey's, Guinness
Cider: Dry Blackthorn

Nearest Tube Station
Clapham Common

·THE SUN·

63 Lamb's Conduit Street, WC1   **405 8278**

'Single women, stay away'

Open
All Week

Hours
11.00–23.00
(12.00–22.30 Sun)
Closed Christmas Day,
Boxing Day

Credit Cards
None

Bar Food Available
12.00–14.30 and
18.00–22.00

Special Features
Wheelchair Access
(but not lavatory)
Tables outside seat 20

Beers Available
Tanglefoot, Adnams
Broadside, Ruddles
County, Brakspear,
Foster's, Holsten,
Guinness

Nearest Tube Stations
Russell Square,
Holborn

The Sun in Lamb's Conduit Street doesn't care what it looks like and truthfully it can look pretty rough. Not just the pub. 'Rough hard men in vests,' reported *Time Out* reviewing 50 West End pubs. 'Single women, stay away.'

Well, it's beer that matters at the Sun and few pubs anywhere take that more seriously. Observe the old U-shaped counter, a bit battered, nothing to write home about, but the hand pumps now, what a sight for sore eyes they are, black and gleaming, seven on one side, nine on the other, 16 cask ales on offer at any one time and often a lot more waiting in the cellars. It likes to claim that no other pub sells a greater range of real ales.

It is its cellars that makes this possible – a labyrinth of vaults and catacombs under the streets of Bloomsbury – and Gary Brown, the manager, might well take you down there if you ask. He often has a group going round in the early evening. If he can't take you for some reason, well, you will have seen a good old London boozer, met some good old boozy Londoners and possibly had a beer you never tried before. They will fit you in for a cellar tour another time.

·THE SUN INN·

Church Road, SW13   **0181-876 5893**

'The perfect object of a walk'

Open
All Week

Hours
11.00–23.00
(12.00–22.30 Sun)

Credit Cards
None

Restaurant Food Available
12.00–14.30

Special Features
Wheelchair Access
Tables outside seat 72

Beers Available
Tetley, Burton Ale,
Young's Ale, Carlsberg,
Lowenbrau,
Castlemaine, Labatts,
Guinness

Nearest BR Station
Barnes Bridge

First find Barnes Green. Note the willow that grows aslant the brook, the avenue of horse chestnuts, the house, on the left, where Henry Fielding lived. Take a turn round the pond and there's the Sun, a pretty Georgian building with a mansard roof, a pergola, window-boxes and hanging gardens.

Before you go in, though, go round the back and have a look at Barnes Bowling Club, still owned by the brewers. It has a very rare, old-fashioned green, a sort of inverse crown with the centre lower than the sides. Here, so the story goes, Elizabeth 1 was taught to play by Drake and Walsingham.

Inside the Sun little seems to have changed since its days as an 18th-century coaching inn. There is a charming warren of little rooms, a jumble of nooks and snugs divided by rails, pillars, stained-glass panels and curious sliding leaded windows. There are wooden floors on different levels, beams, low ceilings, stuffed owls, a huge stuffed pike, old prints, old bottles, old rugs, bric-a-brac of all sorts and a ghost.

This fussy spirit is thought to be a former landlord. He moves plates behind the bar and alters clocks, but no one minds, and during opening hours the Sun couldn't be livelier. Barnes is awash with celebrated persons of a musical and theatrical sort and this is where they drink.

The Sun is really a country pub, the perfect object of a walk. The dog will be welcomed – many are counted among the regulars. They are happy to see children too, at lunchtime anyway.

There is no dartboard at the Sun, no pool table, no juke box or television or other distractions of that kind.

· THE SURPRISE ·

6 Christchurch Terrace, SW3   352 4699

'The surprise about the Surprise'

The *Surprise* was the name of the frigate that took Charles II to safety in France, a voyage commemorated on the pub sign. There is the frigate heaving to, there the king being rowed out to board her. He stands heroically in the prow, his wig understandably askew.

This happened 200 years before this Victorian pub was built and in Falmouth, but the Surprise remains grateful to its namesake and there are lots of pictures of the graceful fighting ship or of others like it in the bar, and the surprise about the Surprise is to find so little changed by the years.

The black oak bar with its painted frieze still serves the public bar with its bare floorboards, its dart board and shove-ha'penny board on one side and the saloon bar with its carpet and most of the windows on the other. Change would be met with outrage. There were even some grumbles when they brought the gents in from the yard.

Open
All Week

Hours
11.00–23.00
(12.00–22.30 Sun)

Credit Cards
Visa, Access

Bar Food Available
12.00–14.30

Special Features
Wheelchair Access
Tables outside seat 20

Beers Available
Bass, Hancock HB, Timothy Taylor Best Bitter, Grolsch, Tennent's Pilsner, Carling Black Label, Caffrey's, Guinness

Nearest Tube Station
Sloane Square

· THE SUSSEX ·

20 Upper St Martin's Lane, WC2   836 1834

'A grim reminder'

This busy West End pub was the scene of a violent and tragic event that put it on every front page. On 12 October 1992 the IRA planted a bomb in the men's lavatory. Five customers were injured, one died days later. It was a grim reminder, if one was needed, that public houses are from time to time in the front line.

The Sussex replaced its windows, mended its shattered bar and got on with it. It remains the decent, friendly, useful pub it has always been.

Open
All Week

Hours
11.00–23.00
(12.00–22.30 Sun)

Bar Food Available
12.00–14.00 and
19.00–21.00

Beers Available
Courage Best, Courage Directors, John Smith's, Theakston Best

Nearest Tube Station
Leicester Square

·THE SWAN·

Open
All Week

Hours
10.00–23.00 Mon–Sat
(10.00–22.30 Sun)

Credit Cards
All major cards except Diner's Club

Bar Food Available
10.00–22.00
(10.00–21.30 Sun)

Special Features
Wheelchair Access (but not lavatory)
Seats outside for 66

Beers Available
Courage, John Smith's, Theakston, Gillespie's, Carlsberg, Foster's, Holsten, Budweiser, Guinness

Nearest Tube Station
Lancaster Gate

66 Bayswater Road, W2   **262 5204**

'No wonder the terrace gets packed'

Tourists love the Swan. They come in time and again during their holiday here and years later come back and tell the barmen about it. They were staying in a hotel just round the corner, they will say, and on their very first day they found the Swan. It was the first English pub they had ever seen...

The Swan is genuinely pretty and genuinely old. It was there in the 18th century, or anyway some of it was, and it looks its age. Pubs try to do that. It was a built as a coaching inn, then became the Floral Tea Gardens, then happily it went back to being a tavern and today, though bigger, it is still a nice domestic size, just two storeys, with a handsome swan painted on the stucco and lanterns and hanging baskets and wooden picnic tables on a deep terrace.

This terrace is a tremendous asset. It stretches to the pavement, much of it sheltered by a glass canopy so let it rain, and the traffic roars by but let it roar. This is London, after all. Kensington Gardens are just across the road and after dark they light the gas lamps and you could almost be back a hundred years. No wonder the terrace gets packed all day long in summer.

The bar is comfortably English, so is the food. There's roast beef and Yorkshire pudding every lunchtime and in the room at the back there is a copy of a big old painting of a typically English scene.

Look closely, there is the Swan and there is Bayswater Road, just a country lane in those days you will notice, and the small tree in the picture could easily be the large tree just outside, and that group of redcoats is allowing felons one last drink before taking them to Tyburn to get hanged.

The locals used to enjoy that and entertainment is still provided at the Swan. Every evening from Monday to Saturday there is a typical English sing-song in the back room. Everyone, whether they are from Tokyo, Texas or Tottenham Court Road, ends up joining in.

·THE SWAN·

Open
All Week

Hours
11.00–24.00 Mon–Wed
11.00–02.00 Thurs–Sat
(11.00–02.00 Sun)

215 Clapham Road, SW9   **978 9778**

'A couple of lagers and the search is on'

The young and free who flock to this massive Irish pub in Stockwell drink fast and hope to score.

From Clapham Road, this report: 'A couple of lagers

and the search is for the opposite sex. You don't have far to look. There's the huge bar downstairs and the Swan's Nest upstairs just as big, lots of room, lots of possibilities, plenty of time. The Swan doesn't close till midnight early in the week and not until 2.00 am from Thursday to Saturday.

'Big-name Irish acts play here, Frances Black and Four Men and a Dog, so check your programme, otherwise every night is Friday night at the Swan. Watch the doormen, though. They failed O-level charm.

'Early-evening dance classes are proving a massive and unexpected hit – Irish step dancing on Tuesdays, country line dancing on Sundays.'

Credit Cards
Barclaycard
Bar Food Available
All opening hours
Special Features
Wheelchair Access
Private Room seats 200
Beers Available
Ruddles Best, John Smith's, Foster's, Carling Black Label, Holsten, Guinness, Beamish
Nearest Tube Station
Stockwell

·THE SWAN·

77–80 Gracechurch Street, EC3   **283 7712**

'Probably the smallest pub in the City'

For 23 years Franco and Maria Ferrer ran the Rossetti in St John's Wood. It was big, sunny and Mediterranean and all seemed well but Franco, Mario and the Rossetti all came to a crossroads together. The pub was being sold and Franco and Maria were homesick for Spain. They went home to Barcelona and new owners took over the Rossetti and pulled it down.

There are 32 new flats on the site now. Franco and Maria have watched them go up because their retirement did not last long. They had a nice house, the beach was nearby and the sun shone but they were bored. They missed their daughters, grown-up and living in Mill Hill. They were homesick for London.

So it is that Franco and Maria are running a London pub again. It is the Swan, cosy, Dickensian and probably the smallest pub in the City of London. If a chap of moderate girth stands at the downstairs bar another chap of moderate girth can hardly squeeze by. One has a strange urge to shout 'move right down the bus please'. Nevertheless, City gents line this bar every lunchtime drinking pints of Fuller's Chiswick and breathing in whenever a newcomer arrives.

I don't believe it, but Franco says he can get 38 people in the downstairs bar and at least another 40 upstairs. Ah yes, upstairs. There is a bar there too, exactly twice the size, a nice bar, rich mahogany, thick carpet and a bit of space.

The cellar is tiny and crammed high with barrels delivered once a week at 6.00 am, and the Ferrers, living above the pub as they have for most of their lives together, say how lovely it is to get so much time off. City pubs close at 9.00 pm and don't open at all at weekends.

Open
Mon–Fri
Hours
11.00–21.00
Credit Cards
Visa, Access, AmEx
Bar Food Available
11.00–20.30
Special Features
Wheelchair Access
(but not lavatory)
Beers Available
London Pride, ESB, Chiswick Bitter, Grolsch, Tennent's Extra, Heineken, Guinness
Nearest Tube Station
Bank

· THE SWAN ·

40 Hammersmith Broadway, W6   **0181-748 1043**

'No money spared'

Open
All Week

Hours
11.00–23.00
(12.00–22.30 Sun)

Credit Cards
Visa, Mastercard, Eurocard

Bar Food Available
9.00–21.00

Special Features
No-smoking Area
Wheelchair Access
Private Room seats 60

Beers Available
Charrington variants, Grolsch, Caffrey's

Nearest Tube Station
Hammersmith

Look at this noble pub on its commanding peninsular, a strong presence on the big battling road junction at the heart of Hammersmith. No money was spared by the Victorians who built it, going to town with marble and etched glass and polished mahogany, and there is no identity crisis here. There are painted swans on the inn sign, a flamboyant swan on the gable, a stuffed swan in a case over the bar.

It has a beady eye, the swan in the bar, but this has not always been enough to keep the peace. The dignified Swan, one of nature's aldermen, got decidedly rough not long ago, takings fell and Victorian worthies turned in graves. But there have been confrontations and draconian bannings and trade has doubled in the past year.

The Swan is not such an early starter as it was. It used to open breakfast at 7.00 am, now it starts at 9.00, but it still does a Very Big Breakfast and there is hot food all day until 9.00 pm. The big kitchen is kept at it. There is a handsome function room upstairs, much used for wedding receptions, annual general meetings, parties and goodness knows what. Hammersmith finds it, and indeed the rest of the pub, very useful.

· THE SWISS COTTAGE ·

98 Finchley Road, NW3   **722 3487**

'It gave its name to the entire district'

Open
All Week

Hours
11.00–23.00
(12.00–22.30 Sun)

Credit Cards
None

Bar Food Available
12.00–15.00

Special Features
Wheelchair Access
Beer Garden seats 100
Private Room seats 100

Beers Available
Sovereign Ale,
Ayingerbrau Pils,
Ayingerbrau Prinz,
Extra Stout
Cider: Cider Reserve

Nearest Tube Station
Swiss Cottage

For about ten minutes when Queen Victoria was very young there was a fashion for pseudo-Swiss chalets. People thought they were romantic and sophisticated and just darling, and Prince Albert brought one over from Switzerland in sections. It was reassembled in the grounds of Osborne and the children had tea parties there.

It is to this distant craze that we owe this agreeably dotty pub, a household name in London. In 1840 Finchley Road was being built and they put a pub in the shape of an outsize chalet on the key junction just north of Regent's Park. They called it the Swiss Cottage and it was the last word in chic. It gave its name to the new bus terminus, then to the Metropolitan Line station when it opened and soon to the entire district.

People always liked it and it was rebuilt on an even bigger scale after the war. It is huge now, 6,000 square feet of public space, four bars, a private pool club, a terrace with picnic tables, a deep wooden balcony around three of its sides.

Samuel Smith bought it in 1986 and there has been lots of refurbishing, of course. The Victoria Bar (with music) and the Albert Bar (without) are now big comfortable rooms with sofas, arm chairs, wing chairs and button-backed chairs, grouped around widely spaced coffee tables.

The Tap Room is plain and pleasant and well used by the locals, and you could give a ball in the vast upstairs bar, now used as a function room. A flight of wooden Swiss-type steps leads up to the wide Swiss-type balcony on the first floor, and a big Swiss-type hall, once a venue for live bands, is now the most accessible of pool clubs. Just £10 gets you membership for life after which it is 70p a game. The six tables are permanently occupied every evening.

I see they have taken to calling it Ye Olde Swiss Cottage now. Dottier and dottier but good old Swiss Cottage all the same. They don't build pubs like this any more.

· T E D INGWALLS ·

11 Camden Lock Place, NW1   **267 0545**

'Dingwalls rides again'

Camden Lock may be the biggest market in Europe. It is London's fourth biggest tourist attraction. On a summer's day it can get a quarter of a million visitors and it sometimes seems that they are all trying to get a drink in T E Dingwalls.

Dingwalls has certainly changed. It used to be a venue, a night club, a disco, the inmost place for clubwise kids. It was famously dark and sweaty and for most of the Seventies and Eighties it got the best dancers in town. Rhythm and Booze, they called it, and every up and coming band had to play there.

With the end of the Eighties a rolling programme of renewal began in Camden Lock and in 1991 it was Dingwalls' turn. The whole building was taken apart and put together again and when it reopened in 1992 the old venue had a pub on top. T E Dingwalls.

It is a light, high, roomy pub, bare boards, bare brick, open rafters, stairs from the bar to a mezzanine, seven real ales on the hand pumps, Tex-Mex food and a sensational terrace. When the sun came out the new T E Dingwalls was a magnet again, customers packing the terrace, the bank of the canal and the pub itself and one day in May, 1994, it made a little bit of history. It became the first pub in Britain to get an all-day Sunday licence.

Open
All Week
Hours
11.00–23.00 Mon–Sat
(12.00–22.30 Sun)
Credit Cards
Visa, Access
Bar Food Available
12.00–17.00 Mon–Sat
Special Features
Wheelchair Access
Terrace Area seats 200
Function Room
seats 500
Beers Available
Adnams, Greene King's Abbott, Wadworths 6X, Theakstons XB, Brakspears, Gales, Ted's Tipple, Foster's, Kronenbourg, Carling, Grolsch, Guinness
Cider: Red Rock
Nearest Tube Station
Camden Town

As for the old Dingwalls of the black walls, black ceiling and ace gigs, it lives on underneath, three times the size and with a big bar, air-conditioning and terrific sound. Discs get launched there, rising bands still play there and at the end of the week it becomes Jongleurs, perhaps the biggest comedy club in town, one show on Fridays, two shows on Saturdays, open till 2.00 am. Dingwalls rides again.

· THE TATTERSHALL CASTLE ·

King's Reach, Victoria Embankment, SW1   **839 6548**

'Unbarnacling her bottom'

For 40 years the Tattershall Castle ferried passengers across the Humber. Now it spends cheerful, sociable days moored at Victoria Embankment near Waterloo Bridge. It is one of London's most unexpected pubs.

There are in fact two floating pubs in central London, old salts both. The Queen Mary worked on the Clyde, and this one made eight trips a day between Hull and New Holland across what can be quite boisterous waters. She was a coal-fired paddle steamer and could carry 1,050 people as well as cars and livestock.

By 1973 the old paddle steamer needed urgent repairs to her boiler. Too costly, said British Rail Sea Link. So the old paddle steamer was replaced and what happened next must have surprised her. Instead of being scrapped she was given a radical refit and a prime mooring in the heart of London with wonderful views from the Palace of Westminster to St Paul's.

She has certainly taken to life in the big city. A million pounds was spent on her, a lot of it on unbarnacling her bottom, and she seems extremely perky now with a new taste for nightlife. During the week she keeps pub hours but at weekends the night club in the stern gets going and stays open until 3.00am. It gets queues.

The pub is the thing, though, and once you are in the saloon bar a pub it unmistakably is. The Tattershall Castle can't keep traditional ales but two lagers and a bitter are piped into ten big tanks in the barge moored alongside. These have to be refilled twice a week in the summer when the decks are crowded and the demand for lager seems insatiable.

There is a buffet downstairs, snacks in the bar, a barbecue on deck on fine days, and on Sunday afternoons they do teas. There is something romantic and rather rakish about a paddle boat. Even on a Sunday afternoon that is how it is on the Tattershall Castle.

Open
All Week

Hours
11.00–23.00
(12.00–22.30 Sun)
Closed Christmas Day, Boxing Day, New Year's Day

Credit Cards
All major cards except Diner's Club

Bar Food Available
12.00–22.00
Set-Price Lunch £5.25

Special Features
Tables outside seat 150

Beers Available
John Smith's, Beamish, Foster's, Kronenbourg

Nearest Tube Station
Embankment

·The Thomas à Becket·

320/322 Old Kent Road, SE1   **252 7605**

'Deeply in the doldrums'

There was a time when the Thomas à Becket was one of London's best-known pubs. It was a renowned boxing pub and for a time every world champion was photographed working out in the gym on the top floor – Muhammad Ali, Henry Cooper, Mike Tyson, Frank Bruno, John Conteh, Dave Charnley, Terry Downes, Alan Minter, Joe Bugner…

Goodness knows what happened to the old pub along the way but time and again the Thomas à Becket has been on the ropes. Each time a rescuer has appeared in the nick of time and we have read stories about the imminent return of the good old days.

At the time of writing the Thomas à Becket has rarely been so deeply in the doldrums. The famous gym with its boxing ring, its punch bag, its tall bright windows, its shower and its sauna is locked and unused. There are no customers to speak of in the big downstairs bar and hardly any beer in the cellar. Things have come to such a pass that the pub opens only two nights a week, on Fridays and Saturdays when local rock bands set up their gear and play to whoever turns up.

A year ago it seemed that rescue could be at hand once more. A local businessman showed interest and a new manager talked of new beginnings. He looked round the empty bar and saw it as a major new music venue. He still does.

Open
Thurs–Sun
Hours
20.30–02.00 Thurs–Sat
(19.00–22.30 Sun)
Credit Cards
None
Bar Food Available
20.30–01.00 Thurs–Sat
(19.00–22.30 Sun)
Special Features
Live rock bands (most nights)
Wheelchair Access (including lavatory)
Beers Available
Kronenbourg, Fosters, Guinness, John Smith's Bitter, Budweiser, Grolsch, Becks
Cider: Scrumpy Jack
Nearest Tube Stations
Elephant and Castle, Newcross

·The Three Greyhounds·

25 Greek Street, W1   **734 8799**

'Glamour and oysters'

Lots of things have been happening at the Three Greyhounds. They closed it down and spent £200,000 on it, redoing the bar, moving the counter, putting in central heating, modernizing the cellar, floodlighting the outside, putting up rows of hanging baskets. But Roxy Beaujolais is still there. That's the main thing.

The Three Greyhounds is the tudory one on the corner of Greek Street and Old Compton Street, a genuinely old pub faked up with half timbering in the 1920s. It was distinctly rough before Roxy took over in 1992.

She brought glamour and oysters, cocktails, interesting snacks and cosmopolitan customers. She won't have music, gaming machines or crowds of lads. She made the white

Open
All Week
Hours
11.00–23.00
(12.00–22.30 Sun)
Closed Christmas Day
Credit Cards
Visa
Bar Food Available
12.00–22.30
Special Features
Wheelchair Access (but not lavatory)
Private Room seats 16
Beers Available
Adnams, Young's, Nicholson's, Carlsberg
Nearest Tube Station
Leicester Square

curtains herself and the recent sprucing-uppers left them strictly alone. When someone pinched her stuffed piranha there was a tremendous rumpus.

Roxy doesn't open till noon but she keeps the food going till 10.30 pm. She is about to publish a cookbook for innkeepers. There's a variety of ales, wine starts at £7.10 a bottle and they serve coffee. If you are going to the theatre this is a good place to begin.

· THE TOTTENHAM ·

6 Oxford Street, W1 **636 7201**

'A distinction of a kind'

Open
All Week

Hours
11.00–23.00
(12.00–22.30 Sun)
Closed Christmas Day

Credit Cards
All major cards accepted

Bar Food Available
11.00–15.00

Special Features
Wheelchair Access
(but not lavatory)
Private Room seats 30

Beers Available
Tetley, Burton, Castlemaine, Lowenbrau, Carlsberg, Carlsberg Export, Guinness

Nearest Tube Station
Tottenham Court Road

London's pub population has been going down for years. Oxford Street used to have 20, now it has only one. This one. A recent *Time Out* survey made it one of the worst five pubs in London. That's a distinction of a kind.

The Tottenham is just opposite Tottenham Court Road underground. Its Victorian architect wanted the best for it and quite a lot of its birthright has survived – some decorated mirrors and carved mahogany, three tapestry panels representing the seasons, a striking skylight.

Traditional pub food is served all day. Has anyone seen the missing tapestry?

· THE TOWN OF RAMSGATE ·

62 Wapping High Street, E1 **488 2685**

'Was this the post on which the pirates died?'

Open
All Week

Hours
11.30–23.00
(12.00–22.30 Sun)

Credit Cards
None

Bar Food Available
12.00–14.30

Special Features
Wheelchair Access
Tables outside seat 40

This dark little pub, the scene of many grisly events, still stands its corner in this narrow cobbled street, pinioned between the mass of Oliver's Wharf and the dank alley known as Wapping Old Stairs. Many terrified men in chains went down those old steps to be tarred and hanged from a post in the river while three tides washed over them. This was the fate of the dashing privateer Captain Kidd. The disgraced Judge Jeffreys, caught in the bar trying to get away to Hamburg, was almost lynched and dragged to his death in the Tower.

Captain Bligh drank here with Fletcher Christian before the Bounty sailed, and press gangs kept their unwilling crews manacled in the cellars until their boats could take them. They just keep the beer down there these days, they say.

The Town of Ramsgate is a listed building now. It is a narrow old pub with a wooden ceiling and a small deck over the river at the back. There is a sinister black post sticking out of the yellow water. Was this the post on which the pirates died? The Town of Ramsgate isn't saying.

Some serious drinking goes on there. 'Don't be a mug, buy it by the jug,' says a notice over the bar, and regulars do. A four-pint jug of Bass is £5.50, a saving of 20p a pint.

Beers Available
Bass, London Pride, Worthington, Caffrey's, Carling Black Label, Tennent's Pilsner, Tennent's Extra, Guinness

Nearest Tube Station
Wapping

· THE TRAFALGAR ·

200 King's Road, SW3   **352 1076**

'For teenagers of all ages'

Vast, lively, deafening, a pub for teenagers of all ages. Bands, DJs, records, big-screen telly, pool, darts, pin-ball, arcade games, beefburgers, jumbo sausages, steakwiches, chips (and extra chips) with everything.

Manager after manager has wrestled with this mettlesome pub. The latest seems to have made a difference. 'Bannings and a strict no-squaddies policy have improved the place no end,' he says. A £120,000 Bass refit must have helped too, a smart new wooden floor, partitions cordoning off the pool table and the big-screen television, a whole new front. This has folding-back glass doors that open half the long bar to the street, inviting passing tourists in. The staff has smartened up and the music has s-l-i-g-h-t-l-y calmed down. Doormen still keep an eye on the Friday and Saturday discos. It hasn't calmed down as much as *that*.

The Trafalgar was built in ancient times, the 1930s. In those days it was a boring pub called the Lord Nelson. Atmosphere, said the *Evening Standard* of the day: provincial hotel. It is hard to imagine.

Open
All Week

Hours
11.00–23.00
(12.00–22.30 Sun)

Credit Cards
All major cards except AmEx

Bar Food Available
11.00–16.00

Special Features
Wheelchair Access (but not lavatory)

Beers Available
Worthington's, Grolsch, Tennent's Extra, Carling Black Label, Carling Premier, Bass, Caffrey's, Guinness

Nearest Tube Station
Sloane Square

· THE TRAFALGAR TAVERN ·

5 Park Row, Greenwich, SE10   **0181-858 2437**

'Even the whitebait dinners are back'

Pub is hardly the word for the Trafalgar Tavern, or tavern either. Seat, perhaps, or Hall would be better, so large it is and imposing, with its parade of noble bars and its great ballroom on the floor above.

They call this the Nelson Room and it is a vast room of quite astonishing splendour with its classical mouldings, elegant windows and curved wrought-iron balconies overlooking the river, much in demand for wedding receptions.

Open
All Week

Hours
11.00–23.00
(12.00–22.30 Sun)

Credit Cards
Visa, Mastercard, Access

Bar and Restaurant Food Available
12.00–15.00 and
18.00–22.00

Special Features
No-smoking Area
Wheelchair Access
Private Room
seats 250

Beers Available
Ruddles County,
Courage Best, Courage
Directors, John Smith's,
Truman's IPA, Foster's,
Carlsberg, Budweiser,
Kronenbourg, Beamish,
Guinness

Nearest BR Stations
Greenwich, Maze Hill

The Trafalgar was built in 1837 in this dashing Regency style to attract free-spending grandees from London, which indeed it did. It was one of a number of what were called whitebait taverns, noted for their whitebait dinners. Whitebait – the fry of herring, did you know that? – were heaved out of the river, seasoned, floured and dumped straight into cauldrons. Whitebait dinners were hugely popular and no one did them better or charged so much for them as the Trafalgar Tavern.

The gallants and the bloods careered down to Greenwich in their four-in-hands, the great and the good came more sedately. Thackeray, Wilkie Collins, Macaulay and Dickens were all regulars, and Ministerial Whitebait Dinners became part of political life, guests, including the Prime Minister of the day, arriving by Ordnance Barge.

The whitebait taverns had a good run but with the turn of the century they went out of business one by one. The Trafalgar lasted longer than most but in 1915 it succumbed too. For the next 50 years it was used as a home for old seamen and as a working men's club. Then in 1965 it was restored, relicensed and reopened and there it is on the river. Even the whitebait dinners are back. The Saints and Sinners Club gives one in the Nelson Room every October – 250 members and guests, the whitebait served with a flourish as the second of five courses and some of the most amusing after-dinner speakers in England doing their stuff.

·THE TUFNELL PARK TAVERN·

162 Tufnell Park Road, N7   272 2078

"Get Raised Up" is the message here'

Open
All Week

Hours
11.00–23.00
(12.00–22.30 Sun)
Good Vibes Disco
20.00–02.00 Fri;
Comedy Club
20.00–02.00 Sat

Bar Food Available
Sandwiches all opening hours; barbecues Sat and Sun lunchtimes

Special Features
Wheelchair Access
(with lavatory)
Beer Garden
Function Room seats 100

Beers Available
Courage, Theakston,
John Smith's, Holsten,
Guinness

Nearest Tube Station
Tufnell Park.

This long, low, stylish pub was built in the 1930s with room for half Tufnell Park. If you are seriously into jazz this is your place. There is live music five nights a week in the big Jazz Bar and it's good stuff too. Most of the jazzmen are professionals.

It's a good setting. Moody black and white photographs of jazz greats cover the walls and posters promise evenings of 'earthy 90s dance-floor funk beamed heavenwards with kicking gospel-jazz grooves'. 'Get Raised Up' is the message here and you pick your genre – modern jazz, trad jazz, ethnic jazz, klezmer jazz, boogie blues on Thursdays, jazz funk every Sunday.

The beer garden at the back is big too, with picnic tables under struggling sycamore trees, there's a late-night disco upstairs every Friday, and the Bound and Gagged Comedy Club upstairs every Saturday. It is a lively pub.

·THE TUT 'N' SHIVE·

235 Upper Street, N1   **359 7719**

'The music flattens you against the wall'

A funny thing happened to the Angel and Crown. This unremarkable high street pub in Islington closed for a couple of weeks and when it reopened it had turned into the Tut 'n' Shive. Old regulars popped in, reeled out and have never been seen again.

The Tut 'n' Shive is a pub that sets out to turn the generation gap into the grand canyon. Clearly a wild party has just finished and temporary repairs have been done before the next one starts. Old doors hold the counter up, graffiti is scrawled on peeling paint, corrugated iron sheets are pinned to the ceilings and piped music gets steadily louder until, about 9.00 pm, it flattens you against the wall.

This, surprisingly, is a Whitbread pub, the first of a chain in its early days. It already has its second pair of likeable young landlords, Mark and Lisa Vickers. Like the first pair they are high-spirited and energetic and seem to like all this.

The Tut is their first pub too, and they are making their mark, keeping the comedy nights, dropping the shipwreck nights, optimistically starting poetry nights, but music's the thing, non-stop music, music as loud as you like. That, at the Tut, means loud.

The Tut's jokes remain too, the life-sized Frankenstein monster stirring on his high shelf in the bar, the open coffin on its end, the lavatories labelled Willy's Room and Fanny's Place. There are fewer cask ales these days, though six is still quite good. Herein lies one drawback about managing the Tut 'n' Shive. You are forever having to explain the name.

Let me try. The tut is the breathing hole in the cask. The shive is the plastic ring around it. I think that's right but it hardly matters. From the start the pub has been just known as the Tut.

Open
All Week

Hours
11.00–23.00
(12.00–22.30 Sun)

Credit Cards
Visa, Mastercard

Bar Food Available
12.00–15.00

Special Features
Wheelchair Access
Benches outside
seat 8
Private Room seats 50

Beers Available
Marston's Pedigree, Boddingtons, West Country Pale Ale (99p a pint), Heineken, Stella, Guinness, Murphy's

Nearest Tube Station
Highbury & Islington

·THE TWO CHAIRMEN·

39 Dartmouth Street, SW1   **222 8694**

'Few pubs sell more pink gins'

Sedan chairs were the taxis of their day. They were slow and swayed a lot and the men who carried them were often drunk, but the streets were foul and dangerous and people threw unspeakable things from the upper windows. Lud Madam, I think I'll take a chair!

The chairmen picked up fares at fixed points in London and this pub was one of them. Most of one wall in the bar

Open
All Week

Hours
11.00–23.00
12.00–17.00 Sat
(12.00–15.00 Sun)
Closed Bank Holidays

Credit Cards
All major cards accepted

Food Available
Bar 11.00–22.30
Restaurant
12.00–22.00

Beers Available
Theakston Best,
Courage Directors,
John Smith's,
Webster's, Holsten,
Foster's, Miller,
Guinness

Nearest Tube Station
St James's Park

is covered by a large painting showing a customer being given a bad time by two red-faced chairmen in the green greatcoats they wore. On second thoughts I think I'll walk.

Those chairmen wouldn't be allowed in the Two Chairmen nowadays, not in that state. It is a well-mannered up-market pub in the heart of St James's, frequented almost entirely by civil servants. Quiet conversation is the thing. You get the agreeable impression that little has happened there lately, not since 1756 when it was rebuilt.

There it is then, a quiet, dignified pub, at ease among its government offices. The small restaurant upstairs is popular at lunchtimes. Few pubs sell more pink gins. Miss Penny Allcorn, the manager, has been there, she says, for 11 happy years

· THE VIADUCT TAVERN ·

Open
All Week

Hours
11.00–23.00
(12.00–22.30 Sun)
Closed Christmas Day

Credit Cards
All major cards
accepted

Bar Food Available
12.00–20.00

Special Features
Wheelchair Access
(but not lavatory)

Beers Available
Tetley, Old Bailey,
Nicholson's, Carlsberg,
Castlemaine, Tennent's
Extra

Nearest Tube Station
St Paul's

126 Newgate Street, EC1   **606 8476**
'Interesting but grisly. You may need a drink'

On your way to the City or possibly to the Old Bailey you will find this most interesting pub, a small gin palace built in 1869, the year Queen Victoria opened Holborn Viaduct. It was the height of fashion, decorated mirrors, neo-classical paintings, a beaten-copper ceiling supported by a cast-iron Corinthian column, an ornate manager's stall behind the bar. The landlord's wife would sit enthroned in it, issuing tokens for drinks. The staff was not trusted with money.

Wan, soulful ladies gaze down from the wall representing banking, agriculture and the arts. The arts has been holed. A drunken soldier from the London Regiment did it in the First World War. Some say he shot it, others say he charged it with a bayonet.

I should warn you that there's something very nasty in the cellars, to whit the debtors' cells. They were once part of Newgate Prison but they are part of the Viaduct Tavern now. The cells are tiny and they used to cram 16 people into each of them. Ventilation holes in the ceilings opened onto the pavement in Newgate Street and prisoners would push their hands through, clutching at passers-by, desperate for food. Two prisoners seem to have been left behind.

The landlord takes groups down there from time to time. It is interesting but grisly. You may need a drink afterwards.

· THE VINTRY ·

30 Queen Street, EC4 **329 8985**

'They reckon there's still time for a quickie on their way home'

This handsome Victorian city pub may not be long for this world. There are plans to demolish its bit of Queen Street and build something else, new offices actually. They will too, the old offices are already emptying. Danuta Dabrowska who runs the Vintry puts this out of her mind and gets on with her job, as do the City gents who lunch there every day. They know demolition is on its way but reckon there's still time to pop in for a quickie on their way home.

The Vintry has a short but classy wine list. You get a choice of eight champagnes including Dom Perignon '85 at £75. Its sirloin steak sandwiches are decidedly swanky too. Danuta's forefathers were Polish, since you ask.

Open
Mon–Sat
Hours
11.00–23.00
Credit Cards
All major cards except Diner's Club
Food Available
Bar 11.00–21.30
Lunch 12.00–15.00
Beers Available
Chiswick Bitter, London Pride, ESB, Summer Ale, Mr Harry, IPA, full range of bottled beers.
Nearest Tube Station
Mansion House

· THE WARRINGTON ·

93 Warrington Crescent, W9 **286 2929**

'How was the Church to know about its raucby double life?'

The Church of England is down to just a handful of pubs now, a shame really. It used to have so many. Still, it could be a troublesome portfolio as the Warrington in Maida Vale showed. How was the Church to know about its double life? It was so stately, how to explain that all those lively young ladies were not, well, ladies?

The Warrington had long since put its past behind it by the time the Church sold it to David and Charles Williams in 1983. Their family had run the Warrington for years. Everyone thought it was their pub. Now it was.

It is a tremendous star turn, regularly appearing in movies and television ads. It plays what you might call walking-in parts. Cameras love the photogenic entrance with its faïence pillars and art-nouveau tiling, its mosaic steps flanked by huge wrought-iron standard lamps made by Biggs and Co of Southwark.

As for the saloon bar, it is a sight to behold, the great high room with its cherubs and marble pillars, the marble-topped counter with its ornate canopy, the frieze, the art-nouveau glass, the handsome fireplace, lofty ceiling, sweeping mahogany staircase... I like the tap room myself but you would not have found Marie Lloyd in there. The main salon was created for great music hall stars and on a shelf over the fireplace you will see an empty champagne bottle, the last she consumed there.

Upstairs, in what was the naughtiest bit in the old days,

Open
All Week
Hours
11.00–23.00
(12.00–22.30 Sun)
Credit Cards
None
Food Available
Bar 12.00–14.30 and 18.00–23.00
Restaurant 18.00–22.30
(19.00–22.00 Sun)
Special Features
Tables outside seat 200
Beers Available
Fuller's ESB, Young's Special, Brakspear Special, London Pride, Marston's Pedigree, Grolsch, Tennent's Extra, Foster's, Guinness
Nearest Tube Stations
Maida Vale, Warwick Avenue

is now in the hands of Mr Songklod Boonyachalayont, known as Ben, whose large smiling staff provides delicious Thai food from 7.00 pm onwards. You have to book.

The Warrington is much admired, not least by English Heritage, which recently made a grant towards its repair. Listed Grade II buildings like this take a lot of looking after. It does not take itself too seriously, though. It remains a lively and popular pub and seems to be under siege on sunny days with crowds outside and the big grassy traffic island covered by its younger customers. I have no hesitation in saying that as often as not this is the most densely populated traffic island in London.

·THE WATER RAT·

1 Milman's Street, SW10   **351 4732**

'For fans of Absolut Mars Bar'

Open
All Week
Hours
11.00–23.00
(12.00–22.30 Sun)
Credit Cards
None
Bar Food Available
12.00–14.30
(12.00–15.30 Sat)
Special Features
Wheelchair Access
Tables outside seat 48
Beers Available
Old Speckled Hen, Yorkshire Bitter, Guinness, Carlsberg, Holsten, Kronenbourg, Foster's
Nearest Tube Station
Sloane Square

You can't miss the Water Rat in high summer. Such masses of flowers spill from windows boxes, baskets and tubs that the Royal Borough of Kensington and Chelsea gives it prizes.

Even without the flowers this is a good-looking pub, three-storeyed, well-proportioned. This comes from being built in the 1830s when they took pains with these things. Inside there is a big bar with a wallful of small-paned windows, taped music and Sky TV for big sports events. It is a freehouse so real ales rule. Absolut Vodkas are big there too, with home-made variations – Absolut Mars Bar, Absolut Hot Chilli Pepper, Absolut Raspberry. You can have one for £1 a slam on Friday and Saturday nights. They certainly seem to get things going.

Should Milman's Street seem a little far flung and the need be great you can make an Absolut Mars Bar yourself. You chop up a Mars Bar, add the vodka and let it stand until the Mars dissolves. This takes about 24 hours. Chill well.

·THE WATER RATS·

328 Grays Inn Road, WC1   **837 7269**

'Dress to sweat'

Open
All Week
Hours
11.30–24.00 Mon–Fri;
19.00–24.00 Sat;
(19.00–22.30 Sun)
Closed Bank Holidays
Credit Cards
None

Regard the two faces of the Water Rats. By day it is a conventional King's Cross local, used by unsuspecting office workers. Then the clock strikes eight and it is goodbye quiet Dr Jekyll.

At 8.00 pm the Water Rats becomes one of the most

influential venues in the music business. With heroic disregard for their hearing, music journalists nightly seek out the next big thing on our behalf here. It is one of their most fruitful staging posts.

One such writes:

'A youthful and lively buzz goes round the front bar. Bands at the top of the indie charts play in the friendly murk of the back room. It is frequently packed to the rafters so dress to sweat. Hugely popular. Twice a month it turns into the most excellently smashing Mint Tearooms. It remains the best music pub in town.'

Food Available
Thai Food 12.00–18.00
Special Features
Private Room seats 60
Beers Available
Young's Ordinary, Young's Special, Courage Directors, John Smith's, Foster's, Kronenbourg, Hoffmeister, Guinness, Beamish
Nearest BR and Tube Station
King's Cross

· THE WATERSIDE ·

82 York Way, N1   **837 7118**

'You find that the Waterside is indeed on the waterside'

A railway needs warehouses and there are some new ones behind King's Cross, a group of modern red-brick buildings of a strictly necessary kind with high railings to keep you out. The end one is rather different. It has a large board inviting you in. 'The Waterside' it says. A pub sign yet.

So go in. This is not what you have been led to expect. There is a large 19th-century Hereford barn inside that red-brick shell, oak frame, roof beams, timber and brick walls, an old black plank floor. Left-over timber has been made into plain tables and benches, and through the big doors at the end is a wonderful sight. You find that the Waterside is indeed on the waterside.

Beyond the deep brick terrace covered in picnic tables is a wide spread of glossy water. This is Battlebridge Basin, a working siding for canal boats. The terrace narrows and follows the basin to its junction with the Grand Union Canal. There is a place behind the railings here where men and boys sit fishing hour after hour.

The pub had its own floating restaurant, a canal boat called Waterside Lady, gaily painted and moored off the terrace. Alas, it has been floated off to Slough whose need was greater. The Waterside now has a Berni Inns food servery in the bar and still has a barbecue on the terrace on sunny Sundays.

It is an excellent and unexpected pub that greatly cheers a glum bit of London.

Open
All Week
Hours
11.00–23.00
(12.00–22.30 Sun)
Credit Cards
Access, Visa, Mastercard
Food Available
New Berni Menu
12.00–15.00 and
17.00–22.30
Special Features
Wheelchair Access (but not lavatory)
Beer Garden seats 120
Beers Available
Boddingtons, Flowers IPA, Adnams, Marston's Pedigree, Heineken, Stella, Murphy's
Nearest BR and Tube Station
King's Cross

·THE WELLINGTON·

351 The Strand, WC2   **836 0513**
'Like the Iron Duke a strong character of its own'

Open
All Week
Hours
11.00–23.00
(12.00–22.30 Sun)
Credit Cards
All major cards accepted
Food Available
Bar snacks all day
Restaurant
12.00–15.00 and
17.00–19.30
Special Features
Wheelchair Access
(but not lavatory)
Tables outside seat 15
Beers Available
Bass, London Pride, Hancock's HB, Worthington Best, Caffrey's, Grolsch, Carling, Staropramen, Guinness
Nearest Tube Station
Charing Cross

The good news about the Lyceum Theatre is good news for the Wellington. The once-great theatre has been rotting away for years. Now it is being restored on a grand scale and could soon be filling the little pub next door again.

It is a small pub but it has an excellent position at the end of the Strand and, like the Iron Duke, has a strong character of its own. Its public and saloon bars each have their own street entrance and there is no mistaking which is which. The public bar has the wooden floor and the saloon bar has the carpet. Hot meals are served in the upstairs bar, a pleasant room with a front window that looks directly across Waterloo Bridge.

Anita Smith is manager now. Her husband Frank was manager before but he has taken over Drummonds opposite St Pancras Station. A massive refurb is turning it back into a pub again and the brewers offered a bottle of champagne for the best new name. The winner: the Cross Fox. Anita's suggestion.

·THE WELLINGTON·

81–83 Waterloo Road, SE1   **928 6083**
'A two-pint glass Wellington boot'

Open
All Week
Hours
11.00–23.00
(12.00–22.30 Sun)
Closed Christmas Day, New Year's Day
Credit Cards
All major cards except AmEx and Diner's Club
Bar Food Available
12.00–22.00
Special Features
Tables outside seat 24
Beers Available
Bass, Boddingtons, Gales, ESB, Adnams, Barleymow, Keens, Greene King IPA, Brakspear, Carling, Foster's, Stella, Grolsch, Caffrey's, Murphy's, Guinness
Nearest Tube Station
Waterloo

Grandeur was what one looked for in a railway hotel. The Midland Grand had a 270-ft-high clock tower, an imperial staircase and 250 bedrooms. The Great Eastern had a ballroom. You would have searched in vain for one of them in the South Eastern Railway's hotel at Waterloo. It was, to speak frankly, a modest affair.

The Wellington, for so it was called, had two floors of bedrooms and some public rooms but the force was not with it. Almost at once they started rebuilding Waterloo Station. The job took 22 years. There was a war, then a depression, then another war at the end of which it is probably true to say that the bloom was off the Wellington Hotel. By the time Regent Inns bought it in 1994 it had become a large and rather rough pub. Furthermore you could hardly fail to notice that two railway bridges came massively across the road and disappeared into the upper floors. Did trains thunder through the bedrooms?

Regent Inns set about a major refurbishing. Architects, designers, builders and decorators descended and in eight weeks it was transformed. Do look at it when you are next at Waterloo. It is a terrific pub now with one vast bar the length of the entire block. There's linenfold panelling, sophisticated lighting, new everything – carpets, sofas, armchairs, plants. A glass dome was uncovered in what had been the hotel dining room and they found that the original lobby had had a fine curved ceiling. A mural was commissioned from John Waldon, the Battle of Waterloo, Wellington on his horse, Blücher with the West Prussians, the Scots Greys attacking the French artillery, Napoleon, surrounded by his Imperial Guards. It is a jolly good ceiling.

The new licensee, Jill Keen, presides over this leap upmarket. There are eight cask beers on the hand pumps. Keen's bitter is served not in a glass slipper but in a two-pint glass Wellington boot. There are proper butcher's sausages on the grill and there are still 12 letting rooms upstairs, single rooms £28, double rooms £46, get your own breakfast.

·THE WESTBOURNE·

101 Westbourne Park Villas, W2   **221 1332**

'The happy marriage of the pub and the bistro'

The Westbourne, deep in Notting Hill Gate, is a big good-looking pub with a priceless natural asset, a big sunny forecourt. In France this would be a grand restaurant with serried white-clothed tables in tight rows shaded by canopies. Here it gets crammed with people standing, sitting, eating, drinking. You can't book a quiet spot. There isn't a quiet spot. This is a pub.

It is strange to think that this, like its near neighbour, the Cow, was a scruffy, old half-empty boozer for most of its life. Now it is one of the new generation of sophisticated born-again London pubs, cheaper, younger and jollier than the Cow but with exactly the same aim: the happy marriage of the pub and the bistro.

The new Westbourne is the creation of Oliver Daniaud and the painter and sculptor Sebastian Boyle. They found the pub in apparently terminal decline with the decrepit bar empty by day and local kids using it for rave-ups. They worked on it for two years, running out of money, facing crisis after crisis, one day meeting the River Westbourne running through the cellars but opening in May 1995, a few weeks after the Cow, to the same phenomenal success, the combination of English beer, continental lager, a sunny staff and Brit-Med food irresistible.

It is said that neighbouring house prices have gone up because the Cow and the Westbourne are there. That is not something house prices usually say about pubs.

Open
All Week

Hours
17.30–23.00 Mon;
11.00–23.00 Tues–Sat
(12.00–22.30 Sun)

Food Available
13.00–15.00 and
19.00–22.00 Tues–Sun

Special Features
Wheelchair Access
(but not lavatory)
Tables outside seat 35

Beers Available
Marston's Pedigree,
Boddingtons, Heineken,
Stella, Kronenbourg,
Dortmunder Union,
Leffe Blond, Guinness

Nearest Tube Stations
Westbourne Park,
Royal Oak

· THE WESTMINSTER ARMS ·

9 Storey's Gate, SW1   **222 8520**

'MPs can find safety in numbers'

Open
All Week

Hours
11.00–23.00
(12.00–22.30 Sun)

Credit Cards
Visa, AmEx, Mastercard

Food Available
Restaurant
12.00–14.30
Wine Bar 12.00–22.00

Special Features
Wheelchair Access
(but not lavatory)
Tables outside seat 15
Private Room seats 40

Beers Available
Westminster Bitter, Brakspear PA, Brakspear Special, Young's, Theakston XB, Wadworth 6X, plus changing guest beers, and lagers

Nearest Tube Stations
Westminster,
St James's Park

There are nine bars in the House of Commons, one for every 72.2 MPs, and they have to share eight of them with visitors and the like. So it's rather a squash. Luckily there are quite a few pubs a short walk away. This is one of them.

Until the new Queen Elizabeth Conference Centre was built the Westminster Arms had a clear view of Big Ben and of Westminster Abbey. Now what it sees is the side of the conference centre, not a good swap. On the other hand it gets wave after wave of custom from the new building, in fact it is extraordinarily busy most of the time and MPs can find safety in numbers and reassurance from the division bell in the bar.

The bar, crowded most of the day, looks much as it did when the pub was rebuilt in 1913, but as the cellar bar was thoroughly done over in the modern manner this year it looks a great deal older. It is now back in the 1850s with a flagstone floor, drinking booths round the walls, old panelling, benches and wooden tables. There is a pleasant restaurant upstairs, a wine bar downstairs and tables and chairs on the pavement outside all summer.

· THE WETHERSPOONS ·

Victoria Station, SW1   **931 0445**

'You can watch your train leaving without you'

Open
All Week

Hours
11.00–23.00
(12.00–22.30 Sun)

Credit Cards
Access, Visa, Delta, Switch

Bar Food Available
11.00–23.00
(12.00–22.30 Sun)

Special Features
No-smoking Area
Wheelchair Access
Tables outside seat 30

Beers Available
Theakston Best, Theakston XB, Younger Scotch Bitter, Courage Directors, Marston's Pedigree, and three guest beers, Becks

Nearest Tube Station
Victoria

This is a rarity, a pub built in the 1990s in the style of the 1990s. It is cool, light and minimalist. There is a life-like hologram of Queen Victoria outside it. She liked trains, though possibly not pubs.

The new Wetherspoons is in the middle of Victoria station on the first floor of the new building it shares with W H Smith. It has its own short escalators to take you up and bring you down again. and there is a terrace on either side. From one you look down on the South Central Concourse and get a full view of the departure board, and from the other you can look down on platforms 6, 5, 4 and 3 and watch your train leaving without you.

It is an unexpectedly quiet and civilized spot in this hectic place.

·THE WHITE HART·

New Fetter Lane, EC4   **583 4876**

'The Stab In The Back no longer'

When the Mirror Group left its red tower in Holborn Circus and decamped to Canary Wharf the White Hart lost nearly all its customers.

Gone, at a stroke, were the entire staffs of the *Daily Mirror*, the *Sunday Mirror*, the *People* and the *Sporting Life*, the last papers to leave in the great Fleet Street diaspora. They had made the White Hart their own ever since it was built. They always called it the Stab In The Back. With their departure it was strangely quiet.

Gone too was the sign of the cockerel above the modest entrance, proclaiming it a Courage house. The pub had been taken over by Scottish and Newcastle some months before and, with the exodus, it fell to an unexpected new manager to build up a new clientele. Gillian Woods had meant to be an actress. She had left Grimsby six years before, at the age of 20, to go to stage school and bar jobs helped to pay the way. Now she had a whole pub to run and she has made it a very different place.

It looks much the same. The library decor with books lined up on high shelves remains, as do some pictures, but occasional *Mirror* people making a sentimental pilgrimage find far more radical changes. Gillian brought in two other young women as her staff and they may be discovered dressed down for the cellar, dressed up for the evening or dressed as the likes of Madonna on charity fund-raising nights. They have live music evenings too, and games. The wearer of the worst tie of the evening can get a prize, that sort of thing.

This is going down well with the new customers from the local offices, and Gillian has won Scottish and Newcastle's Warm Welcome Award. The White Hart is the Stab In The Back no longer.

Open
Mon–Fri
Hours
11.00–23.00
Closed Bank Holidays
Credit Cards
Visa, Mastercard, Eurocard
Bar Food Available
11.00–15.00
Special Features
Wheelchair Access
Tables outside seat 30
Live music fortnightly on Fridays
Beers Available
Theakston Best, Courage Best, Courage Directors, Kronenbourg, Foster's, Guinness, Becks, Budweiser, Buduar, Molsen Dry, Foster's Ice, John Smith's L. A, Kaliber
Nearest Tube Station
Chancery Lane

·THE WHITE HORSE·

1 Parsons Green, SW6 **736 2115**

'The Sloany Pony'

Open
All Week
Hours
11.00–23.00
(12.00–22.30 Sun)
Credit Cards
All major cards except Diner's Club
Food Available
11.00–14.45 and
17.00–22.20 Mon–Sat;
(11.00–22.00 Sun)
Special Features
Wheelchair Access
(but not lavatory)
Beer Garden seats 80
Private Room seats 60
Beers Available
Belgian and Dutch beers, Harveys Sussex, Highgate Mild, Bass, Adnams Extra, Staropramen
Nearest Tube Station
Parsons Green

Old coaching inns, their original occupations gone, often adapt brilliantly to our times. Three hundred years ago the White Horse on Parsons Green was the last stop for a meal and a change of horses before the long hard journey from London to Exeter and Bristol. Now it is itself the destination.

It is a extrovert, cheerful place. The big comfortable U-shaped bar has huge draped windows, leather sofas and eating booths, there is a billiard room upstairs and a regularly changing team of young Australian and New Zealand athletes behind the bar. They arrive for six months or so, live in, work hard and move on, having made friends for life in London.

The charismatic manager, Sally Cruickshank, recently retired to the golf course, and Rupert Reeves is now in charge, with Mark Dorber still leading his double life, by day successful City analyst, by night White Horse cellarman. Dorber is a serious bespectacled man totally enthused by the beer in his charge.

A lot goes on at the White Horse. Big beer festivals have spread its reputation far beyond London – particularly the Old Ale Festival in the last week of November with 60 different ales on tap.

The Sloany Pony, as it is known locally, claims to be the only place in the world to offer all 15 Trappist brewed beers, houses many European lagers and has up to 100 wines on its wine list. Its food gets better all the time.

An *Evening Standard* Pub of the Year.

·THE WHITE SWAN·

14 Vauxhall Bridge Road, SW1 **821 8568**

'The currently modish style known as Old English Ale House'

Open
All Week
Hours
11.00–23.00
(12.00–17.00 Sun)
Credit Cards
All major cards accepted
Bar Food Available
12.00–17.30
(12.00–16.00 Sun)
Special Features
Wheelchair Access
Tables outside seat 70
Private Room seats 60

The White Swan is the big Victorian pub you pass as you drive in heavy traffic towards Vauxhall Bridge. The temptation to stop is sometimes great.

Drastic things have been happening there. It is now one huge bar in the currently modish style known as Old English Ale House, massive weather-worn timbers, bare floorboards, bare brick walls, chopping-board tables, pine benches, ceilings lowered a good yard with introduced bare rafters. The original Victorian ceiling can be glimpsed high above if you look carefully enough.

Real ales, robust traditional food and lots of room make for busy lunchtimes, the latest gaming machines, a juke box and television get a lively young crowd in the evenings, and a large white swan in a glass case keeps a beady eye on all around it.

·THE WILLIAM IV·

75 Hampstead High Street, NW3 **435 5747**

'William IV seems to have been staunchly heterosexual himself. On the other hand...'

Near the top of Hampstead's steep leafy High Street is one of North London's principal gay pubs, prosperous, respectable and middle class, mirroring, as pubs do, the community it serves.

The William IV stands four square on its corner, yellow London brick with black shutters, window boxes and hanging baskets bright with flowers. The interior is very smart, ceiling Lincrusta'd, walls sponged, stippled, papered and panelled. A large notice headed 'Our Fabulous Wines' lists eight.

There is a substantial island counter and a team of cheerful barmen dealing with four separate drinking areas. Seasoned regulars gather in the small bar at the front. Some have hardly budged in 25 years. Younger customers stick to the big open space at the other end. The new Bar Verandah upstairs, launched as 'London's first and only non-smoking gay and lesbian bar', was not a great hit in this role and is now just used for functions and for a set Sunday lunch: £6.95.

The rest of the week there is lunch in the bar with an alternative not far to seek. La Creperie de Hampstead is on the pavement outside. No crepes are allowed in either the pub or the garden but you can have one at the tables on the pavement. The garden, large, pleasant and filled with tables, can count on a busy and sociable summer.

William IV, bluff and red-faced, looks down from the inn sign. He might have been surprised by the William IV of our day. He seems to have been staunchly heterosexual himself, lived for 21 years with the actress Mrs Jordan who bore him ten children. On the other hand, he *was* known as the sailor king.

Beers Available
Courage Best,
Theakston XB,
Theakston Best, John
Smith's, Wadworth 6X,
Kronenbourg, Foster's,
Carlsberg

Nearest Tube Station
Pimlico

Open
All Week

Hours
11.00–23.00
(12.00–22.30 Sun)

Credit Cards
None

Bar Food Available
12.00–14.30 Mon–Sat

Special Features
Wheelchair Access
Beer Garden seats 50
Tables outside seat 16
Bar Verandah seats 30
for private parties

Beers Available
'Pink Willy' bitter,
Courage Best, Courage
Directors, Ruddles
Best, Foster's,
Carlsberg,
Kronenbourg, Holsten
Export, Guinness

Nearest Tube Station
Hampstead

· WILLIAMSON'S TAVERN ·

1 Groveland Court, EC4 **248 6280**

'No place for ravers'

Open
Mon–Fri

Hours
11.30–21.00
Closed Bank Holidays

Credit Cards
All major cards accepted

Bar Food Available
11.30–14.45

Special Features
Private Room seats 50

Beers Available
Tetley, Nicholson's, Adnams, Wadworth, Brakspear, Castlemaine, Carlsberg, Guinness

Nearest Tube Station
Mansion House

You can lose yourself and never be seen again searching for Williamson's Tavern so let me tell you precisely where it is. It is the exact centre of the City of London's square mile. A stone in what was the parlour marks the spot.

What a remarkable history this tavern has. It started off as a grand private house, so grand that it was the official residence of successive Lord Mayors. One of them entertained the King and Queen there, William and Mary, who presented him with a truly royal knick-knack, a pair of wrought-iron gates. These are still in daily use.

The house became Williamson's in 1739 when Robert Williamson bought it and converted it into an hotel. They had just laid the foundation stone of the Mansion House so the Lord Mayors had to stay on for another 13 years until the new building was finished.

It seems to have been a successful hotel. Successive owners worried about fire and one banned matches, which seems to have done the trick. It did not burn down and in the 1930s a new owner made it a pub. It is a distinctly superior pub with a library, two fine panelled bars and the general air of a gentleman's club. It is very popular with City gents who know exactly how to get there, also with City women who like its unpubby atmosphere. Between them they fill all three big bars at lunchtime. There is a charcoal grill in one of them and some say its steak sandwiches are the best in London.

It is very peaceful in Williamson's in the afternoon with everyone back at work. Then it wakes up again as people look in for a snifter on their way home and it closes about 9.00 pm as most City pubs do. Like most City pubs it stays closed at weekends. The City of London is no place for ravers.

· THE WILTON ARMS ·

71 Kinnerton Street, SW1 **235 4854**

'Grand in its own right but knowing its place'

Open
All Week

Hours
11.00–23.00
(12.00–22.30 Sun)

Credit Cards
Access, Visa

Wilton Crescent, Wilton Place, Wilton Row, as good addresses go these are hard to beat and the Wilton Arms, named like the rest after the first Earl of Wilton, stands, most respectfully, in the mews. I see it as the comptroller of the household, grand in its own right but knowing its place.

The mews is Kinnerton Street, rough and malodorous in

its early days with an open sewer and more horses than people. The Wilton Arms hardly knew where to look. Those days are long gone and for many years the Wilton Arms has had most distinguished neighbours.

It has always been a superior public house. It got further improved in the Whitbread manner six years ago, and high settles and bookcases now give the big bar a number of pleasantly separate drinking areas. There are some jolly good books in the bookcases. New Zealand Statutes. Public Acts of Tasmania.

It used to have a garden at the back. This has been replaced by a conservatory to win more tables, and the flowers have moved to the front where new hanging baskets and window boxes, exuberant with fuschias and pansies, have won certificates of excellence.

There is a kitchen with a presiding chef on the first floor and hot food is served all day.

Bar Food Available
11.00–23.00
11.30–16.00 Sat;
(12.00–17.00 Sun)
Special Features
Private Room seats 20
Beers Available
Boddingtons, Flowers IPA, Abbot Ale, Heineken, Stella Artois, Guinness, Murphy's
Nearest Tube Station
Knightsbridge

·The Windmill on the Common·

Clapham Common South Side, SW4   0181-673 4578
'A very genteel and good accustomed house'

You might not like to be called ye olde and some pubs don't either. This famous pub was called Ye Olde Windmill for a while but it is the Windmill on the Common now if you don't mind. It is on the olde side all the same. It has been here since at least 1665. Charles II. Full bottom wigs. Richard Attenborough opening in Mousetrap.

The mid-17th century then and a windmill in open countryside, a miller doubling as an ale-house keeper. Another 100 years and the windmill has gone and the Windmill Inn has replaced it. 'A very genteel and good accustomed house,' a Mr Edwards wrote at the time.

Another 200 years and here we are with the Windmill in terrific form, big wandering bar with tropical fish, spacious conservatory for non-smokers, excellent restaurant and an adjoining hotel that gets three stars from the AA and a highly commended from the English Tourist Board…

Things are always going on at the Windmill – quizzes, fiesta nights, jazz, opera in the conservatory. In the summer drinkers spill out onto the common and in the winter there's an open fire in the bar.

There are cask ales, draught lagers and a plentiful wine list, five reds, five whites, two rosés and two champagnes. The head chef of the attached restaurant does the bar food and makes his own bread.

The Windmill on the Common gets packed in the evenings and at weekends and no wonder.

Open
All Week
Hours
11.00–23.00
(12.00–22.30 Sun)
Credit Cards
All major cards accepted
Food Available
Bar 12.00–14.30 and 19.00–22.00
Restaurant 19.00–22.00
Special Features
No-smoking Area
Wheelchair Access (disabled lavatory)
Beer Garden seats 50
Beers Available
All Young's variants
Nearest Tube Station
Clapham Common

·THE WINDSOR CASTLE·

114 Campden Hill Road, W8　　　　　　　　**727 8491**

'A spectacular run on the Pimms'

Open
All Week

Hours
11.00–23.00
(12.00–22.30 Sun)

Credit Cards
Visa, Access, AmEx

Bar Food Available
All Hours

Special Features
No smoking Sunday lunchtimes
Wheelchair Access
Beer Garden seats 60

Beers Available
Bass, Adnams Extra, Charrington's IPA, Stones

Nearest Tube Station
Notting Hill Gate

When the Windsor Castle was young it was gravel pits, farms and a quiet life up there on Campden Hill. Maids a-milking and ploughman's lunches, I shouldn't wonder. On a clear day you could see Windsor Castle. Now, surrounded by some of the most expensive real estate in London and with no view to speak of, the Windsor Castle is a most up-market London pub.

As the houses were built the pub expanded – three bars, each with its own entrance, one for the local toffs, one for the hoi polloi, a third for anyone who happened to be passing. The bars are still in good order but you don't see much of the hoi polloi there these days. The Windsor Castle is part of what is known as the Eton drinking round, one of a handful of London pubs where Old Etonians meet, and it has never been so busy. The Campden Bar gets so packed in the evenings that movement is impossible, though the staff in their black waistcoats and long white aprons manage somehow.

In the summer the garden opens and the capacity of the pub trebles. It is a splendid garden shaded by an old plane tree – two other trees are coming along nicely for future generations.

The Windsor Castle's kitchen has a high reputation. There is a roster of cooks producing hot prawns, salmon fishcakes, chargrilled steak and such, and from Monday to Saturday there's food all day. You can get half a dozen oysters for a fiver, a bottle of champagne for £16, and there is often a spectacular run on the Pimms. Sunday lunch in the Campden Bar – always roast rib of beef and Yorkshire pudding – is so popular that lunchtime goes on until 4.00 pm.

Should you brave the sherry bar, the approved drink is the huntsman – dry sherry with tomato juice, a milder Bloody Mary.

·THE WOODMAN·

60 Battersea High Street, SW11　　　　　　**228 5949**

'Local horses go for carrots and Guinness'

Open
All Week

Hours
11.00–23.00
(12.00–22.30 Sun)

Credit Cards
Access, Visa, Switch

There is, in Battersea High Street, a little country pub called the Woodman. It is at number 60. A few doors along, at number 44, is another little country pub. It is called the Original Woodman. Hello hello? What's this then?

I don't want to take sides in this Balkan affair but I will nervously say that the Woodman is easily the prettier, with its cottage frontage and hanging baskets, and it certainly wins on size. First comes a little public bar with a sawdust floor, full of real ale and character. Behind it is a saloon bar with a carpet and traditional games – bar billiards, table football, shove ha'penny. Then comes a much newer bit with a modern food counter, and beyond that is a pleasant paved garden with a large pull-out awning. So let it rain.

This is old Battersea, and pre-gentrification locals amicably rub shoulders with the new sort. It makes for an interesting, lively pub. Its regulars send it postcards when they go on hols, there is a pub football team, recently beaten 14–0, empty champagne bottles commemorate marriages and births, and local horses go for carrots and Guinness every Christmas morning.

The Original Woodman does not go in for this sort of thing. It is very much the local boozer, one small bar and no frills. Some like it best.

Bar Food Available
12.00–22.00

Special Features
Wheelchair Access (but not lavatory)
Tables outside seat 90

Beers Available
Badger Best, Tanglefoot, Hard Tackle, Wadworth 6X, Theakston Old Peculier, Eagle IPA, Blackadder.

Nearest BR Station
Clapham Junction

·THE WORLD'S END·

459 King's Road, SW10   **376 8946**

'The end of the world?'

The World's End is a bus terminus, a garden centre, a theatre, a council estate, a district and, of course, the pub that gave them all its name, a big Victorian public house in what used to be the farthest reaches of the King's Road. It had and still has a message for the nervous traveller. You have left nice, safe SW3, it says. You are now in the unchartered waters of SW10.

When it was built in 1890 it was called the World's End Distillery, a name that still appears on the oldest of the surviving windows, suggesting the downward path to Gin Lane. It has had many ups and downs since then, many owners too, some of whom soon decided that this was indeed the world's end. A couple of years ago it became a Harvey Floorbangers but it was soon taken on by Badger Inns and got its historic name back.

For many years now it has had one big bar with an island counter making lots of room for the pinball machine, the table football and the gaming machines. Youngsters on their way to clubs in Chelsea and Fulham meet here for a drink and the music is pumped up late in the evening to get them in the mood. You can get burgers and chips all day.

Open
All Week

Hours
11.00–23.00
(12.00–22.30 Sun)

Credit Cards
Visa, Mastercard, AmEx

Bar Food Available
11.00–22.00

Special Features
Wheelchair Access (but not lavatory)

Beers Available
Badger, Tanglefoot, Smile's. Hard Tackle, Foster's, Holsten, Kronenbourg, Guinness
Cider: Dry Blackthorn.

Nearest Tube Stations
Sloane Square, Earls Court

·THE WRESTLERS·

North Hill, N6   **0181-340 4297**

'No wrestling'

Open
All Week

Hours
11.00–23.00
(12.00–22.30 Sun)

Credit Cards
None

Bar Food Available
12.00–14.30 and
18.00–21.30

Special Features
Wheelchair Access
(but not lavatory)

Beers Available
Draught Bass,
Worthington Best,
Grolsch, Tennent's
Extra, Tennent's Pilsner,
Carling Black Label,
Guinness, Caffrey's
Cider: Strongbow

Nearest Tube Station
Highgate

A plaque on the wall says there was a pub here in 1547 but this clearly was not it. This one was built in 1921, a solid, suburban public house. It recently took on modern times head on with a spell as a Slug and Lettuce but this didn't work and the Wrestlers was soon the Wrestlers again. For a while it made one proud claim to up-to-dateness. 'Only Pub in Highgate with Air Conditioning' said a board outside. Alas, this proved too expensive to run. It is now the only pub in Highgate that used to have air conditioning.

Wrestlers wrestle on the inn sign. Tudor times, apparently. There's no wrestling at the Wrestlers today.

·THE YACHT TAVERN·

7 Crane Street, SE10   **0181-858 0175**

'Charles II liked it'

Open
All Week

Hours
12.00–23.00
(12.00–22.30 Sun)
Closed Christmas Day

Credit Cards
All major cards
accepted

Bar Food Available
12.00–20.00

Special Features
Wheelchair Access
Tables outside seat 50

Beers Available
Theakston Best,
Ruddles Best, John
Smith's, Courage
Directors, Carlsberg,
Holsten, Foster's

Nearest BR Station
Maze Hill

The original Yacht Tavern was a famous old pub. Charles II liked it. He would slip in there when the court was at Greenwich. It had a pleasant riverside garden and was growing old with much grace when, alas, Hitler got it.

In the rebuilt version a modern extension completely covered the old garden and you saw little of the river from the bar. A major new refit, however, is currently under way and promises to improve matters: a terrace overlooking the river, a new place for the bulky bar counter…

The Greenwich Meridian line runs through the building. Some things don't change.

· Eros Awards ·

Babushka
173 Blackfriars Road, SE1
928 3693

Cittie of Yorke
22 High Holborn, WC1
242 7670

Engineer
65 Gloucester Avenue, NW1
722 0950

Hoop and Grapes
47 Aldgate High Street, EC3
480 5739

King's Head
115 Upper Street, N1
226 1916

**Lord Moon
of the Mall**
16–18 Whitehall, SW1
839 7701

Old Bank of England
194 Fleet Street, EC4
430 2255

Orange Brewery
37 Pimlico Road, SW1
730 5984

Pharoah and Firkin
90 Fulham High Street, SW6
731 0732

Spaniard's Inn
Spaniard's Road, NW3
0181-455 3276

TE Dingwalls
11 Camden Lock Place, NW1
267 0545

Trafalgar Tavern
5 Park Row, SE10
0181-858 2437

· Pubs with Theatres ·

King's Head N1
Latchmere SW11
Man in the Moon SW3
Old Red Lion EC1
Orange Tree, Richmond

Other pubs with theatres include:

Bush
 Shepherds Bush Green W12
Duke of Cambridge
 64 Lawford Road NW5
Finborough Arms
 118 Finborough Road SW10
Hen and Chickens,
 109 St Paul's Road N1
Landor
 Landor Road SW9
Oxford Arms,
 265 Camden High Street NW1
Prince Albert
 (The Gate) *11 Pembridge Road W11*
Rose and Crown
 61 High St, Hamton Wick, Kingston.
Three Horseshoes
 28 Heath Street NW3
Union Tavern,
 146 Camberwell New Road SW9
White Bear
 138 Kennington Park Road SE11

· Gay Pubs ·

Black Cap NW1
Champion W11
Coleherne SW5
Earls SW5
William 1V NW3

Other gay pubs include:

Angel
 65 Graham Street N1
Brief Encounter
 41 St Martin's Lane WC2
Brompton's
 294 Old Brompton Road SW5
Comptons
 53 Old Compton Street W1
Duke of Wellington
 119 Balls Pond Road N1
Duke's
 349 Kennington Lane SE11
Edward VI
 25 Bromfield Street N1
Father Redcap
 319 Gamborwell Green SE5
Hudson's
 330 Kennington Lane SE11
King's Arms
 23 Poland Street W1
London Apprentice
 333 Old Street EC1
Market Tavern
 1 Nine Elms Lane SW8
Queen of England
 320 Goldhawk Rd W6
Queen's Head
 27 Tryon Street SW3
Ram and Teasel
 39 Queens Head Street N1
Royal George
 7 Selby Street, Vallance Rd E1
Royal Vauxhall Tavern
 372 Kennington Lane SE11
Salmon and Compasses
 58 Penton Street N1
Two Brewers
 114 Clapham High Street SW4

·Riverside Pubs·

Anchor SE1
Angel SE16

Barley Mow E14
Bell and Crown W4
Black Lion W6
Blue Anchor W6
Bull's Head W6

Captain Kidd E1
City Barge W4
Cutty Sark SE10

Dickens Inn E1
Doggett's Coat and Badge SE1
Dove Inn W6
Duke's Head SW15

Founders Arms SE1

Gazebo, Kingston
Grapes E14

Hornimans at Hays SE1

Mayflower SE16

Old Ship W4
Old Thameside Inn SE1

Prospect of Whitby E1

Queen Mary WC2

River Rat SW11

Rutland W6
Ship SW14
Ship Inn SW18
Star and Garter SW15

Tattershall Castle SW1
Town of Ramsgate E1
Trafalgar Tavern SE10

White Swan, Twickenham

Yacht SE10

Other riverside pubs include:

Barmy Arms
 Riverside, Twickenham
Bishop out of Residence
 Bishop's Hall, Thames Street, Kingston
Gun
 27 Cold Harbour Lane E14
London Apprentice
 62 Church Street, Old Isleworth
Pope's Grotto
 Cross Deep, Twickenham
The Ram
 34 High Street, Kingston
Samuel Pepys
 Brooks Wharf, 48 Upper Thames Street EC4
Three Pigeons
 87 Petersham Road, Richmond
Waterman's Arms
 1 Glenaffric Avenue E14

·Pubs with No Smoking Areas·

Albion N1
Alexandra SW19
Argyll Arms W1

Barley Mow E14
Beehive SW9
Bell and Crown W4
Blackbird SW5

Cat and the Canary E14
Crooked Billet SW19
Crown and Greyhound SE3

Doggetts Coat and Badge SE1
Drayton Arms SW5

Freemasons Arms NW3
Friar and Firkin NW1

Gallery SW1
Gatehouse N6
Guinea W1
Hamilton Hall EC2
Hand in Hand SW19
Hare and Hounds SW14

Hoop and Grapes EC3
Hornimans at Hays SE1

JJ Moon's, Heathrow

Lamb WC1
Lamb Tavern EC3
Lord Moon of the Mall SW1

Man in the Moon SW3
Melton Mowbray EC1
Mitre W2
Moon and Sixpence W1
Moon under the Water WC2

Old Bank of England EC4
Old Bull and Bush NW3
Old King Lud EC2
Old Shades SW1
Orange Tree, Richmond

Paxton's Head SW1
Phoenix and Firkin SE15
Prospect of Whitby E1

Punch and Judy WC2

Rising Sun EC1
Rose and Crown SW19
Rose of York, Richmond

Salisbury WC2
Sherlock Holmes WC2
Stargazey SW10
Swan W6

Trafalgar SW3
Trafalgar Tavern SE10

Waterside Inn N!
Wetherspoons SW1
William IV NW3
Windmill on the Common SW4
Windsor Castle W8

No smoking areas are now allotted 30 per cent of the space in all J.D.Wetherspoon pubs

·Pubs with Live Music·

Albion N16
Alexandra SW19

Babushka SE1
Barley Mow E14
Beaufoy Arms SW11
Black Cap NW1
Blue Anchor W6
Bull and Gate NW5
Bull N6

City Barge W4
Coleherne SW5
Cutty Sark SE10

Drayton Arms SW5
Dublin Castle NW1

Eagle Tavern N1

Falcon NW1
Ferret and Firkin SW10
Finch's SW10
Flask NW3
Flask N6
Flyman and Firkin WC2

Freemasons Arms NW3
Friar and Firkin NW1
Fulmar and Firkin WC2
Fusilier and Firkin NW1

George Inn SE1
Goose and Firkin SE1
Ground Floor Bar W11

Half Moon SW15
Hare and Hounds SW14
Henry Addington E14
Holly Bush NW3
Hobgoblin SW2
Horse and Groom NW3

Jack Straw's Castle NW3

King's Head SW6
King's Head N1

Lamb and Flag WC2

Maple Leaf WC2
Marquess Tavern N1
Mitre W2

Monarch NW1

Narrow Boat N1

O'Hanlon's EC1
Old King Lud EC4
Old Ship W4
Old Bull and Bush NW3
Olde Surgeon W1
Orange Tree, Richmond
Outback WC2
Outpost E3

Phoenix and Firkin SE15
Pharoah and Firkin SW6
Prospect of Whitby E1

Queen's Arms SW3

Railway Tavern E8
Rutland W6

Scruffy Murphy's W1
Ship SW14
Ship Inn SW18
Sir George Robey N4
Slug and Lettuce SW15
Swan SW9
Swan W2
Swan W6

Trafalgar SW3
Trafalgar Tavern SE10
Tufnell Park Tavern N7
Tut 'n' Shive N1

Water Rats WC1
White Horse SW6
Windmill on the Common SW4

Yacht SE10
Ye Olde Swiss Cottage NW3

· PUBS WITH OUTSIDE SEATING ·

Albion N1
Alexandra SW19
Anchor SE1
Anglesea Arms SW7

Babushka SE1
Bell and Crown W4
Black Lion W6
Blenheim SW3
Blind Beggar E1
Bull N6
Bull's Head W6

Camden Head N1
Captain Kidd E1
Cartoonist EC4
Catcher in the Rye N3
Champion W2
Chelsea Ram SW10
Clarence SW1
Cocoanut, Kingston
Compton Arms N1
Cricketers, Richmond
Crooked Billet SW19
Crown and Greyhound SE3
Cutty Sark SE10

Dickens Inn E1
Dog and Fox SW19

Dogget's Coat and Badge SE1
Dove Inn W6

Enterprise SW3

Flask NW3
Flask N6
Founder's Arms SE1
Fox and Pheasant SW10
Fox and Grapes SW19
Freemason's Arms NW3

Gatehouse N6
Gazebo, Kingston
George Inn SE1
Gipsy Moth SE10
Grapes E14
Green Man SW15

Hamilton Hall EC2
Hand in Hand SW19
Hare and Hounds SW14
Henry J Beans SW3
Henry Addington E14
Hillgate Arms W8
Hobgoblin SW2
Hollywood Arms SW10

Jack Straw's Castle NW3

King's Head SW6

Ladbroke Arms W11
Legless Ladder SW11

Marlborough, Richmond
Marquess Tavern N1
Monarch NW1
Monkey Puzzle W2
Morpeth Arms SW1

Narrow Boat N1
Nightingale SW12

Old Thameside Inn SE1
Old Bull and Bush NW3
Old Ship W4
Orange Tree, Richmond
Orange Brewery SW1
Outpost E3

Phene Arms SW3
Phoenix and Firkin SE15
Plumber's Arms SW1
Prospect of Whitby E1
Punch and Judy WC2

Queen Mary WC2

River Rat SW11
Robert Browning W9

Rose and Crown SW19
Rose of York, Richmond
Round Table WC2
Rutland W6

Salutation Inn W6
Scarsdale Arms W8
Sekforde Arms EC1
Shakespeare Head W1
Ship Inn SW18
Ship SW14
Slug and Lettuce SW15
Spaniard's Inn NW3
Sporting Page SW10
Star and Garter SW15
Swan W2
Swiss Cottage NW3

Tattershall Castle SW1
Tufnell Park Tavern N7

Water Rat SW10
Waterside Inn N1
Westbourne W2
Westminster Arms SW1
White Horse SW6
White Swan, Twickenham
William IV NW3
Windmill on the Common SW4
Windsor Castle W8
Woodman SW11